£3.30-

MANAGE WITH ENGLISH

MANAGE WITH ENGLISH

P L Sandler   C L Stott

Oxford University Press
1981

Oxford University Press
Walton Street, Oxford OX2 6DP
London Glasgow New York Toronto
Delhi Bombay Calcutta Madras Karachi
Kuala Lumpur Singapore Hong Kong Tokyo
Nairobi Dar Es Salaam Cape Town
Melbourne Auckland
and associate companies in
Beirut Berlin Ibadan Mexico City
ISBN 0 19 4513173

The authors would like to thank Barbara Clarke and Peter Donovan of OUP for their assistance. P. L. Sandler would like to thank Heather and Flolyn Murray; C. L. Stott would like to acknowledge the encouragement and forbearance of colleagues at York Language Training Associates during the writing of this book.

The publishers would like to thank the following for permission to reproduce photographs:

Ashridge Management College
Stewart Bale Ltd.
Paul Brierley
Canon Business Machines (U.K.) Ltd.
E.M.E. Ltd.
Gate Machinery Co. Ltd.
Gestetner International Ltd.
Hotpoint
Hytec – Oxford
Massey-Ferguson Ltd.
Olympia Business Machines Ltd.
Shell Chemicals Ltd.
Startrite Machine Tools Ltd.
Wellman Engineering Co. Ltd.

The publishers would like to thank the following for their time and assistance:

Boots Ltd., Oxford
Sun-Ray Blinds and Windows, Oxford
University of Oxford

Location photographs by Dafydd Jones.

Set in Compugraphic Sabon by T H Brickell & Son Ltd,
The Blackmore Press, Shaftesbury, Dorset
Printed in Great Britain at the University Press, Oxford by Eric Buckley,
Printer to the University

Contents

Teacher's Notes

1 Aims of the Course

The course is intended for two categories of learner. Firstly, for practising managers in industry and commerce who, for a variety of reasons, need to improve their performance in English. Secondly, for business studies students and management trainees who are studying for an examination in English or who are expected, as part of their second-language training programme, to attain a level of proficiency in English.

This course aims, by employing a wide range of creative activities, to practise and develop the four skills of reading, writing, listening and speaking for business-specific purposes.

The entry level is intermediate, using J. van Ek's Threshold Level* as a basis of reference. The course can be used by (i) learners who have recently been following an English course, (ii) learners who have re-started using English after a number of years without practice, and (iii) learners without a great deal of formal training in English who have nevertheless reached a certain performance level and now need to consolidate their language.

2 Design

The course is designed so that the introduction of language is carefully controlled. One of the principles of the course is that unreasonable demands should not be placed on the learner in the understanding of 'new' language features. Consequently, new lexical items or structures are never introduced or exemplified in terms of more complex elements unless meaning can be deduced from illustration and context. Structural exponents and lexis are introduced in Sections A and B of each main unit and subsequently practised within each unit and, where relevant, in other units. The learner is not faced with any 'new' structures in Sections C-G of each unit.

The principal language work in the course is based on concepts and functions relating to the practice of management skills. Therefore the emphasis is placed on such elements as:

- comparing/contrasting
- quantity
- degree
- the language of graphs and charts
- time reference
- classification
- sequencing
- cause/effect
- reporting
- giving and seeking information
- giving opinions
- suggesting/advising etc.

3 Organization and Teaching Method

There are eighteen units in the course: fifteen main teaching units with accompanying casssettes and a revision unit after units five, ten and fifteen. The fifteen main units cover a wide range of management topics based on personnel, production, marketing and finance. Each main unit follows a topic theme (see Contents List) and is divided into seven sections.

SECTION A Reading

Reading Passage
The reading passages in units one to five are 'neutral' and 'informative' in register. In units six to fifteen, however, the learner is presented with texts in a number of different registers which include: reports, magazine articles, company statements and directives, and letters.

Word Study
This section provides definitions for all the newly-introduced lexical items in the reading passage.

Comprehension
The emphasis in the comprehension section is on the understanding of statements and factual information as presented in the reading passage. The questions are designed to develop such skills as:

- scanning the text for detailed information
- skimming for ideas and themes
- recognizing relevant information
- summarizing information in tabulated form
- incorporating the learner's own knowledge in close reading
- understanding referencing devices which relate different parts of the text.

SECTION B Listening

The listening section follows the topic theme introduced in the reading passage. The dialogues represent authentic settings such as:

- business meetings
- interviews
- training sessions
- telephone conversations
- presentations.

The comprehension questions and activities, some of which are presented to the learner before listening to the tape and some afterwards, are designed for:

- listening for detailed information
- listening for general ideas and themes
- creative engagement in the listening process.

This ability to listen critically is developed through questioning on such points as the role, attitude, and relationship of speakers.

SECTION C Language Study

This section focuses on specific language features which have been exemplified in Sections A and B.

SECTION D Listening

The aim of the second listening section is to consolidate the language work of the unit, though in a different business-specific setting. There are comprehension questions and activities designed to fulfil the same functions as in Section B. However, the emphasis is firmly on listening and therefore the dialogues from this section have not been reproduced in the coursebook.

SECTION E Using Information in Different Ways

The exercises in this section make use of the non-verbal devices which managers must frequently employ in their work such as graphs, charts, elementary networks, flow diagrams and tables. The purpose of the transfer exercises is to provide practice in handling relevant materials and to develop skills in ordering, grouping, classification and so on.

SECTION F Discussion

In each unit, a number of thought-provoking questions on management topics are presented in order that the learners will have the opportunity to bring their own experience and opinions to bear during discussion while practising newly-acquired language skills.

SECTION G Writing

The exercises in this section are designed to develop the learners' skill in making effective presentation of statements and factual information. Emphasis is placed on the ability to structure information by means of exercises based on:

- the sequencing, ordering and classifying of information
- linking devices for relating parts of the text and for providing continuity
- recognizing central information and supporting statements
- expanding notes
- building paragraphs.

The Revision Units

These units are designed to check that the structures and lexis of the five preceding units have been learned and can be used effectively.

4 Classroom Use

The course is designed for up to eighty hours of classroom work on the basis of fifteen main units at five hours each and the three revision units at an average of one and a half hours each. These timings do not represent any hard and fast rule as teachers will adapt the material to their own particular situation. For example, exercise work on writing, discussion and the preparation of the reading passage may be set for out-of-class activity and only the main difficulties brought to the classroom. On the other hand, where language laboratory or 'listening lab' facilities exist, teachers may feel that learners will benefit from longer practice with the taped dialogues of sections B and D.

The following notes on classroom procedures are intended only as a guide. Teachers will find it necessary to adapt to the particular needs of the students. It should be pointed out that students should do the exercises in their notebooks and not in the coursebook.

SECTION A Reading

Spend a few minutes orientating the students to the unit topic by asking questions about their knowledge or experience.

Ask the students to read through the passage silently twice and to use the Word Study notes to check on words they are unsure of. Provide individual assistance. Ask the students a few general questions based on the text. Discuss specific difficulties.

Ask the students to write down the answers to the comprehension questions. Check answers orally with the students. Use the board for answers in tabulated form.

Summarize orally with the students the main points of the passage.

SECTION B Listening

The symbol □ in the coursebook means 'switch off the tape and answer the questions that follow'. Get the students to answer the comprehension questions *while* they listen to the tape. Students should not read the dialogues at this stage. Discuss briefly the answers after the first run of the tape. Allow the students to listen again. Encourage students to listen to the complete dialogue and not small extracts. Discuss the answers. The post-tape questions should be attempted orally without further listening. Discuss the answers, then, where possible, allow the students to listen selectively to check their answers. Allow the students to read the dialogue for a check on understanding.

SECTION C Language Study

Introduce the language teaching points for each exercise, discuss difficulties and provide further exemplification where necessary. Ask the students to write down the answers to the questions and provide individual assistance. Check the answers orally with the students and discuss difficulties.

SECTION D Listening

The procedure is the same as in Section B except that there is no opportunity to read the dialogues in the coursebook.

SECTION E Using Information in Different Ways

Go over the questions with the students in order that they understand the task and the non-verbal devices involved. Ask the students to write down the answers. Provide individual help where required. Discuss the answers with the students, using the board to work through the answer.

SECTION F Discussion

Ask the students to prepare discussion notes, preferably as an out-of-class assignment. Individual students can be asked to prepare a brief introduction to begin the discussion.

Some of the discussion topics require experience and a detailed knowledge of the subject. Whereas this will not, generally, be a problem with practising managers, there will obviously be some topics that are too complex for management trainees. The teacher should use discretion in omitting topics that require specific expertise but should bear in mind that a good discussion can develop between trainees if they are encouraged to produce their own opinions and ideas.

SECTION G Writing

Go over the exemplification or model with the students and discuss any difficulties. Ask the students to write down their answers and provide individual assistance. Get the students to read out answers, and write the correct version on the board.

* The specification of a 'threshold' level of language proficiency was drawn up by Dr J. A. van Ek on behalf of an expert group convened by the Council for Cultural Co-operation of the Council of Europe. Strasbourg 1975.

Self Study Notes

1 Introduction

Intermediate level students can use this course for self-study without the help of a teacher.

The course is intended for practising managers, management trainees and business studies students who need to perform better in the reading, writing, listening and speaking of English for management or business purposes.

The introduction of new language in the course is organized so that you do not meet new words or language use without practice and explanation. The language work in the course is developed through subjects taken from personnel, production, marketing and finance.

2 Contents

There are eighteen units in the course: fifteen main units with tapes and three revision units after units five, ten and fifteen. Each main unit follows a subject such as Sales or Training, and has seven sections.

SECTION A Reading

This section gives practice in reading and understanding information. In the reading passages, there are examples of management reports, letters, magazine articles and company statements. There is a Word Study section which gives explanations of all the new words introduced in the reading passage. A comprehension section checks your understanding of the reading passage.

SECTIONS B & D Listening

These sections give practice in listening and understanding business conversations, meetings, telephone conversations and presentations. Comprehension questions test the understanding of information and that you have understood the ideas and opinions of the different speakers.

The dialogues for Listening B are in the coursebook but the dialogues for Listening D are not.

SECTION C Language Study

This section practises the important language work introduced in Sections A and B of each unit.

SECTION E Using Information in Different Ways

The exercises in this section make use of graphs, charts, flow diagrams, networks and tables in order to practise language work connected with management practice.

SECTION F Discussion

This section presents a number of questions on modern management subjects.

SECTION G Writing

The work in this section gives you practice in presenting written information. There are a number of different exercises which carefully build up your writing ability.

3 Study Guide

Answer all the questions in a notebook and not in the coursebook. Most of the answers to the exercises are in the Key at the end of the coursebook. The symbol △ in the Key means that the answer represents a 'model'. That is, it gives an example of the sort of answer that is required. In the Listening sections, the symbol □ means 'switch off the tape and answer the following questions.'

The Index at the back of the book gives all the words used in Manage With English that are above intermediate level.

The following notes are intended only as a guide to students.

SECTION A Reading

Read the passage without looking at the Word Study notes. Read the passage again and use the Word Study notes to check vocabulary. Answer the comprehension questions. Check the answers with the Key. When an answer is not correct, go back to the passage to make sure you understand the reason.

SECTION B Listening

Answer the questions *while* you are listening to the tape. Listen to the complete tape and do not read the dialogues in the coursebook. If necessary, listen through again. Check the answers with the Key. Listen to the tape again to check any incorrect answers. Where there is a further question after the symbol □, try to answer it without listening to the tape again. Check your answer with the Key and listen to the tape again to check any incorrect answers. Read the dialogue in the coursebook for a final check.

SECTION C Language Study

Do the exercises. Check your answers with the Key. Where the answers are incorrect, do the questions again without looking at the Key.

SECTION D Listening

The same as Section B, but there is no dialogue check in the coursebook.

SECTION E Using Information in Different Ways

Do the exercises. Check your answers with the Key. Where your answers are incorrect, do the exercise again without looking at the Key.

SECTION F Discussion

Make notes on the different questions. Try to think of the arguments on both sides.

SECTION G Writing

Do the exercises. Check your answers with the Key. Where your answers are not correct, do the exercise again without looking at the Key.

The Revision Units

Answer the questions in the same way as Section A and Section C.

Unit 1 Recruitment and Selection

SECTION A Reading

If you meet new words or expressions in the reading passages, first try to understand their meanings from the passage and the illustration. After that, look for them in the Word Study notes.

Read the following passage.

When there is a vacancy in a company, it is the job of the Personnel Manager and his department to manage the recruitment of a new employee. One way an organization can find staff for job vacancies is to recruit in-company. Management can inform people of new appointments by means of the firm's notice board or news bulletin. Another possibility is to ask for recommendations from departmental managers and supervisors. If it is necessary to recruit outside the company, the personnel department may use commercial and government employment offices or consultants. It may prefer to put its own advertisement in a newspaper or magazine.

It is usual for an advertisement to give a short description of the job, conditions of work and salary, and to invite introductory letters from applicants. After studying these, management decides who receives an application form.

In order to assess the applications, managers can work from a personnel specification such as Rodger's Seven-Point Plan. They do not choose applicants who do not have a good profile. For this reason, it is important that the application form requests clear information about such things as the applicant's age, education, qualifications and work experience. It must also ask for references from other employers or people who know the applicant well. This information helps management to make a final decision on the number of applicants they can short-list for interview.

The staff who hold an interview together are called an interview 'panel'. It is important that they know what information they need to get from the applicants. This comes from a careful reading of job descriptions, personnel specifications, and applications. To help the panel in their selection, some companies use an interview assessment form. This is used by the panel during the interview when each applicant is checked under the same point on the form.

Many employers say that the success of a good business begins in the Personnel Manager's office.

Word Study

Read these notes carefully. There is information here that may help you do some of the other exercises in this unit.

vacancy *line 1* If a company needs three secretaries, but has only two, then there is a vacancy for one secretary.

personnel *l.1* The employees of an organization are its personnel. Who are the employers?

recruitment *l.2* finding personnel for vacancies. The verb from this noun is *recruit.*

staff *l.3* personnel.

description *l.10* picture in words. Describe yourself by giving your age, colour of hair and eyes, height (cms) and weight (kgs).

conditions *l.11* Adrian works from 9am to 5.30pm, Monday to Friday, and on one Saturday in every month he must work from 10am until 12 noon. Those are two of his conditions of work.

applicants *l.12* If you want a job, you must *apply* for it; you must make an *application.* A person who applies for a job is known as a job applicant.

assess *l.14* Is the applicant the right age? Does he/she have the necessary education? Why does the applicant want to work for this company? The Personnel Manager assesses an application by asking questions of this sort.

specification *l.15* careful description of each necessary point. *Wanted: Typist. Seventy words per minute and some shorthand.* What are the specifications in that advertisement? Can you think of any other specifications for the same job?

profile *l.16* short description of an applicant's important points. The drawing below *illustrates* (= 'gives a picture of') another meaning of the word *profile*. What are the two meanings of the word *profile* that you see in the illustration?

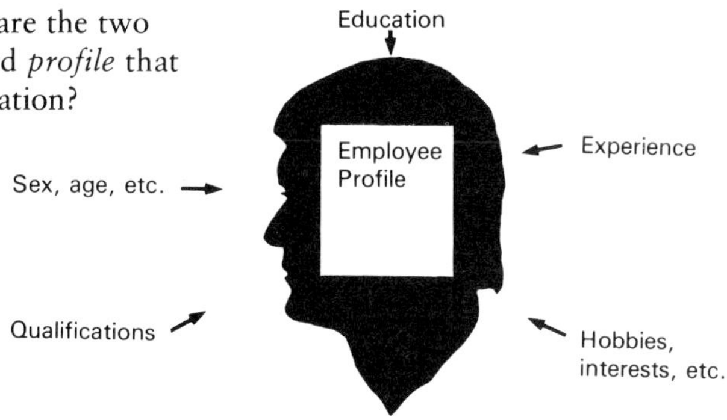

qualifications *l.18* In order to *qualify* for university, you must first finish high school. A high-school diploma is a qualification for entering university.
experience *l.18* Experience is what you get by living through something or by working at it.
references *l.19* Information about the past performance of an applicant.

Comprehension

The information for the exercises below can be either in the reading passage or in the Word Study notes.

1 Complete the table.

Job	*By means of*
a. Recruit staff in-company	1 Firm's notice board 2 . . . 3 . . .
b. Recruit staff outside of company	1 . . . 2 . . . 3 . . .
c. Assess applications	. . .
d. Check past performance of applicant	. . .
e. Assess performance during interview	. . .

2 'It may prefer to put . . .' *(l.8)* What does 'it' refer to?
▷ 'It' refers to the personnel department.

Now do the following in the same way.

a. 'After studying these . . .' *(l.12)* What does 'these' refer to?
b. '. . . that they know . . .' *(l.23)* What does 'they' refer to?
c. 'This comes from . . .' *(l.24)* What does 'this' refer to?
d. 'This is used . . .' *(l.26)* What does 'this' refer to?

3 What is Rodger's Seven-Point Plan?

4 What are the five points that the application form must request information about? Can you think of any more?

5 Complete the following table.

verb	*noun*	*verb*	*noun*
apply	application	specify	. . .
qualify	. . .	. . .	decision
. . .	assessment	. . .	description
refer	. . .	. . .	management
educate	. . .	recruit	. . .
. . .	information	select	. . .
advertise	. . .		

SECTION B Listening

In this section there are things for you to do while you are listening and also questions to answer after listening. This symbol □ at the end of the listening passage means 'switch off the tape and answer the question which follows'. Always try to listen to the tape without reading.

Cassette 1, side 1. While you are listening to the interview on the tape, complete the table below.

Name of applicant	References (very good/good/fair/bad)
Job applied for	
Education	Hobbies . . . .
Qualifications	Which Department is the applicant interested in? . . . .
Work experience (years)	Interviewed by: 1. . . . . 2. . . . .

Linda Excuse me, Mr. Lyle. Here's Mr. Frame to see you.
Lyle Thank you, Linda. Good morning, Mr. Frame. Please come in.
Frame Good morning, Mr. Lyle.
Lyle Please take a seat. May I introduce you to Mr. Coates here, our Training Manager.
Frame How do you do, Mr. Coates.
Coates Good morning, Mr. Frame. I hope you had a pleasant journey? No trouble finding us?
Frame No. No trouble at all, thanks.
Lyle That's fine. Now then, let's look at your application form. H'mm. Well, first of all, Mr. Frame, can you tell us why you want to train as a manager with us here at Galaxy Limited?
Frame It's um . . . it's a job I'm interested in, and I really want to work in industry, Mr. Lyle. And your company is one of the best known.
Coates You say it's a job you're interested in? What do you mean?
Frame Well, of course I have no experience as a manager, and I don't know very much about making chocolates. But the job description you sent me when I applied was very interesting. I mean, I decided I wanted a job like this when I was at university.
Lyle Yes, there's a note about it here. Let's see. That was three years ago. In London, wasn't it?
Frame That's correct. I finished there in 1978 and then I went to business school for two years.
Coates Where you passed your diploma?
Frame Yes. Just last month.
Lyle Well, certainly your references are very good, Mr. Frame. But you say you finished at business school only last month. Is this your first interview?
Frame No, this is my second. And I have two more this week.
Coates Are they all for this sort of job? Same sort of vacancy?
Frame Yes, they are. It's what I want to do for a living.
Lyle Excuse me. Come in? Ah, Linda. Coffee, is it?
Linda Tea, actually.
Coates Oh well, it's hot and wet, right?
Linda Right. Tea, Mr. Frame?
Frame Thank you, yes.
Linda Milk?
Frame Yes, please.
Lyle Thank you, Linda. We can manage from here.
Coates What subjects did you like most at business school?
Frame The work on personnel. I liked that the most, really.
Coates Can you explain why?
Frame I think it's because I like working with people. And I'm very interested in personnel recruitment and training.
Lyle Fine. And what about hobbies?
Frame I enjoy sport. I play football and tennis.
Coates Do you study at all?
Frame I go to evening classes for German lessons.
Lyle Well, I think that's all that Mr. Coates and I want to ask you for now. Is there anything that you want to ask us?
Frame Um . . . yes, there is. How long is the training? Is it a very long programme?
Coates It's a two-year programme. You work with a number of different managers during this time in a number of different offices. At the end of the two years we decide on the work that you're best at.
Frame I see. And what about conditions? Can you tell me anything about holidays and, um, things like that?
Lyle To start, there are four weeks of holiday a year. Then there is the firm's canteen, of course—
Coates —very good value for money, our canteen—
Lyle —and the starting salary for our Trainee Managers is between £4,500 and £5,500 a year. Your starting salary depends on your age, you see, and on your experience, qualifications, and so on.
Frame I understand.
Lyle Good. Is there anything else you want to ask us?
Frame No, I don't think so.
Lyle That's fine, then. Well, Mr. Frame, thank you very much for coming to see us. We hope to be able to let you know about the job in about two weeks . . .

☐ In your opinion, were there any more questions that the panel needed to ask the applicant in order to assess him?

SECTION C Language Study

1 Asking for Information

Examples:
You want to know if I can tell you about my experience.
▷ Can you tell me about your experience?

You want to know where he studied personnel management.
▷ Where did he study personnel management?

In the same way, make questions for the following:

a. You want to know if this is her first interview.

b. You want to know what I mean.

c. You want to know what subjects he liked the most at business school.

d. You want to know if I had a pleasant journey.

e. You want to know if I can explain why I like working with people.

f. You want to know if you may see my letters of reference.

g. You want to know who the Training Manager is.

h. You want to know what the starting salary depends on.

i. You want to know why Frame doesn't have any experience.

j. You want to know where he passed his diploma.

k. You want to know when the new job starts.

2 Nouns as Adjectives

Complete the following.

a. Manager of Personnel	Personnel Manager
b. vacancies for jobs	job vacancies
c. board for notices	. . .
d. forms for applications	. . .
e. experience of work	. . .
f. specification for personnel	. . .
g. plan containing seven points	. . .
h. panel for holding interviews	. . .
i. description of a job	. . .
j. diploma from high school	. . .

3 Ways of Doing Things

Example:
How can a Personnel Manager assess applicants? (interview)
▷ He can assess applicants **by** holding an interview.
or He can assess applicants **by means of** an interview.

Notice that both these answers give us the same information. Answer the following questions in a similar way.

a. How can a company find out about the past performance of an applicant? (references)

b. How can a company inform their staff about job vacancies? (staff bulletin)

c. How can a manager assess application forms? (personnel specification)

d. How can a manager check the performance of a person during an interview? (interview assessment form)

e. How can applicants describe themselves? (age, qualifications, experience)

4 Describing

Here, in short form, is the way one company recruits new staff.

(1) Meeting in personnel . . .
(2) Advertisements in newspapers . . .
(3) Letters from applicants . . .
(4) Application forms to applicants . . .
(5) Application forms checked . . .
(6) Letters to applicants . . .
(7) Interviews . . .
(8) Assessment . . .
(9) Information to interviewees . . .

We can describe the first two parts using the Passive form, like this:
(1) A management meeting **is held** in the personnel department.
(2) Advertisements for a job **are placed** in different newspapers.

Use the Passive form to complete the description.

SECTION D Listening

The conversations for Section D are on the tape; they are not given in the book. Remember, there are questions to answer while you are listening and this symbol □ means 'switch off the tape and answer the following question after listening'.

Cassette 1, side 1. While you are listening to the tape, write down the answers to questions 1–6.

1 What job did Tony apply for?

2 What was the name of the company?

3 What was the starting salary?

4 How long was the training programme?

5 How many weeks holiday were there a year?

6 What were the jobs of the two men on the interview panel?

□ How well did Tony think he performed at the interview?

SECTION E Using Information in Different Ways

1 Read the following paragraph.

Malcolm David Moore works for Litham Inc. as a Personnel Officer in their London factory, where he earns £5,280 a year. He lives near the firm at 22 Norfolk Road, W2. At the age of eleven he went to Holton High School. Then, at eighteen, he began a three-year course at the National Business School, where he received his Diploma in Business Studies. In 1977 he passed the Diploma in Personnel Management. This was in the same year that he left his first job, at Nathan's of London, to join Pinewood Ltd at £4,400 a year. He joined Litham in 1979 in order to get more experience. He was married last week on 24 February, the day after his twenty-ninth birthday. He plays table tennis and badminton. Two evenings a week he goes to evening classes to learn French and Spanish. He now intends to apply for a job as Assistant Personnel Manager.

2 Now complete the application form below, with the help of the information in the paragraph.

OMEGA INCORPORATED

Job application form

Application for the position of . . .

1.	Personal details	
1.1	Surname	Moore
1.2	Forename(s)	. . .
1.3	Date of birth	. . .
1.4	Married/Single	. . .
1.5	. . .	. . .
1.6	Telephone	01-635-3128

		From – To
2.	. . .	
2.1	. . .	1963 - 71
2.2	National Business School	. . .

3.	. . .	
3.1	. . .	1974
3.2	. . .	. . .

4.	Interests
4.1	. . .
4.2	. . .

5. . . .

	Employer	Job	Salary	Reason for leaving	Dates
5.1	. . .	Personnel Assistant	£3,750	More salary	. . .
5.2	. . .	Assistant Personnel Officer	. . .	. . .	. . .
5.3	. . .	. . .	. . .	. . .	. . .

Signature M D Moore

Date 22/3/81

SECTION F Discussion

Use the information in Sections A–E, and your own experience and opinions, to discuss the following.

1 Suppose that you have to recruit the following staff: a secretary, a personnel manager, a trainee manager, an office supervisor, a general labourer. Give your opinions about the best way to find staff for each of those jobs.

2 Say what you think about the advantages (=' good points') and the disadvantages (=' bad points') of using a personnel specification such as Rodger's.

3 Do you believe it is the job of the Personnel Manager to do *all* of the recruitment? Give reasons for your answer.

SECTION G Writing

1 Read this description of Steven Utley's work experience. Notice how the paragraph is built up from the information in the table.

First Steven Utley worked for Robertsons Ltd as a Personnel Assistant at £3,750 a year. He was with the company from 1974 to 1977. **Then** he joined Omega Operations, at £4,610 a year, where he stayed until 1979 in the position of Assistant Personnel Manager. He **now** works for Litho Inc as a Personnel Officer at an annual salary of £5,100.

Steven Utley	Robertsons Ltd	Personnel Assistant	£3,750	1974-77
	Omega Operations	Assistant Personnel Manager	£4,610	1977-79
	Litho Inc	Personnel Officer	£5,100	1979-
Judy Shepherd	Lloyds Bank	Clerk	£2,300	1972-74
	Barclays Bank	Typist	£2,575	1974-76
	Norwich Union	Secretary	£3,000	1977-
B L Davies	Kent Shoes	Shop Assistant	£2,175	1969-71
	Finewear (Leeds)	Assistant Manager	£3,200	1971-73
	Finewear (York)	Manager	£4,460	1974-77
David M Brown	Time Factor Chemicals	Clerk	£3,280	1977-79
	Boyce Chemicals	Accounts Clerk	£3,900	1979-80
	Chemical Engineers Inc	Head Clerk	£4,860	1980-

2 Now write similar paragraphs about Judy Shepherd, B. L. Davies, and David M. Brown. These words may help you: **first, then, now, next, later on, afterwards, following that.**

Unit 2 Training

SECTION A Reading

Remember to try to understand the meaning of new words or expressions before looking in the Word Study notes.

Read the following passage.

Training must have a purpose, which is defined when a firm analyses its training needs. A review of manpower planning should include a training analysis which looks carefully at training from the point of view of the company, its various departments and personnel. This may show that weaknesses exist in some departments and that, as a result, training is needed for their staff. Training needs are based on an analysis of job descriptions and job specifications.

A job description should give details of the performance that is required for a specific job, and a job specification should give information about the behaviour, knowledge and skills that are expected of an employee who works in it. When all of this has been collected, it is possible to make a training specification. This specifies what the Training Department must teach for the successful performance of the job, and also the best methods to use in the training period.

'On the job' training

'Off the job' learning

There are many different training methods, and there are advantages and disadvantages to all of them. Successful training programmes depend on an understanding of the difference between learning about skills and training in using them. It is frequently said that learning about skills takes place 'off the job', in the classroom; but training in using those skills takes place 'on the job', by means of such activities as job rotation and planned experience.

It is always difficult to evaluate the costs and savings of a training programme. The success of such a programme depends not only on the methods used but also on the quality of the staff who do the training. A company can often check on savings in time and cost by examining the manual work performed by operators and technicians who have completed a training programme. The evaluation of management and supervisory training is much more complex than that. In order to test the results of management and supervisory training, many companies have looked at such things as the number of management and supervisory staff who leave their employment and the number who stay away from work for reasons of health.

Word Study

Remember that there is information here that may help you to do some of the other exercises in this Unit.

defined *l.1* described exactly. The noun from this verb is *definition.* Look up the definition of *analysis* in your dictionary.

analyses *l.1* examines and describes the different parts of. The noun is *analysis. Canpan has a staff of 62.* An analysis of that sentence shows the subject *(Canpan),* the verb *(has)* and the object *(a staff of 62).*

manpower planning *l.2* planning for the number of staff needed.

details *l.8* small items (= 'pieces') of information that work together to give a clear, complete picture. Look back at the definition of the word *description* in Unit 1. What details are asked for?

required *l.8* needed; necessary. The noun is *requirement.*

behaviour *l.10* acting, reacting or doing things in a certain way. How does water behave when it is heated to 100°C? How do some employees change their behaviour in the office if the boss is away?

skills *l.10* special abilities. A *skillful* labourer does excellent work and makes very few mistakes.

methods *l.13* ways of doing things. Describe the methods for making copies that are shown in the illustrations below.

carbon paper

spirit duplicator

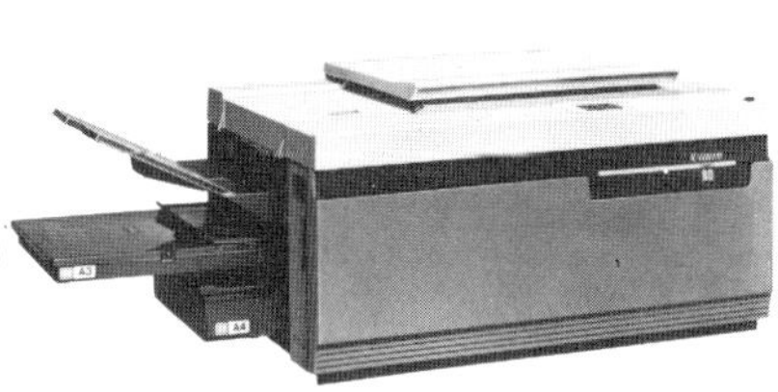
dry copier

job rotation *l.20* moving workers around (= 'rotating them') from one job to another, to widen their experience. The verb *rotate* means 'move around and around'.

planned experience *l.20* You studied the word *experience* in Unit 1. Now say what you think the difference is between *planned experience* and *natural experience.*

to evaluate *l.21* *value* of a thing in money or goods = 'market price'. To evaluate something is to find what a thing is worth not only in money but also in quality, time spent, importance to the company, etc.

complex *l.27* not simple; made up of many related parts, so that much study is needed in order to understand it.

Comprehension

1 Complete the diagram.

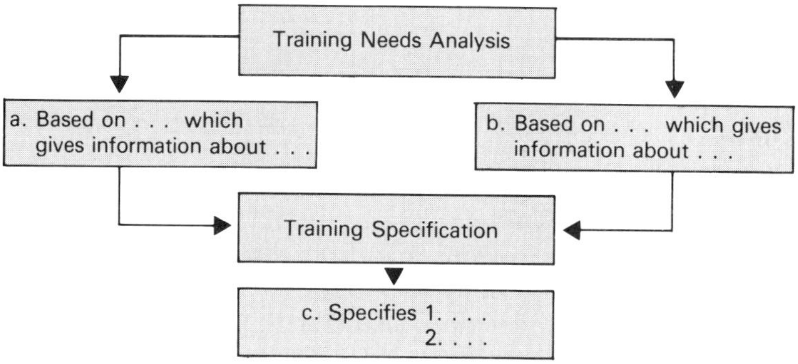

2 '**This** may show . . .'*(l.4)* ▷ **This** refers to the analysis.
a. '. . . who works in **it**.' *(l.10)* ▷ **It** refers to . . .
b. 'When all of **this** . . .' *(l.11)* ▷ **This** refers to . . .
c. '**This** specifies . . .' *(l.12)* ▷ **This** refers to . . .
d. '. . . all of **them**.' *(l.16)* ▷ **Them** refers to . . .
e. '. . . in using **them**.' *(l.17)* ▷ **Them** refers to . . .
f. '. . . than **that**.' *(l.27)* ▷ **That** refers to . . .

3 Explain the difference between 'learning about skills' and 'training in using them'.

4 How can a company evaluate the savings of a training programme?

5 Complete the following table.

verb	*noun*	*verb*	*noun*
define	. . .	. . .	behaviour
analyse	. . .	rotate	. . .
weaken	. . .	. . .	evaluation
perform	. . .	succeed	. . .
. . .	requirement	. . .	employment
. . .	knowledge		

SECTION B Listening

Cassette 1, side 1. Listen to the conversation between Mr. Bates, the Personnel Manager, Mr. Brian Dunn, the Training Manager, and Mr. John Hart, the Management Training Officer. While you are listening to the tape, tick (✓) the correct reasons in the table below.

Trainees did not like the training course for the following reasons:

a. The jobs were very difficult.	...	**f.** There were too many examinations.	...
b. The course was too long.	...	**g.** The course was not well planned.	...
c. The pay was too low.	...	**h.** They had too much responsibility.	...
d. The method of job rotation did not work.	...		
e. The jobs were not interesting.	...		

Bates Well then, gentlemen, are we ready to start? Fine. I'd like to begin with this last course for trainee managers. How did the final interviews go? Brian?

Dunn From the point of view of the trainees, Mr. Bates, not so well. They felt a number of things were wrong with the programme.

Bates What sort of things?

Dunn I suppose the first thing was that two years was too long. And second, they felt they weren't in a real job. I mean they felt they had no real responsibilities during their training.

Bates Perhaps, but I've heard the same thing from trainees for the last twenty years.

Hart Almost all of the trainees on this course felt the same, Mr. Bates.

Dunn And a number of other interesting points were made, too.

Bates Such as?

Dunn For example, they didn't like the method of job rotation in the first eighteen months.

Bates Why not?

Dunn They felt that they received no planned teaching or instruction. There were too many simple manual jobs to do . . . not enough training in skills or knowledge.

Bates That may be true, but trainees always want to run before they can walk. They think they should manage the place in their first year with us. Don't you agree, John?

Hart I know that many of our trainees have thought like that. But I think some of the present points are important. Much of the work given to our trainees is not very interesting.

Bates Anything else?

Hart Yes. They thought that our department should plan their training with them, from the beginning.

Bates I see. And if I'm right, you both agree with the trainees.

Dunn Up to a point, Mr. Bates. I think we should have a careful look at our training methods.

Hart I think I agree with Brian. There are many departmental managers and supervisors who have said the same.

Dunn And we know that many of our trainees have left the company a short time after the end of their training.

Bates Yes, I know that. And I agree it's an important point. So. Where do we go from here? Do you want to make specific recommendations?

Hart I think we should have a review of our training managers' programme.

Bates That's a big job. Are you sure of the weaknesses in our present programme?

Hart I think so, yes. And in my view, we should discuss them now.

Bates What about you, Brian?

Dunn I go along with John, Mr Bates.

Bates Very well, let's talk about it. But we must remember, gentlemen, that Wrights are here, first of all, to make lifts, not just to educate management trainees.

Hart Of course. I'm sure we all agree about that.

Bates Good. So. Where do you want to start?

Dunn Can we define the problem? Then, perhaps, we can go away and give it more thought.

Bates All right, Brian.

Dunn It seems to me that the real problem is our programme of job rotation. It just doesn't work.

Bates Fine, that's one thing we need to look at. Now what else do you think we should examine?

Dunn I think we should look carefully at reserving some management jobs for the trainees. These are real jobs, and this sort of rotation can give real supervisory experience.

Bates If you can find the right sort of jobs. And we mustn't forget that the other staff in a department don't like it very much when certain jobs are reserved for trainees.

Dunn You've got a point there. That is a problem.

Hart What about thinking of the trainees as assistants to existing managers? That way they can get experience of many different jobs, and at the same time they can practise real management skills.

Dunn The problem there is that the existing managers may be no good as teachers and trainers. Or they just, um, may not like to have trainees for assistants all the time.

Bates Of course, Brian, but there's no training method that I know of that doesn't have its disadvantages. Now this is what I want . . . by next week . . . a complete analysis of our present methods, together with your recommendations for any changes that you think may be necessary. Can you get that ready for me?

Hart All right, Mr. Bates.

Dunn Fine.

Bates Now, let's see what's next here for today . . .

☐ In the opinion of the speakers, what is the most important problem with present training methods?

SECTION C Language Study

1 Sentence Links

Notice how we can *link* these two sentences by using **not only** and **but also:**

(1) The success of such a programme does not depend just on the methods used. (2) It also depends on the quality of the staff who do the training.

▷ The success of such a programme depends **not only** on the methods used **but also** on the quality of the staff who do the training.

In the same way, link the following pairs of sentences.

a. (1) To evaluate something is not just to find what a thing is worth in money. (2) It is also to find what a thing is worth in quality, time spent, importance to the company, etc.

b. (1) Companies must not look just at the number of management and supervisory staff who leave their employment. (2) They must also look at the number who are absent from work for reasons of health.

c. (1) Wrights are in business not just to educate management trainees. (2) They are also in business to make lifts.

2 Present and Past Time

Notice how it is necessary to change the verbs from the Present Perfect tense to the Simple Past tense when **exact past time** is used in the following sentences.

I have heard about the training problem.
I heard about the training problem **yesterday.**

She has seen the report.
She saw the report **a week ago.**

Examples:
Have you seen the assessment forms? (yes/yesterday)
▷ Yes, I have. I saw them yesterday.

Yes, he has. He completed it last week. (training programme)
▷ Has he completed the training programme?

Complete the following questions and answers in a similar way.

a. Has he assessed the new application forms? (yes/last week)

b. Have you received the recommendations from the Personnel Department? (yes/yesterday)

c. Yes, I have. I applied for it two days ago. (the job of Training Officer)

d. Yes, we have. We sent them to the trainees last week. (letters)

e. Have you recruited a new Training Manager? (yes/in week 34)

3 Completed Actions

Compare the two pictures of the office below. In the second picture, notice how many things have been done.

Example:
desk drawer (shut)
The desk door **has been shut.**

We are interested in **what has been done** and not in the person who was responsible. It is not necessary to know exactly who shut the drawer.

Use the Passive form to make more sentences comparing the *before* and *after* pictures.

Before

After

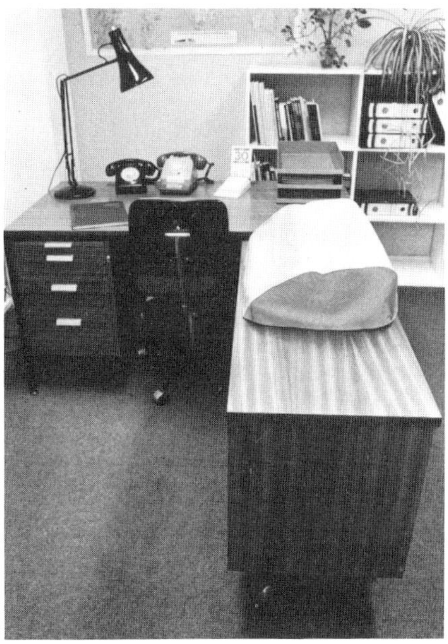

4 Advice and Necessity

a. Look up the words 'advice' and 'wise' in your dictionary.

b. In this unit, **should** is used to express advice, to make a recommendation, or to show that it may be wise to do a certain thing. **Must** is used to express the necessity or importance of doing something.

c. **Should** and **must** have been used a number of times in Sections A and B. Find examples of the uses of **should** and **must** and say what ideas you think are expressed by each one. Give your reasons.

SECTION D Listening

Cassette 1, side 1. While you are listening to the conversation between Robert Lutz and Stan Jacobs, use the table below to show whether they agree or disagree about their management training course.

Subject	*Agree* (✓)	*Disagree* (✓)
a. The training in the personnel department		
b. The responsibilities given to trainees		
c. The length of the training course		
d. The interest of the jobs given to trainees		
e. The quality of the trainers		

SECTION E Using Information in Different Ways

1 Read this description of a training programme.

After the behaviour, knowledge and skills of its staff have been analysed in order to define training needs, a company should look at the performance of personnel and the performance that is required for each job. From this information, it is possible to make a training plan. Next, there are several things to specify. The Training Department must decide where the training is done and who does it. The same department must also decide which training methods are used and the timing of the training programme. Following these decisions, it is necessary to collect materials for the courses. Afterwards, when the courses have been completed, the trainees are tested to find out what they have learnt. Finally, the Training Department should evaluate the training programme.

2 Now complete the following diagram with the help of the information in the description on the previous page.

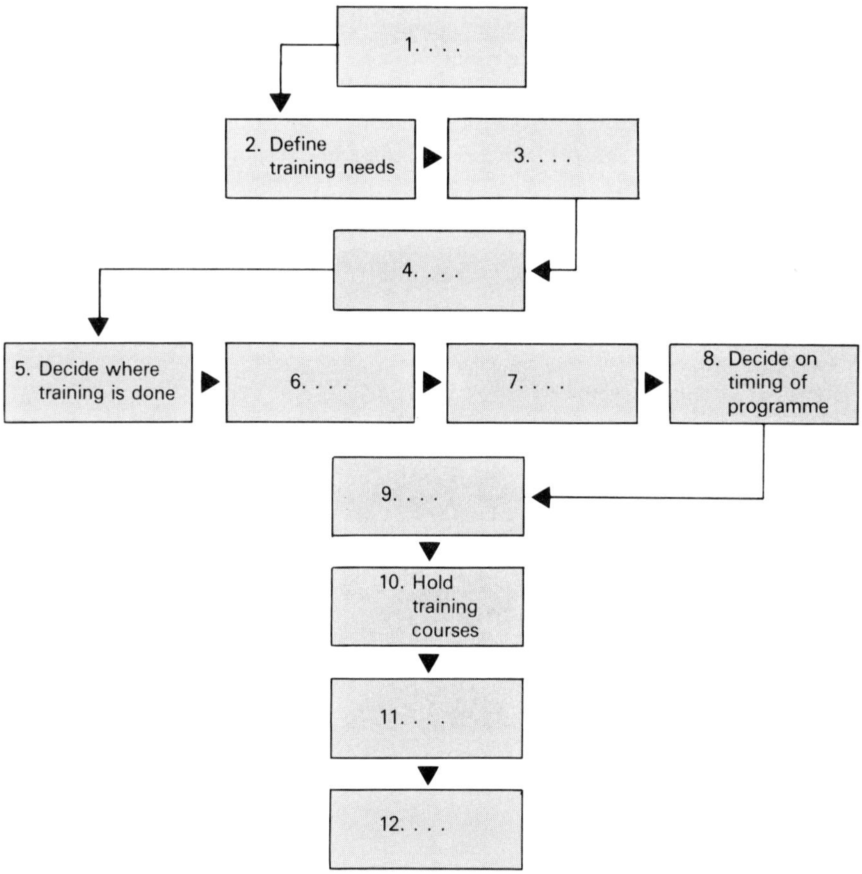

SECTION F Discussion

Use the information in Sections A-E, and your own experience and opinions, to discuss the following.

1 Job rotation is sometimes used as a means of training managers. What are the advantages and disadvantages of this method?

2 Discuss the ways in which we can evaluate management training.

3 Some firms prefer to recruit staff who have received their training in other companies. Is this a good idea?

SECTION G Writing

1 Read this description of Wrights' training programme. Notice how the paragraph is built up from the information in the diagram.

In order to complete Wrights' Management Training Programme, the trainees must **first** follow a one month's introduction course. **Then** they take a three month's general course on management skills. **Next,** the technical trainees go **either** to the Production Department **or** to the Research Department. Non-technical trainees go **either** to Personnel **or** to Marketing. **At the end of** one year, all trainees take a one month's course at the Management Training Centre **before** completing the programme.

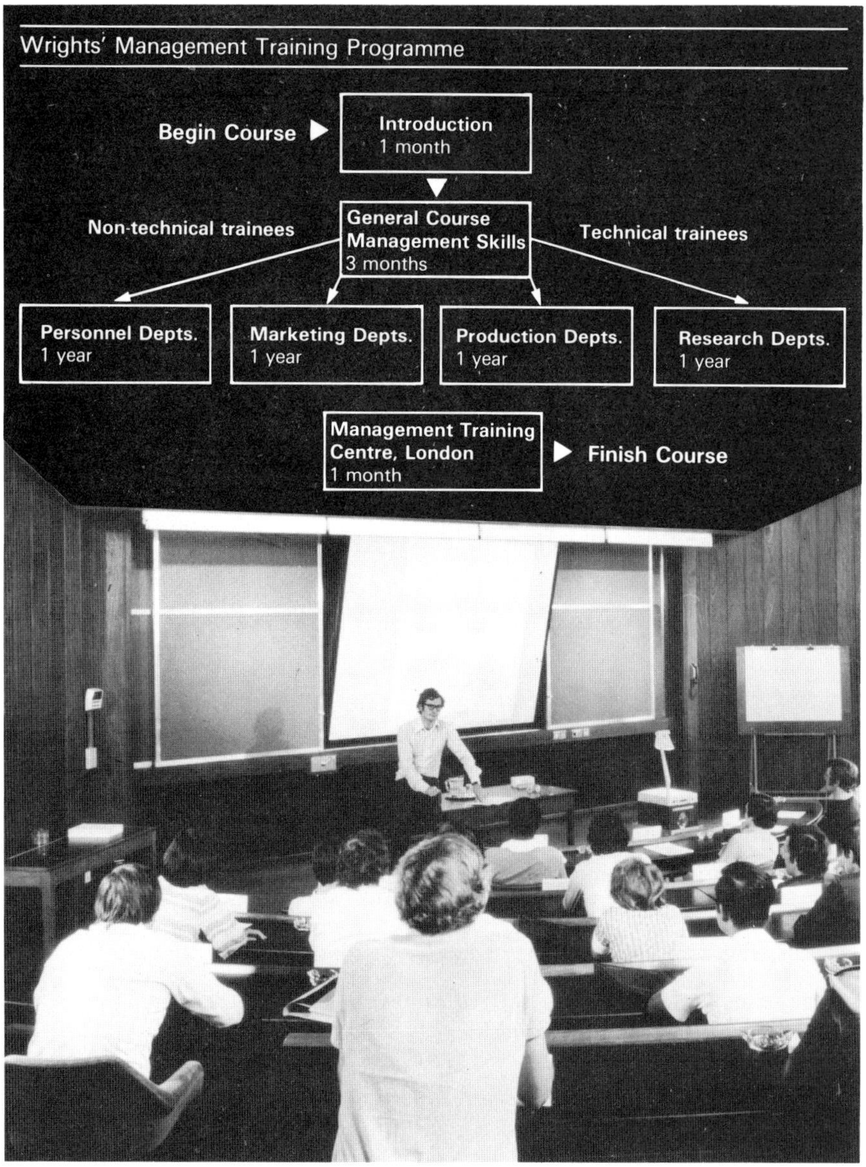

2 Now write a similar description of Lawson's recruitment procedure. In addition to the words you practised in Section G of Unit 1, these words may help you: **in order to/to, either . . . or, at the end of, before.**

Lawson's Recruitment Procedure

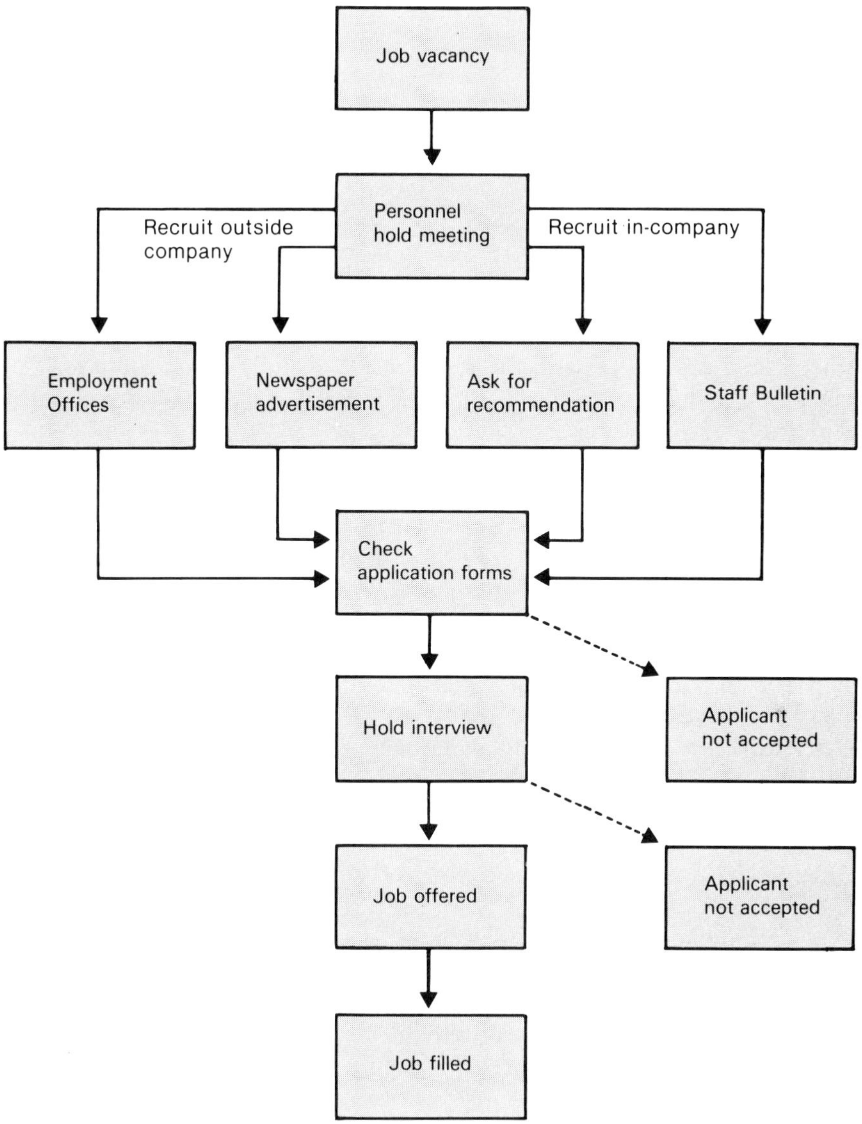

Unit 3 Wages and Salaries

SECTION A Reading

Read the following passage.

The organization and administration of wages and salaries is complex and varied. In some companies, the Personnel Department has more responsibility for wages and salaries than the Accounts Department. In others, the Accounts Department is responsible for calculations of pay, while the Personnel Department is more interested in negotiations with staff about pay.

If a firm wants to introduce a new wage and salary structure, it will have to decide on a method of job evaluation and ways of measuring the performance of its employees. In order to be successful, that pay structure will need agreement between Trade Unions and management or a clearly defined system for dealing with problems.

In job evaluation, all of the requirements of each job are specified in a detailed job description. Each of these requirements is given a value, usually in 'points' or 'factors', which are added together to give a total value for the job. To pay each job what it is worth, the values are linked to the firm's salary structure. For middle and higher management, a well-known points method is the Hay System. This evaluates personnel on their knowledge of the job, their responsibility, and their ability to solve problems. Because of the difficulty in measuring administrative work, however, job grades there are often decided without reference to an evaluation system based on points or factors.

In attempting to reach a salaries policy, the Personnel Department should compare the value of each job with those in the job market. It should also analyse economic factors such as the cost of living and the labour supply.

It is said that payment for a job should vary with any differences in the way that job is performed. Where it is simple to measure the work done, as in manual work, monetary incentive schemes and merit awards are often selected. For indirect workers, where measurement is difficult, methods of additional payments include bonus schemes based on the performance of the company.

Non-financial incentive schemes are becoming more popular for all grades of staff. Fringe benefits such as sickness and pension schemes, sports clubs, housing and canteens are all an accepted part of the conditions of work.

Word Study

varied *l.2* of different kinds; not of the same type. Wages and salaries vary from company to company.
calculations *l.4* using mathematics to find correct quantities and amounts. The verb is *calculate*. To calculate a worker's wages, multiply the number of hours worked (eg., 40) by the rate for the job (eg, £3.00 per hour) = 40 × £3.00 = £120.00.
negotiations *l.5* discussions which try to reach agreement on difficult points.
structure *l.7* way in which all of the parts are put together.
measuring *l.8* evaluating; finding out the quality, quantity (= 'amount') or importance.
system *l.11* method or plan for linking different parts, or for measuring and evaluating them. What is the metric (SI) system?
dealing with *l.11* working with a problem or question in order to find an answer.
factors *l.14* values (eg, factor of 1, factor of 2, etc.) which a company places on each requirement.
to solve *l.18* to make clear; to find an explanation or an answer for. The noun is *solution*.
grades *l.19* steps or degrees (eg, Grade I, Grade II, etc.) which show how jobs vary in importance, value to the company, etc.
attempting *l.22* trying
policy *l.22* special method of action to help in making decisions.
supply *l.24* any quantity of anything which is available for use. The verb is also *supply*. What is meant by the *law of supply and demand*?
monetary *l.27* This is the adjective from *money*.
incentive schemes *l.27* plans or systems which offer workers more in the week or the month in which they produce more.
merit awards *l.27* increases in wages or salaries that are especially given (= 'awarded') as job performance becomes better.
bonus *l.29* any payment to a worker in addition to his or her required wages, salary or holidays. What is a Christmas bonus?
fringe benefits *l.32* valuable things, eg, free housing, company cars, given to employees in addition to their wages, salaries and holidays.
pension *l.32* weekly or monthly payments by an employer or government for past service. Ordinarily, workers receive pensions when they retire (= 'leave their jobs because of age or after a certain length of service').

Comprehension

1 Complete the table.

Financial Incentives	*Non-financial Incentives*
. . .	sickness schemes
. . .	. . .
. . . etc.	. . . etc.

2 What does each of the words in **bold face** refer to?
a. 'In **others** . . .' *(l.3)*
b. '. . . **it** will have to decide . . .' *(l.7)*
c. '. . . **which** are added together . . .' *(l.14)*
d. '**This** evaluates . . .' *(l.17)*
e. '. . . job grades **there** . . .' *(l.19)*
f. '**It** should also . . .' *(l.23)*

3 Explain the difference between an incentive, a bonus, and a merit award.

4 How are job 'factors' calculated?

5 How does the Hay System calculate its job 'points'?

6 Explain the difference between a 'direct' and an 'indirect' worker. For which of those workers is it more difficult to calculate their output and salary or wage? Why?

7 Two workers doing exactly the same job may not receive the same wages or salary. Why not?

8 Complete the following table.

verb	*noun*	*adjective*
vary	variety	varied/various
. . .	. . .	negotiable
calculate	. . .	calculable
benefit	. . .	beneficial
. . .	. . .	soluble
pension off	. . .	pensionable
. . .	measurement	measurable
. . .	. . .	agreeable

SECTION B Listening

Cassette 1, side 1. While you are listening to the conversation between Mr. Renard and Mr. Larsen, note down the answers to the following questions.

1 What do you think is Mr. Larsen's job?

2 When was the company bought by Dillon International?

3 How many people does the company employ at the moment?

4 How many people does the company expect to employ by the end of the year?

5 About how long will Mr. Larsen take to review the wage and salary structure?

6 About how long will it take for a new salary system to operate well?

Renard As you know, Mr. Larsen, the reason we've called you in is to advise us on this question of our wages and salary structure.
Larsen Right. Tell me then, Mr. Renard, what kinds of problems are you experiencing at the moment?
Renard All kinds. I'm afraid there's no clear policy at all. We're very disorganized.
Larsen Can you be more specific?
Renard Yes. For example, because we have no system of job evaluation, it's becoming more and more difficult to assess the value of new jobs.
Larsen Have your employees expressed dissatisfaction about this?
Renard They most certainly have, yes. Many of our staff feel they are paid lower than others who do the same kind of work.
Larsen Is this happening a lot?
Renard More and more.
Larsen Can you tell me something about the history of the company?
Renard Yes, five years ago we were a medium-sized pharmaceutical company. Then in 1976 we were bought by Dillon International. Since then, the company has grown very quickly—
Larsen —and not changed its administration to deal with this growth.
Renard Exactly.
Larsen What is the company going to do?
Renard First, we're going to review the salary structure and pay policy. Then we're going to make the necessary changes—
Larsen —which means introducing a system of job evaluation.
Renard Yes. And it's here that we will require your advice. After you've had time to examine the different departments, we will want your recommendations on the best methods to apply.
Larsen How many employees are there in the company?
Renard Seven hundred and fifty.
Larsen And last year?
Renard About six hundred.
Larsen Does the company expect to grow as quickly this year as it did last year?
Renard Our manpower planning is based on a staff of eight hundred by the end of this year.
Larsen Are there detailed job descriptions in existence?
Renard Not for every job. And for new jobs, we're writing descriptions now. A lot of this work is made easier by using Dillon's experience.
Larsen How are these job descriptions written?
Renard They're done in consultation with our department and the various staff representatives.
Larsen Good. That will make my job easier.
Renard How long do you think you will need?
Larsen I'll be able to have some recommendations for you in about three weeks.
Renard That's excellent. Now that we have decided to make changes, we are in a hurry.
Larsen I should say that the review will not take very long, but in my experience you must allow time for the introduction of any new scheme. There will always be problems.
Renard What kind of problems?
Larsen Let me explain. After we have completed our analysis, I'm sure that we will find many employees who are receiving higher salaries than we think they should—
Renard —and others less.
Larsen Right. Now, I don't have to tell you what this will mean.
Renard We can't take money away from people.
Larsen Nor can you give a lot more to some and not to others.
Renard What will this mean in practice?
Larsen Well, we have to accept that the system will take a few years before it operates the way we want it to. Secondly, after we have introduced the system we must be careful to supervise the way it is working and to review it from time to time.
Renard Fine, Mr. Larsen, I'll remember that. Now, where would you like to start?

☐ Why do the employees feel dissatisfied about wages and salaries?

SECTION C Language Study

1 Plans, Intentions, Possibilities

Study the Personnel Manager's diary below.

Week 24	Plans	Intentions	Possibilities
Monday	Meeting: 10.00 Jones – Training Mngr.	Assessment of applications	See Supply Officer: new desks
Tuesday	Interview: 09.00 Trainee Mngr.	Letters to job applicants	Check progress of job evaluation
Wednesday	Admin: all morning Monthly Report	Visit Safety Officer	Meet Bob for lunch
Thursday	Visit: 11.00 Business Exhibition	Telephone for references	Prepare for wage negotiations
Friday	Lunch: 13.00 Personnel Director	Evaluation of training course	Write to Employment Office

Example:
At ten o'clock on Monday **I am meeting** Mr. Jones, the new Training Manager. During the afternoon, **I am going to assess** the latest application forms and perhaps, if there is time, **I will see** the Supply Officer about the new desks.

Notice how the Present Continuous is used for appointments or fixed plans, the 'Going to' form for intentions, and the Simple Future for possibilities.

Now write similar sentences to describe Tuesday-Friday.

2 Comparing

Study the graph below.

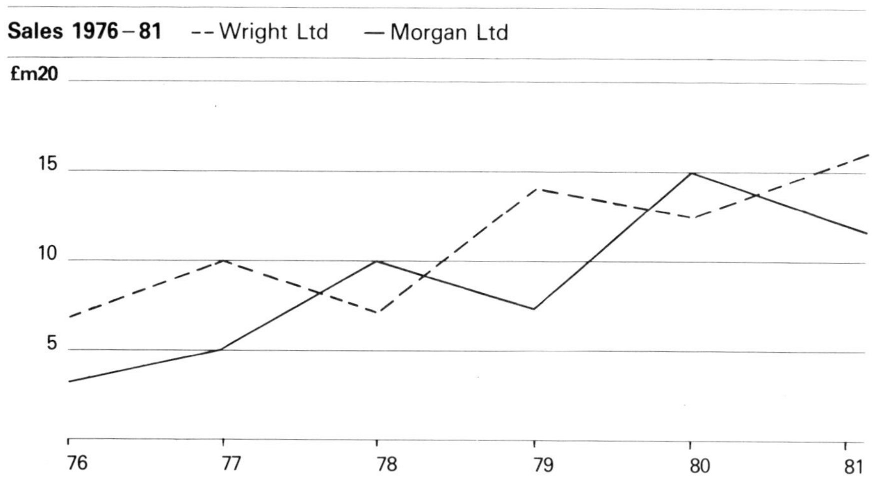

Example:
In 1978, the sales of Morgan Ltd. were **better than** the sales of Wright's. / In 1978, the sales of Wright Ltd. were **worse than** Morgan's. / In 1978, the sales of Wright Ltd. were **not so good as** Morgan's.

Notice that these three sentences give us the same information . Now write similar sentences to compare the other years on the graph.

3 Prepositions

Choose from the following prepositions to complete the paragraphs below: **on, in, for, to, with, without, between.**

If a firm wants to introduce a new wage and salary structure, it will have to decide . . . a method . . . job evaluation and ways . . . measuring the performance . . . its employees. . . . order to be successful, that pay structure will need agreement . . . Trade Unions and management or a clearly defined system . . . dealing . . . problems.

. . . job evaluation, all . . . the requirements . . . each job are specified . . . a detailed job description. Each . . . these requirements is given a value, usually . . . 'points' or 'factors', which are added together to give a total value . . . the job. To pay each job what it is worth, the values are linked . . . the firm's salary structure. . . . middle and higher management, a well-known points method is the Hay System. This evaluates personnel . . . their knowledge . . . the job, their responsibility, and their ability to solve problems. Because . . . the difficulty . . . measuring administrative work, however, job grades there are often decided . . . reference . . . an evaluation system based . . . points or factors.

SECTION D Listening

Cassette 1, side 1. While you are listening to the conversation between Ken Rill, a Personnel Manager, and Dennis Murray, an Assistant Personnel Manager, complete the diagram below.

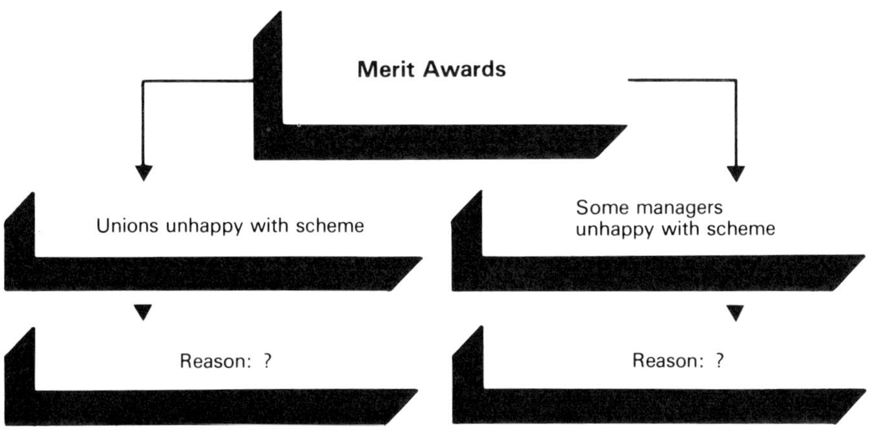

SECTION E Using information in Different Ways

1 Read this description of the grading system at Zirmart Limited.

As a result of job evaluations at Zirmart Limited, the Personnel Department has defined three types of staff and has named them Grades I, II and III. Grade I is used for Zirmart's factory workers and is divided into two categories: (1) skilled workers, such as machine operators, and (2) unskilled workers, such as labourers. Grade II refers to Zirmart's indirects, and here there is a division between supervisory and non-supervisory staff. For the management, the system is more complex, with four sub-grades in Grade III itself. For example, a Personnel Assistant is Grade III(A), and a Production Manager is Grade III(D).

Salaries for Grade I workers range from a minimum of £2,950 (for a labourer) to a maximum of £5,200. The lowest earnings in the company go to the canteen assistants, in Grade II, and these are £2,200. The highest (except for the Directors' salaries, which are not graded) are £12,500.

2 Now complete the following diagram with the help of the information in the description above.

Job Grading at Zirmart Limited

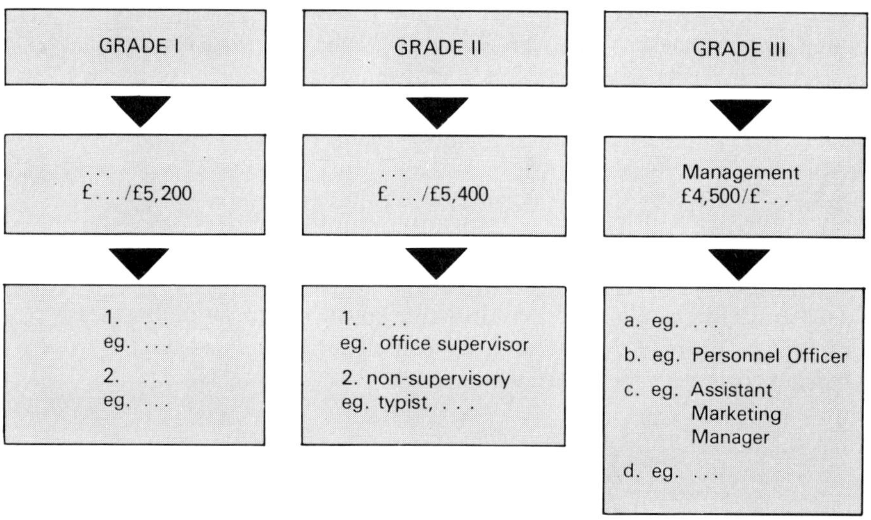

SECTION F Discussion

1 Do you agree that any incentive scheme will only be useful for a limited period of time? Give your reasons.

2 Discuss the problems of evaluating management jobs.

3 What kinds of problems will a company meet when it introduces a job-evaluation system for the first time?

SECTION G Writing

1 Study the following table, which describes some important moments in the history of Lind Incorporated.

The Lind Corporation

Company founded (100 employees)	1910	Produces motor-car parts
	1920	Becomes public company
Production line automated Staff at Lind now 500	1925	
	1931-38	Develops heavy lorries and farm machinery
(Second World War) Produces tanks and aeroplane parts Production and staff greatly increase	1939-45	
	1947	Buys Airframe Ltd, manufacturers of light aeroplanes
Builds 3 new factories, 1 of them in France	1948-56	
	1958	Profits reach £20 million
Unsuccessful export policy	1960-62	
	1963	Profits fall to £8 million
Bought by Runcorn Industries	1964	

2 Complete the following paragraph, basing your work on the information in the table above.

The Lind Corporation was founded in 1910 in order to produce parts for motor cars. In 1920 it became a public company, and five years later its production line was automated. During the company's first fifteen years of operation, the number of employees increased from one hundred to five hundred. Between 1931 and 1938, . . .

Unit 4 Administration

SECTION A Reading

Read the following passage

The function of the office is to perform administrative work. First, it must provide the necessary communications with customers, banks, government departments, and other outside organizations. Second, it must service the information requirements within the company itself. In order to meet these needs efficiently, the Office Manager must employ the most appropriate business methods, systems and equipment.

In an efficient administrative structure, clerical operations are organized so that they add to the profitability of the business. However, in many countries the number of clerical staff has increased while the total of workers employed in production has fallen. In Britain, for example, the total workforce in the years 1919-1976 went up by 25%, while the number of people who were employed in clerical work increased by 150%. For a country such as Britain, which depends on a manufacturing base, that can mean inefficiency.

To ensure that office services run smoothly, there must be the means to check, sort, copy and file correspondence and other paperwork. Today there is a growing range of machines that can be used to do such jobs. The size and resources of a company will determine how mechanized or computerized its office systems are.

The office must give maximum service at minimum cost. A balance must be kept between production, marketing, and administration. As a company develops and grows, the contribution of administration will vary in kind and in value.

The most important objective in modern offices is the processing of data in order to provide a means of business control, but in many companies there are weaknesses in the ability to manage communications efficiently. For example, some data are often used only by individual managers, and different departments in the same company may use different data processing systems. In order to contribute to business efficiency, however, data processing must be a centralized service. The system which is required is one that looks at the total needs of a business and therefore assists management in making appropriate decisions quickly.

Word Study

function *l.1* special duty (= 'necessary action in a job or position') which is required in the performance of work, activity, etc. What is the function of the office? Does the word *office* here refer to rooms and furniture or to personnel?
communications *l.2* information sent out and received.
efficiently *l.5* An *efficient* system produces maximum output for minimum input. *Efficiency* is output divided by input.
appropriate *l.5* having the special qualities required; right; fit; suitable.
equipment *l.6* necessary things, such as machines, furniture and supplies, for doing a job.
clerical *l.7* This is the adjective from *clerk*.
workforce *l.11* number of people in work.
sort *l.16* put into groups according to kind or type.
copy *l.16* make another or others of the same. What is carbon paper used for? What does the abbreviation *cc* at the bottom of a business letter stand for?
range *l.17* line of similar things to choose from.
resources *l.18* plant, personnel, equipment, money and property which can be employed usefully.
will determine *l.18* will set limits to.
mechanized *l.18* given to machines to perform.
computerized *l.19* given to computers to perform. A computer is an electronic machine which performs calculations by means of stored instructions or information.
balance *l.20* equal weight or importance.
contribution *l.22* amount of useful or valuable input.
objective *l.24* intended result of activity.
processing *l.24* preparing by a special method.
data *l.24* things which are known; facts (= 'true statements'), figures, items of information, etc. The singular form, *datum*, is not often used.
individual *l.27* working alone, without referring to others.

Comprehension

1 Complete the table.

a. Office manager must employ most appropriate business system	*in order to*	. . .
b. There must be means to check, sort, copy and file correspondence	*in order to*	. . .
c. Data processing must be centralized service	*in order to*	. . .
d. Manager must have processing of data as most important objective	*in order to*	provide means of business control

2 What do the words in **bold face** refer to?

a. '. . . **it** must provide . . .' *(l.1)*
b. '. . . **these needs** . . .' *(l.4)*
c. '. . . so that **they** add . . . *(l.8)*
d. '. . . **that** can mean inefficiency . . .' *(l.13)*
e. '. . . to do **such jobs** . . .' *(l.17)*
f. '. . . **one** that looks . . .' *(l.31)*

3 Define *efficiency*. How can an office manager measure the efficiency of his staff?

4 Does an increase in the number of people employed in clerical work in a country necessarily mean inefficiency? Why?

5 What is the function of the office manager?

6 In what way are some companies inefficient in managing communications?

7 What sets limits to the degree of mechanization or computerization in a company's office systems?

8 Complete the following table.

verb	*noun*	*verb*	*noun*
communicate	. . .	. . .	. . .
equip	. . .	comprehend	. . .
. . .	mechanization	administer	. . .
. . .	computerization	. . .	service
contribute	. . .	correspond	. . .
. . .	process	balance	. . .

9 True or False?
If any statement below is false, correct it. The first two have been done for you.

a. An office telex is part of a communications system. *True.*
b. The word *office* in line 1 refers to rooms and furniture. *False. It (The word 'office' . . .) refers to personnel.*
c. Efficiency is input divided by output.
d. The value of the contribution of administration varies with the size of the firm.
e. If an office system is efficient, its cost to the company is less than the value of the work it does.

SECTION B Listening

Cassette 1, side 1. Listen to the conversation between Dieter Hermann, Management Services Director, Jane Cooper, General Office Supervisor, and Liam Halligan, Administration Manager. While you are listening to the tape, complete the description of the new video typing system.

Video Typing System *Method of Operation*

1 Reports and correspondence are sent to the video typist.
2 . . .
3 The words appear on the video screen.
4 . . .
5 The video typist instructs the computer.
6 . . .

Video Display Unit

Hermann Come in, Mrs. Cooper. I'd like you to meet Liam Halligan, our new Administration Manager.
Cooper How do you do, Mr. Halligan.
Halligan I'm very pleased to meet you, Mrs. Cooper.
Cooper Welcome to Aberdeen. You've come from Hamburg, I believe?
Halligan That's right. I was with Lambert's International there for, oh, five and a half years.
Cooper From shipping to heavy chemicals. Quite a difference.
Halligan In the product, Mrs. Cooper. I hope the methods and systems in administration won't be too different.
Cooper I'm sure they won't.
Hermann Let me pour you a coffee.
Cooper Thank you, Mr. Hermann.
Halligan Does anybody mind if I smoke?
Hermann Not at all.
Cooper No, please do.
Halligan I'm sorry. Would you like a cigarette, Mrs. Cooper?
Cooper No, thank you. I don't smoke.
Hermann I've asked you up, Mrs Cooper, to meet Liam here and to tell him a little about the way we organize things.
Cooper Where would you like me to start, Mr. Halligan?
Halligan Um, let's see. What about the general office services? What's the system there?
Cooper Well, about eighteen months ago we changed our office over from a typing pool to a video typing system.
Halligan Yes, I've heard about it. Could you explain how it works?
Cooper The typewriters were replaced with VDUs, which have videoscreens but normal keyboards.
Halligan What's the difference in the method of operation?
Cooper All reports and correspondence are sent to the video typist in the normal way, just as in the old system. But now, as a letter is typed, the words appear on the VDU screen. They can be corrected and added to, or their order changed. The size of the page can also be changed, at the press of a key.
Halligan How then is the end copy typed out?

Cooper Each VDU is linked to our central computer, which is connected to an electronic typewriter in the office next to mine. When the video secretary is ready, she instructs the computer, and the end copy is then typed out automatically.

Hermann The computer also stores information, of course, and can reproduce any of our past reports or correspondence on request—

Cooper —except for certain things, naturally, which only I can call up.

Hermann And another advantage from Mrs. Cooper's point of view is that she can check on just how much work is done by the individual VDU operators.

Halligan I see. But tell me, why did you choose this system and not a fully computerized one?

Hermann We didn't want to have to change over from typists to computer operators. Why let good staff go?

Cooper I agree, especially since this system is easy to learn, and finding skilled computer staff is so difficult.

Halligan How successful do you think the system is?

Hermann Very. We calculated the number of lines typed by each typist each day on the old system, and compared that to the daily output of each typist on the new system. Everyone's glad we made the change.

Halligan What's the increase in efficiency?

Hermann Oh, about 130%.

Cooper And we've found that typing speeds have improved, too.

Harrigan How's that?

Cooper Typists generally work more slowly as they near the end of a page, because they're afraid of making mistakes. Now that mistakes can be corrected quickly and easily, typing speeds are much better.

Halligan And what about costs?

Hermann We have five video typists doing the work of nine ordinary typists—

Cooper —and we now do 75% of the typing that the managers' secretaries were once responsible for.

Hermann This means they have more time to help their managers in administrative work, so the managers themselves have more time to spend on such things as . . .

□ How successful, in terms of efficiency, has the new video system been?

SECTION C Language Study

1 Fractions and Percentages

Examples:

$\frac{3}{4}$ = **three quarters** = 75% = **seventy five per cent**

$\frac{2}{5}$ = **two fifths** = 40% = **forty per cent**

$\frac{1}{8}$ = **one-eighth** = 12.5% / 12$\frac{1}{2}$% = **twelve point five per cent/twelve and a half per cent**

Read the following aloud, first as fractions then as percentages:
$\frac{2}{3}$, $\frac{3}{8}$, $\frac{1}{5}$, $\frac{5}{8}$, $\frac{1}{10}$, $\frac{1}{20}$, $\frac{3}{10}$, $\frac{1}{3}$, $\frac{3}{5}$, $\frac{7}{8}$.

2 Short Forms

The short form or abbreviation for 'Limited' is 'Ltd'.

a. Give the abbreviations for Mister, Incorporated, Street, United Kingdom, Avenue, Video Display Unit.

b. What do the following abbreviations stand for? ad, EDP, cc, etc, pm, am, ie.

3 Phrasal Verbs

'I **go along with** John, Mr Bates.'
'We're going to **look at** the problem very carefully.'
Hermann **called** Mrs Cooper **in** to introduce her to Halligan.

Choose from these verbs to complete the sentence below: **call up, stands for, changed over, built up, switched off, taken away,**

a. EDP . . . 'electronic data processing'.

b. The video typists can . . . information . . . from the computer store.

c. About eighteen months ago they . . . from a typing pool to a video typing system.

d. The paragraph was . . . from the information in the table.

e. The letters have been . . . and the light has been . . . .

4 Expressing Sentences in Different Ways

Adjective	*Adverb*
efficient	efficiently
automatic	automatically
good	well
bad	badly

Notice in the following examples how the sentences are written with either an adjective or an adverb without the meaning of the sentence changing.

Examples
The system works **efficiently**. (efficient)
▷ It is an **efficient** system./The system is **efficient**.

The typing-out of the end copy is **automatic**. (automatically)
▷ The end copy is typed out **automatically**.

Use the adjectives and adverbs in parentheses to re-write the sentences below.

a. The video typing system operates smoothly. (smooth)

b. John Masters, the new management trainee, is a very good worker. (well)

c. The Administration Manager's secretary types quickly and efficiently. (quick . . . efficient)

d. The Union Representative is a bad negotiator. (badly)

e. Mrs. Cooper supervises her office staff very carefully. (careful)

f. Evaluation of the training programmes is regular. (regularly)

SECTION D Listening

Cassette 1, side 1. While you are listening to the conversation between the two secretaries, Jane Court and Marie Blake, note down the answers to questions 1 and 2 below.

1 What reasons does Marie Blake give for wanting to leave her job at Eastcote's?

2 Why does Jane Court think that Marie Blake should not leave her job?

SECTION E Using Information in Different Ways

1 Here is a selection of the kinds of letters received by the Personnel Department at Eastcote's one morning. Notice that the letters are listed alphabetically by the names of the senders.

John Adams	application for the post of Personnel Officer
B Cooper	request for travel costs for a trip to an engineering exhibition
Lon Francis	notice of the new opening times of the bar at the Sports Club
Pam Francis	question about pay negotiations
R Hines	Safety Officer's report on F Department
David Johns	request from the Trade Union for a meeting on the annual pay discussions
D Marlow	specification for the technicians' training programme
R B Parks	medical certificate
P Spellman	article for the staff bulletin
Larry Thomas	notice of the annual medical examination for all staff
Paul Trench	request for operator training for D Department
T Underwood	disagreement about job grading in his department
Tom Watson	request for a reference for a job applicant
Sue West	request for a meeting with the Trade Union on Sunday about working conditions and pay

2 Suppose that you are asked to sort these letters under the different subjects to which they refer (eg, **Training, News Items**, etc.). List the different subjects that you will need and then group the letters under them. Give reasons for the groupings that you choose.

3 List the following names in alphabetical order: D. J. Brown, Hilary Brown, D. F. Brown, Mark Xavier, T. Siemens, M. T. M. Sidebottom, P. D'Youville, Marie Goldscheider, S. Hertz, Yousef Al Diwani, Dino Bertolucci, K. Patel, N. Brieger, G. Frank Forbes-Eliot, Harvey L. Meyer, V. G. Mastorakis, Kerstin Klasson, Chuntana Metha, Laura M. Bryce, Peter Mackechnie, Antonio Sanchez.

SECTION F Discussion

1 'One of the main reasons why managers are sometimes inefficient in making the right decisions is that full information fails to reach them.' Do you agree or disagree with that? Why?

2 How do you think computerized systems may change the office of the future? Will you be happy to see these changes? Why?

3 Do you agree that most companies employ more office staff than they need? Give your reasons.

SECTION G Writing

1 Read this description of the performance of five video typists who work for Eastcote's. Notice how the paragraph is built up from the information in the bar chart.

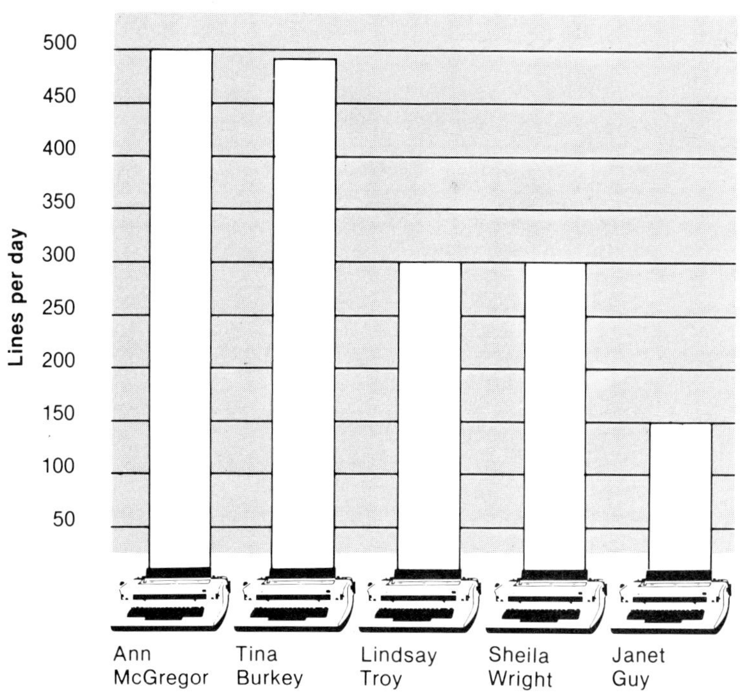

At Eastcote's an analysis of the performance of five video typists working in the General Office gave some interesting results. The bar chart shows that Ann McGregor was the most productive of the five typists, completing 500 lines per day. Second fastest was Tina Burkey, who produced only twenty lines fewer than Anne did. Tina was much faster than Sheila Wright and Lindsay Troy, who both completed 300 lines per day. The slowest and least productive of the five was Janet Guy, who completed only 150 lines. The total number of lines completed by the five typists was 1,730, making an average of 346 lines per day.

2 Now write similar paragraphs for (1) the bar chart illustrating the performance of the typists at Canpan Ltd and (2) the table listing the price and output of the copiers.

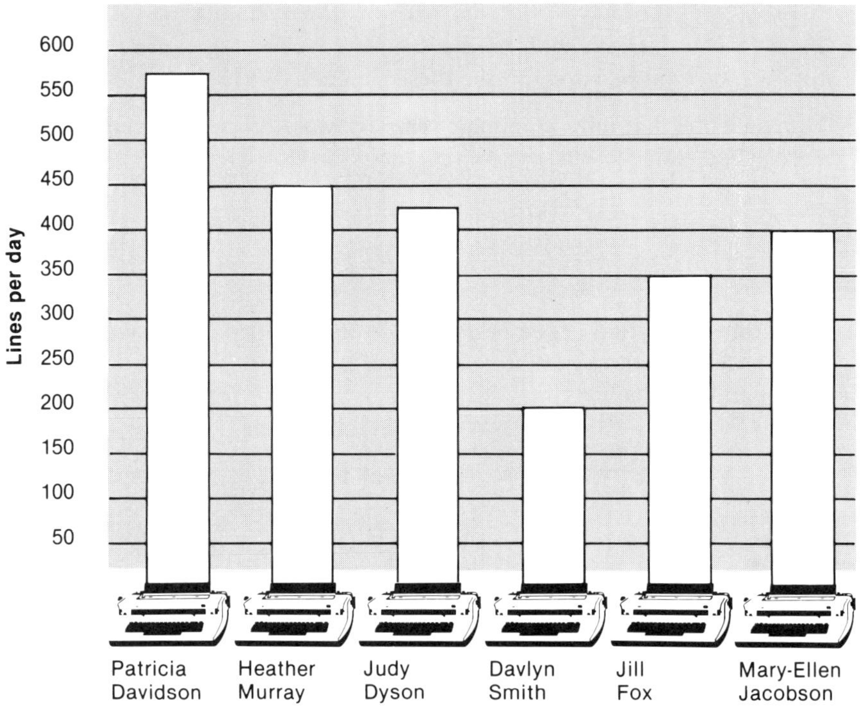

Type of copier	*Copies per minute*	*Price (£s)*
Setti XTG	17	700
Setti 5	21	900
Zanu LT	16	750
Sampson 3	17	900
Rennit Kwik	14	600
Drycopy IV	11	280

Unit 5 Research & Development

SECTION A Reading

Read the following passage

All R&D executives have two major responsibilities: (1) they must ensure that the company is supplied with technically successful projects, and (2) they must select the most promising schemes and ideas for the expenditure of R&D resources. This work is complicated by numerous uncertainties, inasmuch as commercial research and development must be based on market forecasts.

If R&D management can provide a regular flow of new and updated products, the company will benefit in a number of ways. First of all, it will be able to make full use of expensive departmental resources, development engineering and available marketing capacity. In addition to that, a flow of new market winners will provide the business with steady growth in income and profits. This can also be important psychologically, for it is often on this basis that those outside the company assess the quality of its management.

The R&D department's job is made more difficult because of the length of time required to complete its research. In the chemical and pharmaceutical industries, for example, it may take five to ten years before a product is a technical success and a further six to eight years before it reaches full commercial potential.

To achieve results, R&D must define both the areas that should be investigated and the objectives that should be achieved in each area. For this reason, the R&D department must take an interest in all aspects of design, application, efficiency, and use of appropriate materials. There is a difference, however, between the development of new consumer products and the development of new industrial ones. In consumer markets the search for a new product often begins after a statement of a specific need, and development is tailored to meet it. In many industrial markets, product development is the result of work done in the research laboratory. This work is often aimed at a general need, such as a new kind of medicine or higher operating speeds for machines. When the new industrial project has been developed, its performance can be analysed in terms of customer needs.

Word Study

major *l.1* of greater importance than others. The opposite is *minor* = 'of lesser importance than others'.
projects *l.2* schemes for things to be done.
ideas *l.3* thoughts; pictures in the mind.
expenditure *l.3* spending; using up of time, money, etc.
inasmuch as *l.5* because; since; for; for the reason that.
forecasts *l.6* ideas about how things may be in the future.
regular *l.7* according to a fixed plan, schedule or arrangement.
flow *l.7* plentiful supply.
updated *l.7* brought up to date; made more modern.
available *l.10* that can be used, had or reached. What may workers do if they are told that no money is available for a pay increase?
capacity *l.10* ability to contain, hold or receive. What is the capacity of a normal wine bottle?
steady *l.11* smooth and continuous; not changing suddenly.
psychologically *l.12* the way people think. *Psychology* is the science that deals with the mind and behaviour. What is the importance of psychology in advertising?
potential *l.19* ability to come into being; possibility. A potential customer is one who *can* buy, but has not yet actually bought. List some potential dangers on the average factory floor.
to achieve *l.20* to do successfully. The noun is *achievement*.
areas *l.20* subjects. *Area* also means the surface measurement. To find the area of your desktop in cm^2 (square centimetres*), multiply the length by the width.
*There is no agreement yet on the English spelling of the metric (SI) units, and in this book *both* forms are used, ie, gram/gramme, liter/litre, meter/metre.
investigated *l.21* studied; looked into.
aspects *l.22* different appearance when something is seen from different points of view.
search for *l.26* looking for.
tailored *l.27* made to fit specific measurements.
research laboratory *l.28*

aimed at *l.29* directed towards.
in terms of *l.31* relative to. Suppose that two boys have the same father. How are the boys *related*? What is the *relation* between daughter, sister and parent companies?

Comprehension

1 Complete the table.

Statement	*Reason*
R&D Manager's work is complicated by uncertainty	**a.** Based on market forecasts **b.** . . .
Company benefits from a regular flow of new and updated products	**c.** . . . **d.** . . . **e.** . . .

2 What do the words in **bold face** refer to?

a. '**This** work . . . *(l.4)*

b. 'In addition to **that**, . . . ' *(l.10)*

c. '**This** can also be . . . on this basis . . . ' *(l.12)*

d. '. . . **those** outside the company . . .' *(l.13)*

e. '. . . **its** management.' *(l.13)*

f. '. . . new industrial **ones**.' *(l.25)*

g. '. . . to meet **it**.' *(l.27)*

3 What is the difference between the development of new consumer products and the development of new industrial ones?

4 How may it be possible for a product to be a technical success but a commercial failure?

5 Why must R&D take an interest in all aspects of design, application, efficiency and use of appropriate materials?

6 Explain what is meant by (1) promising schemes, (2) a flow of new market winners, and (3) tailored product.

7 Complete the following table.

verb	*noun*	*adjective*
. . .	benefit	beneficial
. . .	basis/base	basic
lengthen	. . .	. . .
widen	. . .	. . .
. . .	. . .	definitive
. . .	. . .	applicable
specify	. . .	. . .
. . .	. . .	additional
. . .	. . .	relative

8 True or False?

a. The area of a desktop which measures one point eight metres by zero point eight metres is fourteen point four square metres.

b. The development of new industrial products depends on forecasts of consumer needs.

c. In some industries it may take from eleven to eighteen years before a product achieves full commercial potential.

d. Product development for industry is often aimed at specific needs.

e. R&D for consumer markets is usually aimed at general needs.

SECTION B Listening

Cassette 1, side 2. While you are listening to the conversation between Dwight Stone, an American R&D Manager, and Clive Smallwood, an R&D Manager from Britain, make notes to answer the following questions.

1 In the last year, United Chemicals has experienced some financial difficulties. What has been the result for Clive Smallwood's R&D Department?

2 In what way do you think Dwight Stone would try to improve the commercial strength of United Chemicals?

Stone Hi, Clive. It sure is good to see you again.

Smallwood Hello Dwight. This is a pleasure. How are you?

Stone Same as usual. And you?

Smallwood Well, my golf's no better than it was the last time we played, I'm afraid.

Stone Hey, maybe we can find time to play again this week, if we're not too busy.

Smallwood Fine, but it will have to be before Friday.

Stone You're leaving the conference early?

Smallwood I am, yes, I'm going back on Friday morning. I have an important meeting in London on Saturday.

Stone: Too bad, but let's see what we can do about getting a game in between now and then, right?

Smallwood I'd like to, yes, if we can manage it.

Stone Great. Now, what's new? How are things going at United Chemicals?

Smallwood Up and down a little. Good and not so good. You know how it is.

Stone That's business, Clive.

Smallwood Have you heard about the, um, minor difficulties that United is experiencing just now?

Stone Can't say I have. Where? In your department?

Smallwood That's part of the problem, certainly. They've given us very much less for R&D expenditure this year, so we won't be able to take on as many new projects as we wanted to.

Stone Bad news. And there's nothing you can do about it?

Smallwood Oh, I've put my point of view, of course, but there are stronger voices in the company than mine.

Stone They have to spend some to get some, Clive. Don't they understand that? If United spent more on R&D, it would be stronger commercially.

Smallwood You don't have to tell me that.

Stone Did you know that real spending on R&D in Britain fell by 11% in the 1970s? Why not point that out to those 'stronger voices'?.

Smallwood Oh I've told them, don't worry. I've also told them that in the 1970s real spending on R&D increased by 29% in Japan, by 28% in West Germany, and by 12% in France. I think you and I read the same article.

Stone Well, this conference needed some preparation, right? It helps to have the facts and figures ready.

Smallwood By the way, which floor is it on? I forgot to bring my programme with me.

Stone Floors, not floor. Seventh and eighth, Clive. Hey, there's an elevator going up. Come on.

Smallwood Lift, not elevator.

Stone Come on . . .

☐ How does R&D spending in Britain compare with other countries?

SECTION C Language Study

1 Advice and Possible Results

Study the following sentences which give advice and recommendations.

a. Potentially dangerous equipment on the factory floor **should be limited** to experienced operators.

b. The company **should tailor** its development programme to meet specific needs.

c. Certain data **should be limited** to the General Office Supervisor.

d. More money **should be spent** on United Chemicals' R&D programme.

e. The R&D Department **should supply** the company with a flow of technically successful projects.

f. A company **should assess** its training programme regularly.

Now consider the things that **may happen** if the advice given above is not followed.
Example:
If the advice about dangerous equipment is not followed, serious accidents **may happen**, (or) the Trade Union Representative **may want** to speak to management.

Write similar sentences for b-f above. In each case, as in the example, there is the possibility of more than one answer.

2 Supposition

Example:
Suppose that United Chemicals spent more on R&D. **What would** the result **be?** (the company/be stronger commercially)
▷ If United Chemicals **spent** more on R&D, the company **would be** stronger commercially.

Write similar answers for the following:

a. Suppose that United Chemicals did the necessary research. What would happen to their products? (their products/improve)

b. Suppose that there was a vacancy for a Training Manager. Where would the company advertise? (company/advertise in the national press)

c. Suppose that there was a need to reduce expenditure. Which department would have to make cuts? (R&D Department/have to make cuts)

d. Suppose that the training programme was not a success. What would the Training Manager do? (Training Manager/analyse and assess the training methods)

a. Suppose that there was an accident in the factory. Who would the Personnel Manager inform? (Personnel Manager/inform the Safety Inspector)

3 Suggesting

Example:

Potential Problem—a vacancy in the Training Department

Possible Action—(1) advertise in the newspapers, (2) advertise in the staff bulletin, (3) ask for recommendations.

If there **was*** a vacancy in the Training Department, the company **could advertise** in the newspapers or the staff bulletin or it **could ask** for recommendations.

* Remember that some English speakers feel that **were** is more formal than **was** in this type of conditional statement. In business letters, therefore, **were** is often chosen: **If** there **were** a vacancy in the Training Department, the company **could . . .**

Do the following in a similar way.

a. *Potential Problem* An increase in manufacturing costs
Possible Action (1) raise prices, (2) improve efficiency, (3) reduce staff.

b. *Potential Problem* Young managers leaving the company
Possible Action (1) improve the training programme, (2) pay more money, (3) give them more responsibility.

SECTION D Listening

Cassette 1, side 2. While you are listening to the interview between Art Shaw, a journalist with Business Eye, and Dr. Roy Sanders of the European Business Institute, note down the answers to questions 1 and 2 below.

1 Dr. Shaw says that when many companies face a new product, they reduce expenditure on their own product research and spend the money saved on their own existing products. What does Dr. Shaw think is (a) the advantage and (b) the disadvantage of this practice?

2 Dr. Shaw says that companies spend a lot of money on products that fail. What two reasons does Dr. Shaw suggest for this failure?

☐ Why does Dr. Shaw think that it is better not to spend a great deal of money on developing completely new ideas?

SECTION E Using Information in Different Ways

1 Read this description of the amounts spent by Associated Chemicals on R&D between 1970 and 1979.

In 1970 Associated Chemicals spent forty million pounds on R&D. In the following year that figure went up by ten million pounds to fifty million.

Over the next two years, 1972 and 1973, total expenditure on R&D increased by a further twenty-five million pounds. This upward trend continued in the following year when the figure reached ninety million pounds. In 1975, however, company spending on R&D remained the same as in the year before, and in the next twelve months it fell by ten million pounds. There was a further increase in 1977 of ten per cent on the previous year's spending. This two-year trend ended in 1978 with a sudden increase to one hundred and twenty-five million pounds. In the final year of the period under review, the amount spent on R&D went up again to one hundred and fifty-five million pounds.

2 Now complete the following bar chart with the help of the information in the description above.

Associated Chemicals R&D Expenditure 1970 – 79

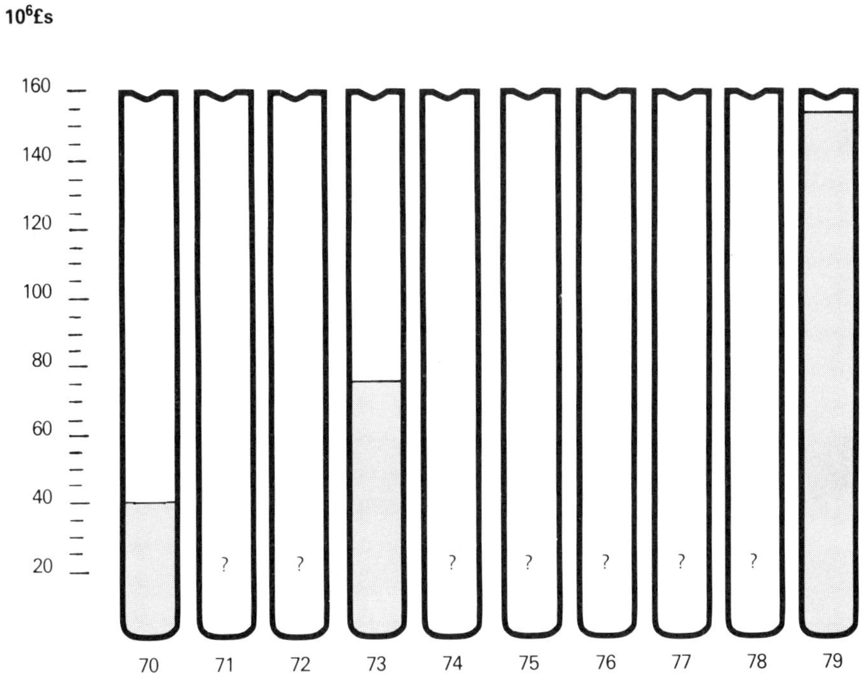

SECTION F Discussion

1 'One of the greatest industrial needs is R&D into better management techniques.' Do you agree? Why?

2 Do you think that all R&D should pay for itself in terms of better processes and improved products? Give your reasons.

3 When faced with new products in their markets, many companies put more money into their old products. Why do you think this happens? Why don't they put money into new products?

SECTION G Writing

1 Use the bar chart to write a paragraph similar to the one in Section E.

White Cross Pharmaceuticals R&D Expenditure 1960 – 69

2 Notice how the paragraph below has been built up from the following notes.

— R&D management to provide regular flow of new products/ company benefits in a number of ways
— full use of expensive departmental resources/full use of development engineering/full use of available marketing capacity
— flow of new market winners/steady growth in income and profits
— psychological importance/often on this basis people outside company assess management

If R&D management can provide a regular flow of new and updated products, the company will benefit in a number of ways. First of all, it will be able to make full use of expensive departmental resources, development engineering and available marketing capacity. In addition to that, a flow of new market winners will provide the business with steady growth in income and profits. This can also be important psychologically, for it is often on this basis that those outside the company assess the quality of its management.

3 Cover the paragraph. Then, using the notes, try to re-write it exactly as it is.

4 Using the notes below, write a similar paragraph on the advantages of investment in R&D (*investment in* = 'putting money and other resources into'). These words may help you: **first, first of all, to begin with, second, next, in addition, additionally, also, finally.**

— country invests successfully in R&D/country benefits in a number of ways
— achieves increase in profits/increase in employment/increase in national income
— flow of successful new products/cuts down on quantity of goods brought in from other countries
— social importance/often on this basis people outside assess industrial achievement

Review Unit 1 Company Organization

This unit is designed to help you to practise the grammar and special vocabularly that you have learned from Units 1-5. There are no new words or structures in this unit.

1 Read the following passage.

Company Organization

In this technical business world, the process of management decision-making has grown more complex. There is, however, a limit to the number of decisions that can be made by one person. In practice, this means that every company must limit the amount of responsibility that is given to individual employees. There are various opinions about the number of people that one person can manage directly in an efficient way; but, for higher executives (eg., Heads of Departments), it is generally agreed that the maximum number should be eight.

People operate in groups in order to achieve objectives that they can not achieve by working individually. In an efficiently-run company, the activities of the various groups and the responsibilities of the individuals who work within them must be carefully defined in an organization structure. For management, the purpose of this organization is the achievement of company policy.

Product Organization (Manufacturing Company)

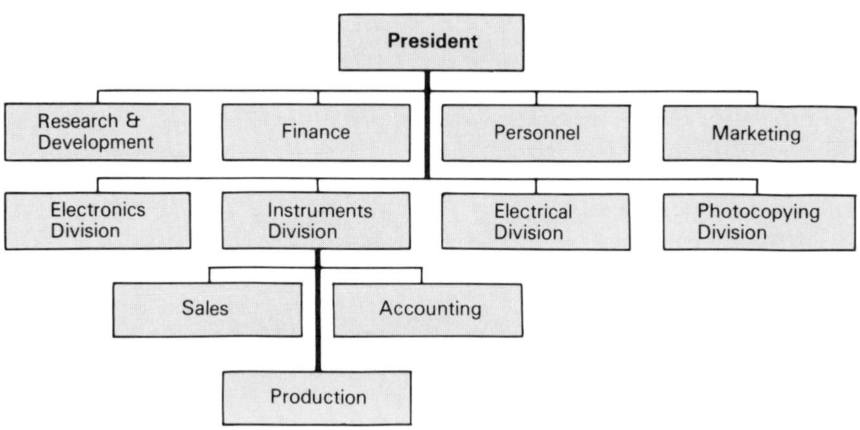

A company organization structure should aim at providing an efficient work system, a means of communication, and satisfaction for the company personnel.

First, in terms of efficiency, a business must try to maximize the output of products and services which result from a given input of resources. This is possible only when company organization functions smoothly. Second, the success of a company depends on a steady flow of full and correct information. Therefore, an appropriate communications system must exist to ensure that the right information reaches the right people. Finally, a well-defined organization provides the means for individuals to assess their relations with others who work for the same company. In a system which is suitably organized, this should serve as the basis for job satisfaction.

Functional Organisation

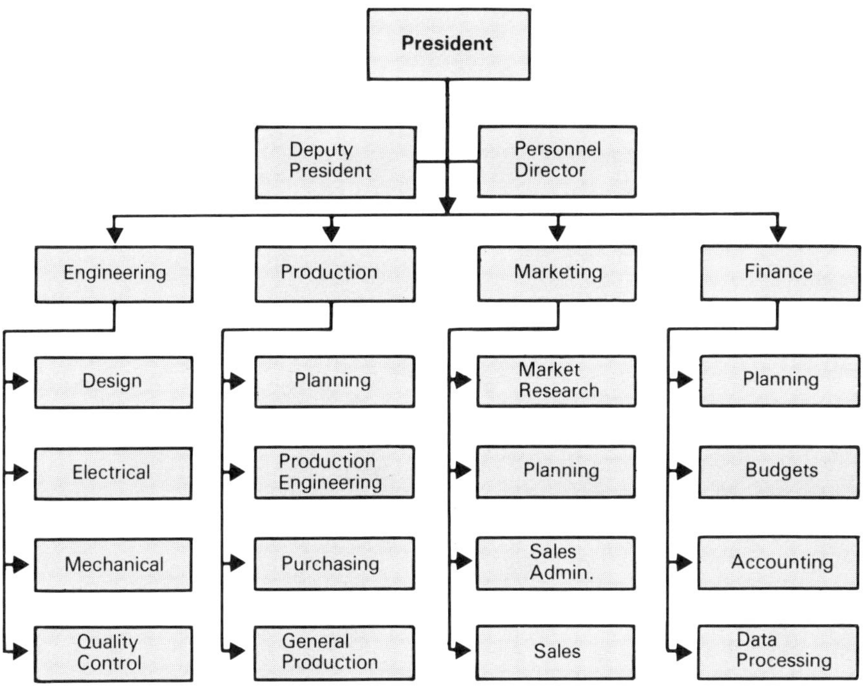

2 Now do these exercises based on the passage.

a. Say what the words in **bold face** refer to.
'In **this** technical business world . . .' *(l.2)*
'. . . **this** means that every company . . .' *(l.4)*
'. . . the maximum **number** . . .' *(l.11)*
'. . . the individuals who work within **them** . . .' *(l.12)*
'. . . the purpose of **this** organization . . .' *(l.14)*
'**This** is possible . . .' *(l.20)*
'. . . **this** should serve . . .' (l.27)

b. In what kind of business world was decision-making simpler?

c. Why must individual responsibility be limited?

d. Why are decision-making groups formed?

e. Why must management define group activity and individual responsibility within it?

f. If an appropriate communication system doesn't exist, what will happen?

g. What will the result be if an organization is not defined well?

h. What advantages should employees get from a suitably organized system? Why?

i. How is it possible to maximize the output from a given input?

j. Describe the different methods of company organization in the diagram on Product Organization and Functional Organization.

3 True or False?

Unit Sales in Thousands, 1980 – 81 (Canpan)

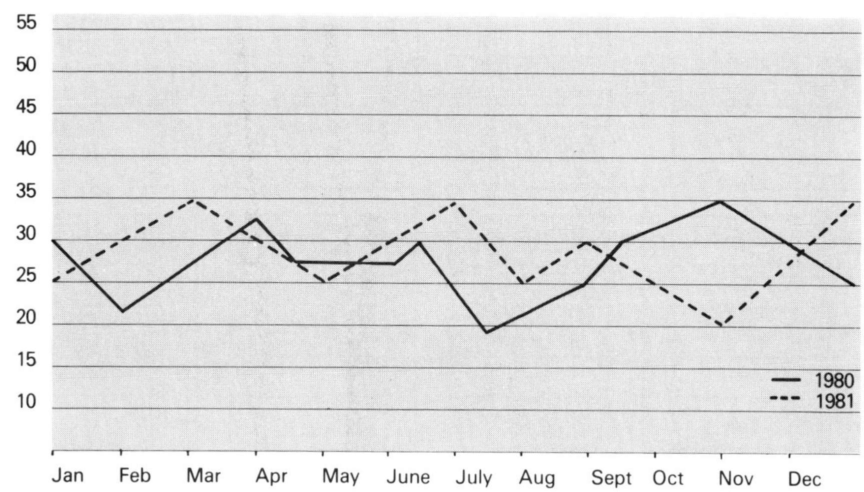

Compare the statements below with the data on the graph. Correct the false statements.

a. Performance in 1980 was generally steadier than in 1981.

b. Between January and the beginning of March, 1981, there was an upward trend in unit sales.

c. In 1981 there was a steady improvement in unit sales between the middle of July and the end of October.

d. In 1980 unit sales remained steady from mid-April until about the beginning of June.

e. The figures for maximum sales in both years are the same.

f. Minimum sales were worse in 1980.

g. The graph is not designed to show why the figures for the two years are different.

h. If the latest trend continues, performance will improve.

i. If the graph were larger, it would contain more information.

j. The graph would contain the same information if it illustrated unit sales only between 15,000 and 35,000.

4 Complete the following paragraphs using suitable prepositions.

A job description should give details . . . the performance that is required . . . a specific job, and a job description should give information . . . the behaviour, knowledge and skills that are expected . . . an employee who works . . . it. When all . . . this has been collected, it is possible to make a training specification. This specifies what the Training Department must teach . . . the successful performance . . . the job, and also the best methods to use . . . the training period.

There are many different training methods, and there are advantages . . . all . . . them. Successful training programmes depend . . . an understanding . . . the differences . . . learning . . . skills and training . . . using them. It is frequently said that learning . . . skills takes place '. . . the job', . . . the classroom, but training . . . using those skills takes place '. . . the job', . . . means . . such activities as job rotation and planned experience.

5 Complete the following table.

verb	*noun*	*adjective*
. . .	. . .	knowledgeable
. . .	weakness	. . .
. . .	. . .	wide
define	. . .	. . .
succeed	. . .	. . .
vary	. . .	. . .
negotiate	. . .	. . .
. . .	calculation	. . .
. . .	benefit	. . .
. . .	. . .	soluble
. . .	pension	. . .
measure	. . .	. . .
. . .	. . .	agreeable
. . .	. . .	long
apply	. . .	. . .
. . .	. . .	specific
add	. . .	. . .
. . .	relation	. . .
. . .	. . .	basic
. . .	. . .	decisive

6 Put the verbs in parentheses into appropriate Passive forms.

After the behaviour, knowledge and skills of its staff (analyse) in order to define training needs, a company should look at the performance of personnel and the performance that (require) for each job. From this information a training plan (can make). Next, there are several things that (must specify). It (must decide) where the training (do) and who does it. The Training Department must decide which training methods (use) and the timing of the training programme. Following these decisions, materials (must collect) for the courses. Afterwards, when the courses (complete), the trainees (test) to find out what they have learned. Finally, the training programme (should evaluate) by the Training Manager.

7 Complete the following.

a.	vacancies for jobs	job vacancies
b.	plan containing seven points	. . .
c.	analysis of training needs	. . .
d.	development of products	. . .
e.	negotiations about pay	. . .
f.	training programme for management	. . .
g.	engineering to achieve development	. . .
h.	products designed for consumers	. . .
i.	forms for applications	. . .
j.	board for notices	. . .
k.	experience of work	. . .
l.	system of data processing	. . .
m.	laboratory for doing research	. . .
n.	capacity for marketing	. . .
o.	programme for a computer	. . .
p.	making decisions in management	. . .
q.	structure of an organization	. . .
r.	satisfaction in a job	. . .
s.	flow of information in a company	. . .
t.	activity of a group	. . .

8 Choose the correct word to complete the following sentences.

a. The job applicant had three years . . . in industry. (qualification/experience/knowledge)

b. The performance of the operators was analysed in order to . . . the training programme. (calculate/measure/evaluate)

c. The company have introduced a new wages and salary . . . (process/policy/requirement)

d. The Personnel Department has a . . . of twelve.
(staff/manpower/capacity)

e. The training . . . were defined in the training specification.
(structures/methods/instruments)

f. The successful applicant was . . . from a short-list of four.
(specified/selected/checked)

g. The new training specifications were . . . accurate job descriptions and job specifications. (based on/relative to/in terms of)

h. The . . . of pay for skilled mechanics was £3 an hour.
(grade/rate/degree)

9 Notice how the ideas are linked in these three sentences.

He got the job **because of** his excellent references.
The system was changed **because** it was inefficient.
The staff bulletin can be used **in order to** recruit in-company.

Now make as many reasonable sentences as possible from the table below.

A personnel specification is used		train in the Accounts Dept.
Their training methods were changed		define training needs.
Data processing must be centralized		the uncertainty of the future.
An interview was held	*because (of)* *in order to*	assess applications.
Staff skills are analysed		improve business efficiency.
He had to qualify in EDP systems		they were inappropriate.
Research work is uncertain		its poor market performance.
He attended the negotiations		take a job closer to home.
She left Galaxy Limited		choose a new manager.
The range was discontinued		it depends on forecasts.
		put his views to management.
		the rather low salary.

10 Make questions relative to the words in **bold face.**

Examples:
The Training Department is located **near the R&D Laboratory.**
▷ Where is the Training Department located?

The interviews were completed **yesterday**.
▷ When were the interviews completed?

a. Dwight Stone works **in R&D.**

b. **Annette Fischer** has been made Director of Research.

c. We changed over to a computerized system **for reasons of efficiency**.

d. Production has increased **by 14.5%**.

e. Sheila Wright is going to work for **the Reynolds Group**.

f. The plane for New York leaves **at seven forty-five**.

g. A consultant was called in **to solve the company's training problems**.

h. Canpan is recruiting **six** additional marketing staff.

i. Canpan is recruiting six additional **marketing** staff.

j. Canpan became a limited company **in 1954**

k. The average salary in management at Canpan is **about £6,300 a year**.

l. The new computer system took **eighteen months** to develop.

m. He takes the Financial Times **in order to get up-to-date business information.**

n. He'll give us the details **as soon as he receives the report.**

o. Complex objectives can be achieved **by group decision-making.**

p. The trouble happened because of **a computer error**.

q. The process was first developed **by Karl Hospers.**

r. The machines are cleaned and checked **once a month**.

s. The vacancies have been advertised **in the staff bulletin**.

t. The idea for dividing responsibilities between the two departments was **Harvey Frankfurter's**.

11 What ideas are the speakers expressing? Follow the example, and remember that there may be more than one possibility in each case.

a. **Lyle** Thank you, Linda. We can manage from here.
▷ Lyle is saying that they don't require any more help from Linda, *or* he's politely asking Linda to leave the room.

b. **Tony** The interview wasn't so bad.

c. **John** I go along with Frank's idea.

d. **Sheila** What did you think of the panel?

e. **David** I'm sorry I didn't send the report in sooner, but some other work got in the way.

f. Godfrey That sounds interesting. Go on.

g. Paul You say production has dropped? How's that?

h. Margot You need a few weeks off, Jane.

i. Gareth Sometimes it's wiser to be a quick second.

j. Mary I don't think you should give up your job.

k. Peter Would you mind if we discussed that later?

l. Cooper Why let good staff go?

12 In the research laboratory illustrated below, there are several things that **should be done** before the lab is closed for the day. Explain what should be done in each case, and why.

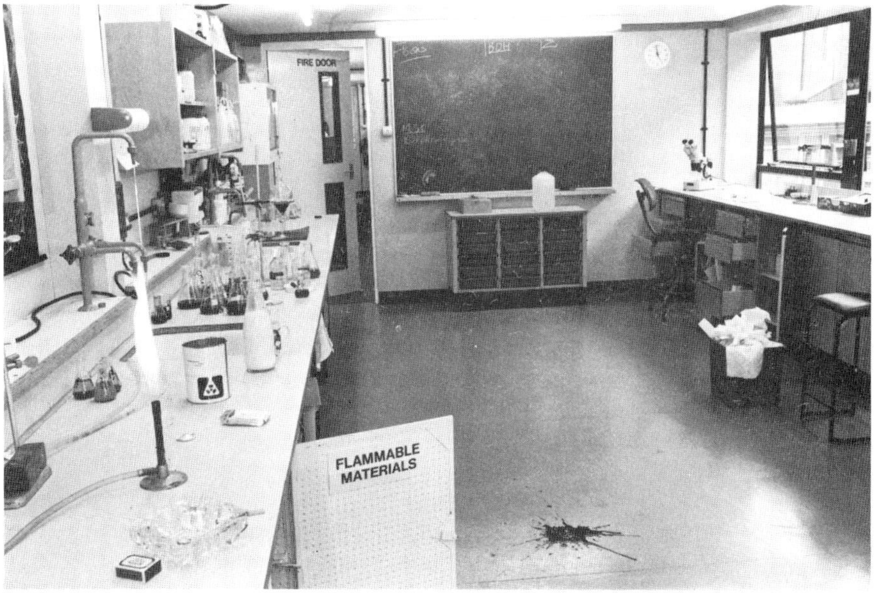

Unit 6 Factory Location

SECTION A Reading

Read the following statement that Mr. Leonard Soames, who is the Chairman of Keynsworth International, gave to the management team of Keynsworth (UK) Ltd.

The Manufacturing Division of Keynsworth (UK) Ltd has been situated in Wembley, London, since 1957. During this time, the Company has achieved a record of steady growth. Indeed, since 1975, output has increased by over three hundred and fifty per cent. This has put increasing pressure on the facilities at the Wembley factory. The Board of Directors, which includes the Managing Director of Keynsworth (UK) Ltd, is aware of the difficult working conditions that all personnel have experienced for many years. The problem is serious because we must have the potential to expand our productive capacity in order to keep our competitive position in the market.

For the past year, we have been examining the possibilities of expanding our UK operations. If we had been able to purchase more land in Wembley, we would have expanded our present site. Our attempts to do this have failed. Consequently, a number of alternative locations have been considered. The important factors in these location studies have been the availability of skilled labour, transport, materials, and government grants.

The Board of Directors has now reached a decision. The new location of the Manufacturing Division will be at Peterhead, Scotland. The Wembley site will be kept only as a service and warehouse centre, and the Company will do its best to limit the number of redundancies by offering to the staff alternative employment where this is possible. Unfortunately, the majority of the workforce cannot be offered new jobs.

The Board hopes that its successful management team will transfer to Peterhead. We fully understand the effect that such a move will have on your lives. However, we would not have taken this difficult decision if there had been any viable alternative.

Peterhead, which is a very pleasant town, has excellent housing, schools and sports facilities. The Company intends to give as much help as it can in order to make relocation as smooth as possible. We hope that you will all join us in this move and that you will play an important part in the future development of the Company.

Site of New Factory

Word Study

situated *l.1* located; sited. The noun *situation* refers especially to the place where a person or thing is, in relation to other persons or things. It can also refer to a position of employment. What information would you expect to find in advertisements under *Situations Wanted* and *Situations Vacant?*

record *l.3* performance reached and written down.

pressure *l.5* demand; high requirement.

facilities *l.5* means by which something can be done more easily, eg, workforce, equipment, machinery, space, etc.

is aware of *l.6* knows about; sees and understands.
serious *l.8* causing deep thought. Suppose a speaker says something, and laughs, and then begins his or her next statement with the expression 'Seriously, now, . . .'. How do you think the speaker's next statement will differ from the one before?
expand *l.9* Increase. Metals expand when they are heated; when cooled, they contract. The expansion and contraction of the metal mercury (Hg) are used to show temperature in degrees Fahrenheit (°F), Centigrade (°C) or Kelvin (°K). What is the name of the instrument that uses this method?
competitive *l.9* Running is a *competitive* sport. Athletes in the same race *compete* against each other. How do businesses compete?
purchase *l.12* buy. The noun is also *purchase.*
consequently *l.14* as a result; therefore.
alternative *l.14* another (location) to choose from. The noun is also *alternative.* An alternative generally limits a choice to one of two possibilities.
considered *l.15* thought about carefully.
grants *l.16* sums of money requested and given.
warehouse *l.19* building in which goods are stored.
redundancies *l.20* jobs lost. A *redundant* worker is no longer needed by his or her employer.
offering *l.20* presenting for acceptance.
transfer *l.23* change place or position.
effect *l.24* result brought about by a cause. *The effect at Wembley of the factory relocation was a loss of jobs.* What was the cause?
viable *l.26* likely to succeed.

Comprehension

1 Complete the table.

Cause	*Situation*	*Effect*
a. . . .	Pressure on Wembley facilities	Board examined other locations
b. . . .	Re-location of manufacturing facility to Peterhead	c. . . .

2 What do the words in **bold face** refer to?
a. 'During **this** time . . .' *(l.2)*
b. '**This** has put increasing pressure . . .' *(l.4)*
c. '. . . **we** must have the potential . . .' *(l.8)*
d. '**Our** attempts to do **this** . . .' *(l.13)*
e. '. . . where **this** is possible . . .' *(l.21)*
f. '. . . **such a move** will have on **your** lives . . .' *(l.24)*

3 Why must Keynsworth's have the ability to expand their output?

4 What factors made the Board choose Peterhead as a new location?

5 What choice do the management team face?

6 What is meant by (1) location study, (2) service and warehouse centre, and (3) viable alternative?

7 Complete the following table.

verb	*noun*	*verb*	*noun*
locate	. . .	. . .	situation
divide	. . .	record	. . .
press	. . .	expand	. . .
facilitate	. . .	consider	. . .
compete	. . .	. . .	transfer
. . .	offer	alternate	. . .

8 Assessment of Alternative Factory Locations

weight = importance expressed as a number between 1 (least important) and 8 (most important).

After the factors have been weighted, each location is assessed on a scale of 1 to 5, and this number is then multiplied by the weight. Eg, location B is best in terms of labour and therefore merits 5, which, when multiplied by the weight, gives 40.

Factor	**Weight**	**Alternative Locations** a	b	c	d	e
Labour	8	2/16	5/40	1/8	3/24	4/32
Housing	6	3/18	4/24	2/12	1/6	5/30
Transport	7	1/7	5/35	3/21	2/14	4/28
Materials	2	3/6	4/8	5/10	2/4	1/2
Services	4	4/16	5/20	2/8	3/12	1/4
Planning	4	3/12	1/4	4/16	5/20	2/8
Expansion	3	3/9	5/15	2/6	1/3	4/12
Cost	4	5/20	4/16	2/8	3/12	1/4
Market	3	1/3	4/12	5/15	2/6	3/9
Port Facilities	2	2/4	3/6	5/10	4/8	1/2
Government Grants	1	1/1	2/2	4/4	3/3	5/5

Which is the best location? Give your reasons.

SECTION B Listening

Cassette 1, side 2. While you are listening to the conversation between Stanley Hymes, a Methods Engineer, and Raymond Stack, a Production Supervisor, complete the table below.
In the following table some information refers to Stanley Hymes and some to Raymond Stack. Place a tick in the appropriate column.

Hymes Well, Ray? What do you think of the news?
Stack I'm not very surprised. Are you?
Hymes Yes I am, a little.
Stack Why? We've known since last year that the company had plans for expansion.
Hymes Expansion, sure. But I didn't expect the company to close down completely here in Leeds.
Stack At least they want people like you and me to make the transfer with them.
Hymes Is that what you're going to do? Transfer to Forningsby?
Stack I'm not really sure. My wife's not happy about the idea. She has her own job, and all of her friends are here. Then too there's the problem of her mother, who's almost seventy-five now. That puts pressure on us to stay in Leeds.
Hymes It won't be easy to find another job, you know.
Stack I know it won't.
Hymes There's a lot of unemployment in engineering at the moment.
Stack I know that, too. And I'm fifty-one, remember. Not the best age to, er, start looking around for a new job.
Hymes Does that mean you may make the move, after all?
Stack I really don't know, Stan. Really I don't. I've lived here since I was a child. It would be difficult for me to make a change like that at my time of life.
Hymes Well, they've given us year to make up our minds. That's something, anyway.
Stack What about you, Stan?
Hymes I'll tell you one thing. I wouldn't have joined Masterson's if I had known about the possibility of relocation.
Stack How long have you been working here now?
Hymes Two and a half years.
Stack Yes, well, you're young. You'll be all right.
Hymes That's not the point. I could have joined Talbot's.
Stack I'm not with you.
Hymes When I left college two and a half years ago, both Talbot's and Masterson's offered me a position. I accepted this one, unfortunately.
Stack Oh well, that's all in the past. It's the future you should think about.
Hymes In Forningsby?
Stack Why not? The company is providing good grants for housing, and transport, and things like that. And special bonuses will be given to those who say yes to the transfer early.
Hymes But I like Leeds.
Stack Forningsby is not a bad place.
Hymes How do you know? Have you been there?
Stack Okay, no, I haven't. But according to the information in the company statement, it seems to be quite a nice place. If you want my advice, Stan, for someone of your age, well, I think you should relocate with the company.
Hymes Should I?
Stack Yes. If you don't, you may find that there's no alternative work in this area. After all, you have been doing your job for only about—what?—thirty months? That's not a lot of experience.
Hymes But I have done very well since I joined. I've learned a lot, Ray, you can't say I haven't.
Stack You have, but will it be enough if you leave? If you go out to look for a new job, you'll have to compete against engineers who have a lot more experience than you.
Hymes True.
Stack And there's another point you should consider. If you go along with the company on this, you'll be in an excellent position in your department, with a much better chance of becoming a manager.
Hymes Years and years from now, maybe.
Stack Time flies, Stan.
Hymes True, Ray.

Information	*Hymes* (✓)	*Stack* (✓)
a. He is not surprised at the news of re-location.	. . .	. . .
b. His wife is not happy about the re-location.	. . .	. . .
c. He has a mother of seventy five.	. . .	. . .
d. He will find it difficult to find another job in Leeds.	. . .	. . .
e. He has lived in Leeds for over forty years.	. . .	. . .
f. He has worked for Masterton's for less than three years.	. . .	. . .
g. He has a good chance of becoming a manager in Forningsby.	. . .	. . .

☐ On balance, do you think Ray will stay in Leeds or make the transfer to Forningsby? Why?

SECTION C Language Study

1 Past Time

Notice, in the following examples, that we use the Simple Past tense to refer to completed past time, the Present Perfect tense with **since** to refer to a particular point in time, and the Present Perfect tense with **for** to refer to a particular period or length of time.

Keynsworth (UK) Ltd. built their Wembley factory in 1957.
Keynsworth (UK) Ltd. has been situated in Wembley **since 1957.**
Keynsworth (UK) Ltd. has been situated in Wembley **for twenty four years.**

Complete the following sentences where necessary using **since, for** and **in.**

a. There has been talk of re-location . . . years and years.

b. Stack has lived in Leeds . . . he was a child.

c. He was recruited into the Training Department . . . 1976.

d. They began work on the computer break . . . last month.

e. Output has increased by 25% . . . the new procedures were introduced.

f. The negotiations have been going on . . . more than twelve hours.

g. We have been waiting for a decision from management . . . the 14th of last month.

h. New working methods were introduced . . . two months ago.

i. They have been discussing the new factory site . . . I joined the company.

In sentences **f**, **g** and **i** above, notice how the Continuous form of the Present Perfect is used in order to express the idea of incompleteness and continuation.

2 Past Intentions

Notice how the Conditional form is used to re-write the example.

Example:
We were not able to purchase more land in Wembley in order to expand the present site.

▷ If **we had been able** to purchase more land in Wembley, **we would have expanded** the present site.

Change the following sentences in a similar way.

a. Since we were not able to call in a consultant, the problem of the salary structure has not been solved. (If, however, we . . .)

b. We were not able to employ more staff, and as a result the training programmes did not improve. (If, however, we . . .)

c. The company was not able to increase its production in order to improve the supply position. (If, however, we . . .)

d. As we were not able to introduce a computer system, the administration remained inefficient. (If, however, we . . .)

3 Adding Information

Notice how we can combine these two sentences by using **who**:
(1) Relocation for a middle-aged employee such as Raymond Stack is always a problem.
(2) Raymond Stack is fifty years old.
▷ Relocation for a middle-aged employee such as Raymond Stack, who is fifty years old, is always a problem.

Using **who** or **which**, combine the following sentences in a similar way.

a. (1) The Board of Directors is aware of the difficult situation.
(2) The Board of Directors includes the Managing Director of Keynsworth (UK) Ltd.

b. (1) Peterhead has excellent housing, schools and sports facilities.

(2) Peterhead is a very pleasant town.

c. (1) The pay offer made by the Personnel Director has not been accepted by the Union Representatives.

(2) The Personnel Director leads the negotiating team.

d. (1) The various redundancy payments were negotiated and agreed with the Unions in April.

(2) The various redundancy payments can be seen on the notice board.

SECTION D Listening

Cassette 1, side 2. While you are listening to the telephone conversation between Marie Pinet, an Administration Manager, and Charles Bond, a Marketing Manager, do the following exercise.

During the telephone call there are only two important subjects of conversation. In as few words as possible, describe (a) the subject introduced by Marie Pinet and (b) the subject introduced by Charles Bond.

☐ When he arrives in Paris, Charles Bond will have to stay in a hotel for two months. What advantage does Marie Pinet think this will have?

SECTION E Using Information in Different Ways

1 Read the following list of activities that are required for the planning and building of a new factory. Notice that the time required to complete each activity is also given.

Activities	*Time in weeks*
a. Get planning agreement	5
b. Get builders	2
c. Get services (gas, water, etc.)	4
d. Make roads and paths	3
e. Build car park	2
f. Get design drawings	3
g. Paint factory	4
h. Build factory	17
i. Purchase land	5
j. Plant gardens	3
k. Negotiate for land	4

2 Place the eleven activities in an appropriate order of operations.

3 Using the information above, complete this simple network analysis diagram.

Planning & Building a Factory by Network Analysis

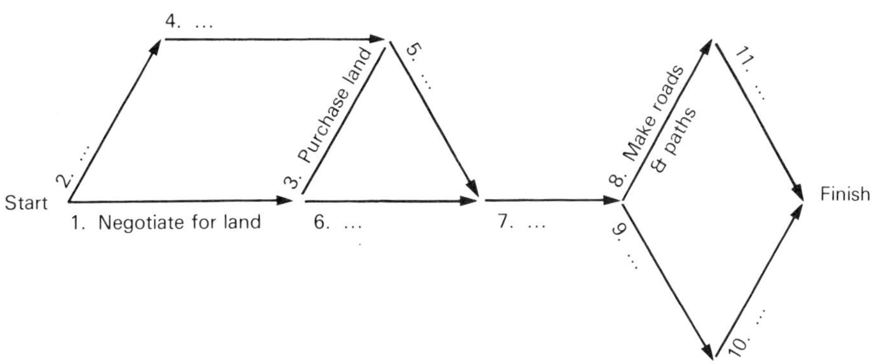

SECTION F Discussion

1 An expanding engineering firm needs to move to a new site. What factors should be considered in the choice of location?

2 'No company executive should expect to be employed in one location all of his working life.' Do you agree? Give your reasons.

3 How may the location of a plant have an effect on a company's profitability?

SECTION G Writing

1 Read this paragraph about Lamont Engineering's location plans.

Lamont Engineering requires additional plant capacity because of the pressure on the facilities at its factory in London. **Therefore**, the Board of Directors has considered a number of alternative locations. **As a result**, it has decided to relocate the factory at Ayr, in Scotland. **However**, the company has also decided not to keep any productive capacity at its present site. **Consequently**, there will be a large number of redundancies. Some skilled workers and managers, **however**, will be offered jobs at the new location.

2 Now put the statements below into their appropriate order and build them up into a paragraph. These words may help you to link the various sentences smoothly: **therefore, however, consequently, as a result.**

a. David and his wife visited Bristol in order to look at the schools and housing facilities.

b. Leemax Ltd. have requested David Crampton, a Personnel Officer, to transfer from their Birmingham office to the Bristol headquarters.

c. They found that Bristol did not compare very well with Birmingham.

d. David has been investigating a number of managerial vacancies in the Birmingham area.

e. He is undecided whether to move to Bristol or to take an alternative job near home.

f. He does have six months to make up his mind.

Unit 7 Manufacturing

SECTION A Reading

The following passage is an example of the descriptive English which is used in business textbooks.

It is usual to classify types of production as job production, batch production and flow production. In job production, products are supplied to the special requirements of a customer, and the whole project is undertaken as one operation which is completed before passing on to the next. A good example of this kind of work is shipbuilding. In job production a single item is produced at a time, whereas in batch production a number of similar items are produced in order to meet a continuing sales demand. Batch sizes vary, but the quantity which is produced amounts to more than immediate requirements, and the surplus production is stored. Finally, in flow production, the manufacture of a product proceeds from one operation to another at a planned rate of output.

It is argued that the type of production method which is employed depends on the development of an individual company. That is to say, many factories begin manufacturing on a job production basis and proceed, as the volume of production increases, to batch and flow production methods. This is not always the case, however, since the type of production is not necessarily determined by the product volume which is aimed at. In fact, in the car industry, tools are produced by jobbing methods, components are produced by batch methods, and the final product is assembled by flow methods.

Flow production is associated with flow layouts, whereas job and batch production are associated with process layouts. In a process layout, machines of a similar type are grouped together in the same section of the factory, and work in progress is moved from one part of the factory to another. In a flow layout scheme, the manufacturing equipment is arranged in the same sequence as the operations performed on the product. Each of these operations must be capable of processing work at the rate required for assembly of the final product, and the output for each operation must be balanced in order to provide a smooth flow of work.

There are advantages in both types of layout. In a process layout system there is more flexibility, and a greater specialization of machines and labour is possible, while in a flow layout system it is not necessary to maintain a high level of stocks or to demand great skill in the workforce.

a. Flow Layout

b. Process Layout

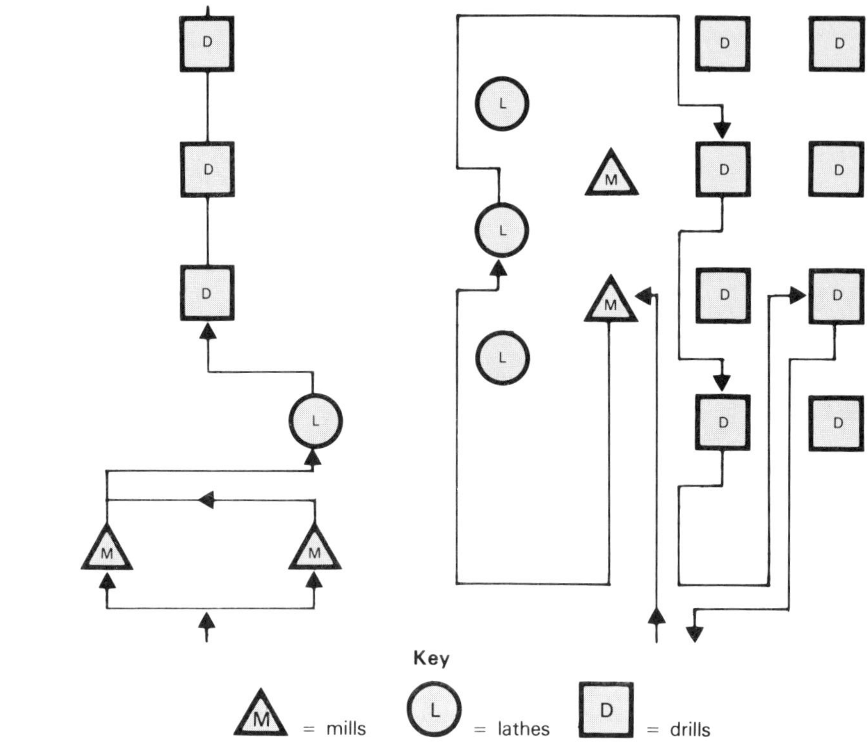

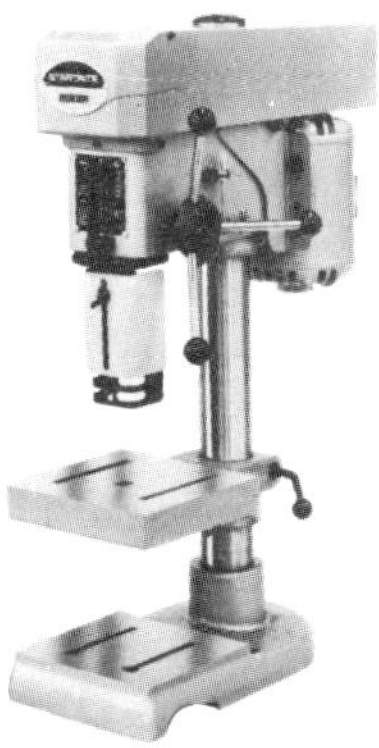
drill

lathe

mill

Word Study

classify *l.1* arrange in groups according to a system. Classify these words: *classify, classification, rotate, rotation, produce, production.*

batch *l.1* number of things made in one operation.

whereas *l.6* She is tall, *whereas* he is short. The management team will be asked to relocate, *whereas* most other staff will be made redundant.

quantity *l.8* amount; number of things referred to.
amounts to *l.8* adds up to.
surplus *l.9* quantity over and above the quantity which is needed.
proceeds *l.10* goes on; continues (in a certain process).
argued *l.12* The verb *argue* here means 'try to show that something is true by giving reasons'.
volume *l.15* quantity; amount. A storage container is 1.2 cm long by 80 cm wide by 50 cm deep. What is the *volume* of the container in cubic centimetres (cm^3)?
This . . . the case *l.16* *This is not always the case* = 'This is not always the situation'.
determined *l.17* defined and decided on.
components *l.19* various parts which make up the whole.
assembled *l.20* put together. What is an assembly line?
associated *l.21* connected; linked; in relation.
in progress *l.24* moving forward to completion.
sequence *l.26* order in which one thing follows another; continuous or related steps in a process.
flexibility *l.31* capability of change or easy alteration. A *flexible* object is able to bend without breaking. Why are the necks of some desk-lamps flexible? What are *flexible working hours*?
maintain *l.32* keep from falling; keep up.
level *l.33* measured quantity or amount.
stocks *l.33* total amounts of goods in store.

Comprehension

1 Complete the tables.

Types of production	*Industry*	*Method*
Job	a. . . .	b. . . .
Batch	c. . . .	Number of similar items produced, above immediate requirements
Flow	Car	d. . . .

Types of production	*Associated layout*	*Method*
e. . . .	f. . . .	Equipment arranged in manufacturing sequence
Job + Batch	g. . . .	h. . . .

2 Say what the words in **bold face** refer to.

a. '. . . before passing on to **the next**.' *(l.4)*
b. '. . . **this kind of work** . . .' *(l.5)*
c. '. . . but **the quantity** which is produced . . .' *(l.8)*
d. '. . . **this** is not always the case . . .' *(l.16)*
e. '. . . one part of the factory to **another**.' *(l.24)*
f. 'Each of **these operations** . . .' *(l.26)*

3 What disadvantages are there in the two layout schemes?

4 Explain why the type of production method is not dependent on the development or size of an individual company.

5 True or False?

a. Job production is aimed at the manufacture of a surplus.
b. A single product requires a single production method.
c. Process layouts are appropriate to both job and batch production.
d. The author argues that production methods depend on individual company development.
e. Manufacturing which begins on a job production basis may, if production volume increases, proceed to batch and flow production methods.

SECTION B Listening

Cassette 1, side 2. While you are listening to the conversation between Mr. Pearson, a Production Director, Mr. King, a Production Manager, and Mr. Cairns, a Senior Process Engineer, complete the diagram below.

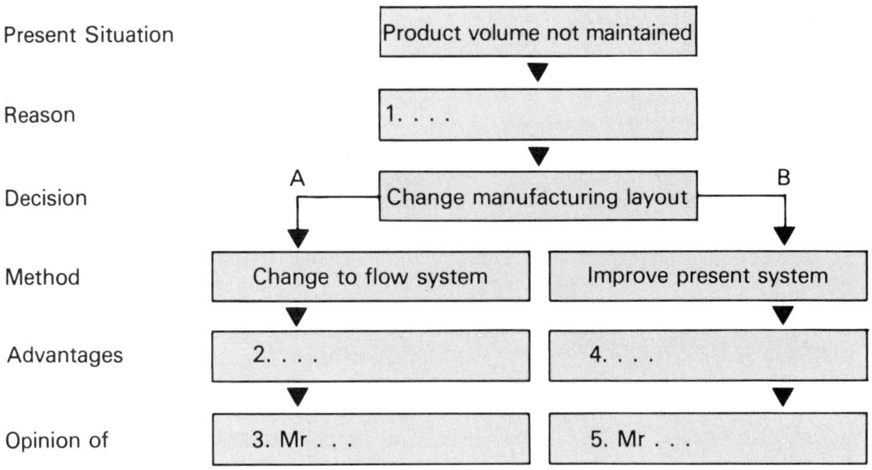

Pearson Well, gentlemen, I take it that you have both read the consultant's report on our production methods and processes?

King Yes, sir, we have. Mr. Cairns and I have been giving it a lot of thought over the past few days.

Pearson And what are your feelings about it, Mr. King?
King I must say that I agree with the findings.
Pearson Mr. Cairns?
Cairns The report makes good sense, er, generally speaking.
Pearson But?
Cairns It is stated here that we have difficulty in meeting our product volume because our production processes are, it is pointed out, inefficient . . . er . . .
Pearson And you disagree?
Cairns Not disagree, no. It's just that this is, um, nothing new. I mean, we have been aware of this situation for a very long time, after all.
King I think I see what Mr. Cairns is getting at. He means, I think, that the report gives a good description of the present situation, but it does not say very much about the future.
Pearson Perhaps not, but it would be impossible for us to make decisions about the future if we did not have a detailed analysis of the system as it is now. We would not have called the consultant in, gentlemen, if we had been able to define the problem ourselves.
King Quite so, Mr. Pearson. But can we take it that, as a result of these findings, the company is going to make a decision about the reorganization of the manufacturing layout?
Pearson That's right. And I think, in a way—if you don't mind my saying so—that you have both misunderstood the purpose of this report. We aim to use it as the basis for some immediate future decisions. Immediate ones.
King I see.
Pearson Now notice that it is, um, recommended in the report that we change over, for example, from a process system to a flow system. Mr. Cairns, what do you think about that one?
Cairns From the point of view of systems, um, all right, I suppose. I think I agree that our industrial pumps could all be manufactured more efficiently if we employed flow methods.
King That's true from the demand point of view as well. We have a high and steady demand for our products. We would be able to work at capacity, and what's more—
Pearson Just a moment, Mr. King. Mr. Cairns, I have the feeling that you don't agree one hundred per cent with the idea of such a changeover.
Cairns I do have some worries, sir.
Pearson Let's hear what they are.
Cairns In my view, the report gives an unbalanced opinion about the advantages that a flow system would bring, if one was introduced. We all know that in a flow system we don't need to maintain a high level of stocks, we don't need to provide such a large manufacturing area, and we don't need to train our personnel to such a high degree of skill.
King And production control is easier, too. That all sounds very advantageous to me, I must say.
Pearson Now then, Mr. Cairns, what is it that you, um, seem to think would be disadvantageous to us if the new scheme came in?
Cairns Well, as I said, in a flow system a highly skilled labour force isn't necessary. But here at Renco, that's exactly what we've got. It seems reasonable to me that we should use the skills and resources that the company has built up over the past several years.
Pearson Ah, but the question is, how? As you yourself have pointed out, everybody has been aware of our inefficient methods, but very little has been done about them.
King Sir. If a system is basically inappropriate, then it is very difficult to make it work better by changing minor aspects of it.
Pearson So you would go along with the recommendation in the report and change over completely to a flow layout, Mr. King.
King Certainly. I see no reason why it can not be done.
Pearson What about Mr. Cairns's point about the use of the skilled labour which we already have?
King I don't see that as a great problem. Naturally, there will be some de-skilling over the years. But we can manage any problems that come up as a result of that.
Cairns Sorry, but I can't agree. First, I think we would face serious problems associated with job grades, responsibilities, salaries, et cetera. But more importantly, I really do think we should look at our present factory layout again.
King Again? We have tried to do that—what?—four or five times already?
Pearson Excuse me, Mr. King. What exactly do you have in mind, Mr. Cairns?
Cairns To begin with, I think we should re-group the mills and drills in F Department, as, um, here, in this diagram I've prepared. As you can see, if this were done . . .

□ What do you think King means by *de-skilling*? When would de-skilling be necessary?

SECTION C Language Study

1 Impersonal Reporting

Examples:
Some people argue that the type of production method which is employed depends on the development of an individual company.
▷ **It is argued** that the type of production method employed . . .

The consultant recommended that we change over from a process system to a flow system.
▷ **It was recommended** that we change over from a . . .

Now use the Passive form to change the following sentences in a similar way.

a. The report states that we have difficulty in meeting our product volume requirement.

b. People have said the Renco are considering a production system changeover.

c. The writers of the report pointed out that the system was inefficient.

d. People generally felt that the recommendations could cause serious difficulties with the workforce.

e. Everybody understands that the company will do everything in its power to keep redundancies to a minimum.

f. The management hoped that the changeover would be smooth and trouble-free.

g. People generally believe that government grants will be increased from the beginning of the year.

h. People thought that the increase would be between 12% and 15%.

2 Comparing

Notice how we can link the following sentences using **whereas** or **while:**
(1) In job production a single item is produced at a time. (2) In batch production, however, a number of items are produced in order to meet a continuing sales demand.
▷ In job production a single item is produced at a time, **whereas** in batch production a number of items are produced in order to meet a continuing sales demand.
(1) In a process layout system there is more flexibility. (2) In a flow layout system it is not necessary to maintain a high level of stocks.
▷ In a process layout system there is more flexibility, **while** in a flow layout system it is not necessary to maintain a high level of stocks.

Use **whereas** or **while** to link the ideas in each of the following.

a. (1) She is tall. (2) He, on the other hand, is short.

b. (1) The management team will be asked to relocate. (2) Most other staff, however, will be made redundant.

c. (1) In 1971, the index of industrial production was 100 in the UK. (2) In Germany, during the same period, the figure was two points higher.

d. (1) King agrees with the consultant's recommendation. (2) Cairns, on the other hand, would like to see a regrouping of operations under the system as it is.

e. (1) At Renco last year investment in R&D was up by £2m over the year before. (2) Continuing the trend, the company this year increased it by £1.2m.

3 **Defining or Limiting with 'who' and 'which'**

a. Use **who** or **which** to connect each idea in the left-hand column with an appropriate completion in the right-hand column.

The whole project is undertaken as one operation . . .	. . . is required is one that looks at the total needs of a business.
The quantity . . .	. . . is available for use.
Supervisors are experienced employees . . .	. . . is completed before passing on to the next.
A person . . .	. . . is produced amounts to more than immediate requirements.
A 'supply' is any quantity of anything . . .	. . . improve their job performance.
The system . . .	. . . applies for a job is known as a job applicant.
Bonuses are awarded to workers . . .	. . . are in charge of complete operations.

b. In Unit Six you studied this example of combining ideas with **who:** Relocation for a middle-aged employee such as Raymond Stack, **who** is fifty years old, is always a problem.

In this unit you have studied this example of defining with **who:** A person **who** applies for a job is known as a job applicant.

Notice the use of commas in the first example but not the second and explain in what way you think these two examples are different.

SECTION D Listening

Cassette 1, side 2. While you are listening to the conversation between Mr. Banks, a Production Manager, and Jim Carter, a Production Foreman, complete the table below.

Subject: G Department

Problem	*Excuse/reason*
a. Last Week: Held up final assembly twice	1. . . . 2. . . .
b. Last month: Unsatisfactory performance	1. . . . 2. . . .

SECTION E Using Information in Different Ways

1 Read this passage on industrial production in the UK, Germany and Italy.

In 1971, the index of industrial production was 100 in the UK, while in Germany the figure was two points higher. For that year, Italy had the same index number as the UK. By 1973, the figure for the UK amounted to 110; for Germany, 113; and for Italy, 114. In 1974, both the UK and Germany experienced a decrease, with the UK figure down by 4 points and Germany's down by 2 points. Italy, however, had a 6 point increase in 1974 but in the following year the figure was 12 points lower. In 1976, the index figure showed an increase in all three countries. In the UK, the increase was the smallest at only one point more than the 1975 figure. Italy and Germany both performed better in 1976, with the Italian figure 14 points higher than the year before and the German figure up nine points on 1975.

2 Using the information from the passage above, complete the following table.

Index of Industrial Production*

	1971	1972	1973	1974	1975	1976
United Kingdom	. . .	103	. . .	. . .	101	. . .
Denmark	102	110	115	109	103	114
Germany	. . .	106	. . .	. . .	105	. . .
Italy	. . .	104	. . .	. . .	. . .	. . .
Japan	103	110	127	124	110	125
USA	102	111	120	120	109	122
USSR	108	115	123	133	143	150

* EEC statistics (EEC = European Economic Community)

3 Now use the table that you have just completed to fill in the lines for the UK, Germany and Italy in the following graph.

Industrial Production 1971 – 1976

SECTION F Discussion

1 When laying out a factory, what would you take into consideration in order to maximize production?

2 'There is a link between the demand for a product and the method used in its production.' Do you agree? Why?

3 'Flow production is efficient only when a large number of requirements have been met.' What are the important requirements for efficient flow production?

SECTION G Writing

1 Complete the following paragraph to compare the index of industrial production in Japan with that of the USSR. The information can be found in the table in Section E.
In 1971, the index of industrial production in Japan showed a figure of 103, while the figure for the USSR was 108. In the next year both countries showed an increase. In Japan, the figure reached 110 and in the USSR it went up to 115. In 1973, the upward trend continued . . .

2 Use the table again to write a paragraph comparing the index of industrial production in Denmark, Japan and Belgium.

Unit 8 Control of Production

SECTION A Reading

Read the following report on the use of computer facilities for the control of production at Lindquist Limited.

Summary of the report on the use of real time computing for the control of production

1 *Terms of Reference*
On the instructions of the Production Director, to report on the failure of real time computing facilities to improve the control of production.

2 *Procedure*
The report was made after investigation and analysis of all the production functions and the Management Services Department.

3 *Findings*

3.1 *Background*
Five years ago the company had a real time EDP system installed in order to (1) make the measurement of performance against established standards more efficient and in order to (2) have any deviations from those standards corrected quickly. The availability of data on such things as the status of production programmes and the number of labour hours worked were expected to improve the control of production.

3.2 *Present Situation*
The real time system has provided good measurement data and it has been able to identify deviations from standards. Although this quick identification of problems has been a valuable service, the development of corrective programmes has still been required. What is more, the implementation of these programmes has been a time-consuming job. For example, in the simple case of quality control, although factory rejects have been quickly noticed, it has taken a lot of time to identify the causes of those rejects and to implement corrective programmes.

4 *Conclusions and Recommendations*
It is suggested that there has been too much dependence on statistical data. Secondly, there has been too little consideration of the cost of collecting real time data and not enough savings in terms of time to justify the cost.

Information on the results of a programme is not good enough. Management require a system of control that will inform them of how to deal with potential problems. This means altering our methods to more future-directed means of control.
It is recommended that more consideration is given to the status of the company's network planning techniques, such as critical path analysis and programme evaluation and review technique (PERT).

Word Study

summary *l.1* short statement of the main points.
real time computing *l.1* computing which allows the data of an event to be processed and used while the event is *taking place* (= 'happening').
terms of reference *l.3* statements that limit or define the area under discussion or report.
instructions *l.4* orders; directions.
improve *l.5* make better; raise to a better condition or quality.
background *l.10* events leading up to something; information which will help to explain something; brief history to explain a present situation.
installed *l.11* fixed in position, ready for use.
established *l.12* accepted or recognized; set up. Explain what is meant by *Morris Tobacco Ltd. (Est. 1847).*
standards *l.13* rules of comparison for measuring quality, value, quantity, etc. Which monetary standard is the *gold standard?* In the SI system, what are the standard units of measurement?
deviations *l.13* movements away from the correct course, standard, definition, etc.
status *l.15* existing position, condition or situation.
identify *l.20* show who or what somebody or something is. In many countries, although not in the UK, *identification cards* must be carried at all times. An ID card has a photograph on it and shows a person's name, date of birth, place of birth, etc.
what is more *l.22* in addition; additionally; besides that.
implementation *l.23* putting into practice; putting into operation.
rejects *l.26* things thrown away as useless, worthless, substandard, etc.
conclusions *l.27* decisions or opinions which are formed after thought, consideration or investigation.
suggested *l.28* put forward as a possibility.
justify *l.31* show to be right or reasonable.
altering *l.34* changing.
critical path analysis *l.37* technique for determining the minimum project length.

Comprehension

1 Why did the Production Director request the report?

2 Say what the words in **bold face** refer to.
a. '. . . **those standards** . . .' *(l.14)*
b. '. . . **these programmes** . . .' *(l.23)*
c. '. . . **those rejects** . . .' *(l.26)*
d. '. . . to justify **the cost**.' *(l.31)*
e. '**This** means . . .' *(l.34)*

3 How long have Lundquist's been using a real time system?

4 What has the real time system been able to do? Has this been enough for Lundquist's? Why?

5 What is needed in addition to programme results? Why?

6 What conclusions does the report come to?

7 What recommendations are made in the report?

8 Complete the following table.

verb	*noun*	*verb*	*noun*
. . .	identification	. . .	suggestion
. . .	improvement	. . .	justification
. . .	installation	consider	. . .
deviate	. . .	instruct	. . .
implement	. . .	sum up	. . .

9 True or False?

a. If the real time computing facilities at Lundquist had improved their control of production, there would have been no justification for *this* report.
b. If the real time computing facilities at Lundquist had improved their control of production, there would have been no justification for *a* report.
c. The real time system at Lundquist has identified problems quickly.
d. The real time system at Lundquist has enabled the quick implementation of corrective programmes.
e. PERT is one of the techniques in Lundquist's network planning.

SECTION B Listening

Cassette 1, side 2. While you are listening to the conversation between Jeff Lyon, a Methods Engineer, and Tom Francis, a Production Foreman, complete the table.

Job number	*Part description*	*Problem*
272D	b. . . .	c. . . .
a. . . .	Small covers for J2 Pump	1. Difficult to perform 2. . . .

Lyon Hello, Tom. What seems to be the problem?
Francis Two things, Jeff. First, job 272D, these small end-plates here. They're not meeting the specifications.
Lyon Let me see one. H'mm. They don't look too bad to me.
Francis Well, they're not good enough for the quality control inspector. He rejected the whole of the last batch we did.
Lyon Didn't we have trouble with this part the last time it came up? I seem to remember we did.
Francis You're right. It was about three months ago.
Lyon We had the tooling changed in order to correct the trouble, I remember.
Francis Now it's happening again.
Lyon Are you sure that you had the right tool put on the press this time?
Francis I think so.
Lyon Let's check it to make sure.
Francis Just a second . . . Here. The tool number is T219973.
Lyon That's the correct tool according to the job card, Tom.
Francis Do you want to have a look at it?
Lyon Tell me, um, who's been operating the press for this job?
Francis Oakes. John Oakes.
Lyon Experienced?
Francis He's an experienced press operator, although he is new to this department.
Lyon Okay, Tom. Could you run a few pieces through the press? I'd like to have a quick look at them.
Francis Here we go . . . There. Have a look.
Lyon H'mm. Yes. I think I've got it. There's too much pressure coming down on this side of the plate. See? Here.
Francis What can we do about it?
Lyon We'll send the tool up to the toolroom and have some minor alterations made to it.
Francis Will it take long?
Lyon No, I've just said, there's not a lot of work required.
Francis All the same, you know what they are like in the toolroom. It may be a week before I get it back.
Lyon Don't worry. I'll have a word with the foreman up there, see what I can do for you. Okay? Right. Now what else did you want to see me about?
Francis We're having problems with job 764B.
Lyon What's 764B?
Francis The small covers for the J2 pump.
Lyon What's the trouble?
Francis The operators are having great difficulty in keeping the work up to standard.
Lyon You think it's a methods problem?
Francis I do, yes. It's a very difficult job to perform on the press, and it's very time-consuming.
Lyon Can you give me a few more details?
Francis It's hard to position the material on the press and hold it in line. We have to work very slowly, if we don't want rejects all the time. In fact, the tooling doesn't seem right to me.
Lyon What's wrong with it?
Francis It's hard to tell. Perhaps the press is too light for the job.
Lyon What kind of press are we using?
Francis Forty tons. You think that's heavy enough?
Lyon I think so, although I'll need to check the job in order to be 100% sure.
Francis Could you come down next time the job is running and see if you can put your finger on the problem?
Lyon I'll do that. Next time you have a batch ready, give me a call.
Francis Thanks very much, Jeff.
Lyon It's what I'm paid for, Tom. See you later.
Francis See you later.

☐ Why does Lyon ask about the press operator?

SECTION C Language Study

1 Getting Things Done

There are different ways of expressing the idea of ordering, instructing or arranging for someone else to perform a service for us. Notice how the examples have been re-written using the Causative form.

Examples:
The Methods Engineer arranged for the improvement of the tooling.
▷ The Methods Engineer **had** the tooling **improved.**

Lundquist's instructed a specialist computer firm to install the real time system.
▷ Lundquist's **had** a real time system **installed** by a specialist computer firm.

Now change the following sentences in a similar way.

a. The foreman ordered some minor alterations to the tooling.

b. The company instructed a Business Consultant to write a report.

c. The Production Manager arranged for an outside company to repair the press.

d. The Production Director instructed management to introduce a new production control system.

e. The foreman instructed the operator to do the job again.

2 Sentence Links

Notice how we can link these two sentences by using **although**:

(1) The real time system has been able to identify problems quickly.
(2) The development of corrective programmes has been a time-consuming job. ▷ Although the real time system has been able to identify problems quickly, the development of corrective programmes has been a time-consuming job.

Use **although** to link the following sentences.

a. (1) The tooling has been changed twice. (2) The end-plates are still not meeting specifications.

b. The Production Manager instructed D Department to clean the components. (2) The Foreman in D Department did not remember to schedule the work.

c. (1) Raymond Stack was rather old. (2) Raymond Stack was able to find a new job in Leeds.

3 Degree

If, for example, we want to describe the weight of a press, we can say:

It is a **fairly** heavy press.
It is a **very** heavy press. ↓ STRONGER
It is an **extremely** heavy press.

If, however, we want to show that the weight of the press is not acceptable for a certain job, we can say:
The press is **too heavy.**/The press is **not light enough.**

Now complete the following sentences using **very, too,** or **enough.**

a. The new operator is a . . . hard-working member of the department.

b. The matter was not given . . . consideration to make a reasonable decision.

c. The system was . . . complicated for the staff to operate efficiently.

d. Although the applicant had . . . good qualifications, they were not good . . . for the job.

e. The company did not allow . . . time to complete the job.

f. The scheme has failed to work because there has been . . . much dependence on statistical data.

SECTION D Listening

Cassette 1, side 2. While you are listening to the conversation, answer questions 1, 2 and 3 below.

1 *Names of Speakers* — *Job Titles*

Names of Speakers	*Job Titles*
Mr. Fanfoni	Management Services Manager
Mr. Simms	Production Director
Mrs. Barnett	Production Manager

Decide the job title for each of the speakers.

2 In the diagram below, decide if the relationships between the speakers are friendly, unfriendly, neither friendly or unfriendly.

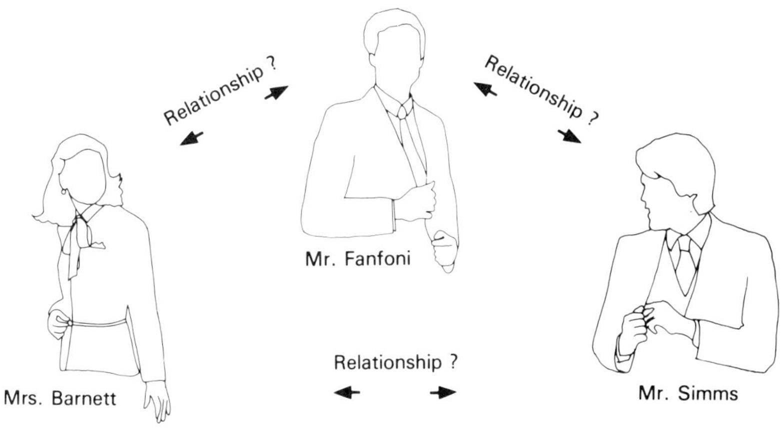

3 What is the purpose of the meeting?

☐ What is the important point of disagreement during the meeting?

SECTION E Using Information in Different Ways

1 Read the following description of Mr. Eriksonn's morning work activities.

After Mr. Eriksonn has entered his office, he assesses the paperwork waiting on his desk. On those mornings when there is a lot of it, he generally sorts it into groups before making a start. Then, if his secretary is in, he calls her into his office in order to discuss his programme for the day as a whole. Every morning, except on Tuesdays, he works until lunchtime on daily administrative jobs such as correspondence, report writing and consulting with various members of staff. Production meetings are held on Tuesday mornings. Sometimes these are quite short, in which case Mr. Eriksonn is able to return to his office and continue with his office work until lunchtime. At the production meetings, however, it sometimes happens that there are serious problems which require immediate sorting out. If this is the case, Mr. Eriksonn spends the whole morning at the meeting.

2 Using the information in the passage above, complete the following programme of Mr. Eriksonn's morning work activities. Notice that each **Yes** or **No** is the answer to a preceding question in a diamond-shaped box.

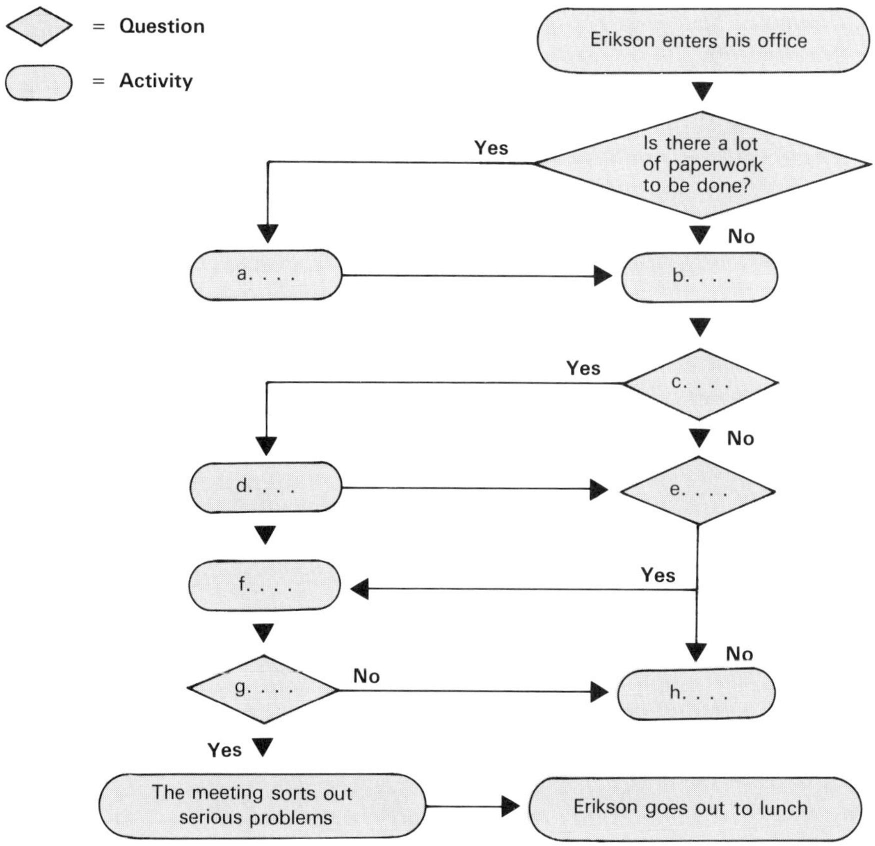

3 Choose from the following to complete the diagram below, and give your reasons for classifying each expression as INPUT or OUTPUT:

updated working file	**stock file**
working file	**programmes and schedules**
layouts/material requirements/ job cards	**stock control data**
	progress documents
completed orders	**alterations to orders**

The Computer for Production Planning

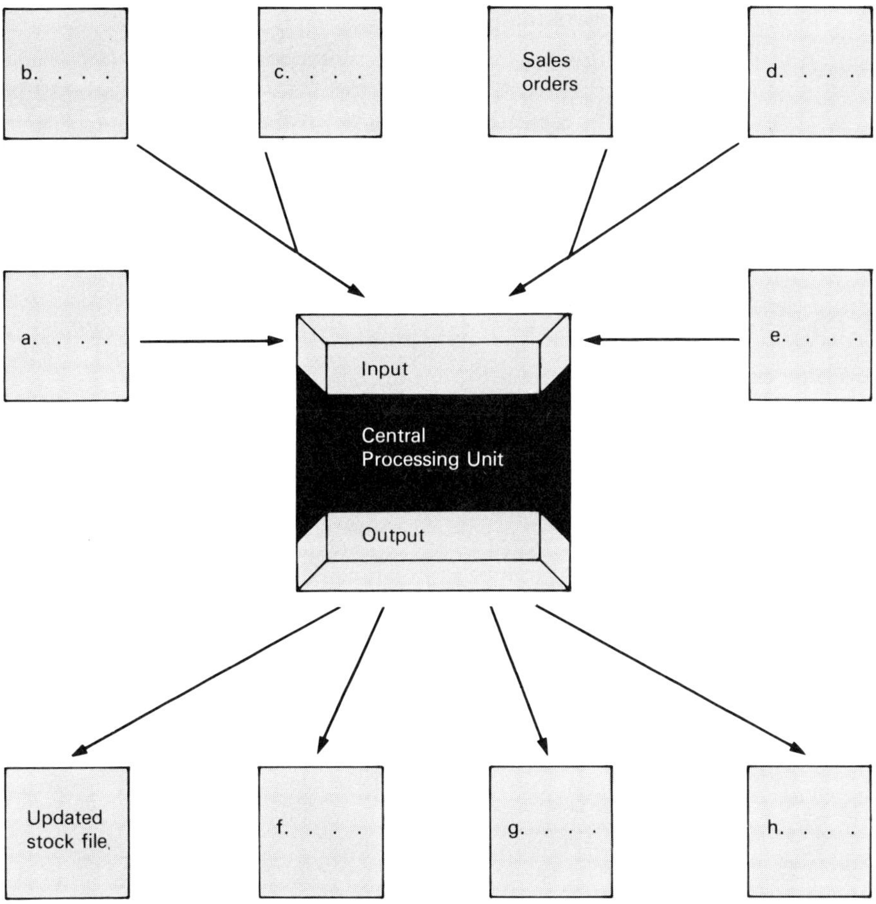

SECTION F Discussion

1 How are planning and control related to each other? What are the similarities and differences between them?

2 What techniques and procedures are useful in the process of executive control?

3 Why is real time information not good enough for effective control of production?

SECTION G Writing

1 Notice how the paragraph below has been built up from these notes.

— real time computing system can help to improve control of production/measures standards of performance/indicates ways of correcting deviations from standards
— system can provide valuable service/skilled staff needed to run it/expensive to install and maintain
— in order for real time system to be efficient, important that appropriate skills available in workforce/important that potential savings from system greater than cost of operation

A real time computing system can help to improve the control of production by measuring standards of performance and by indicating ways of correcting deviations from these standards. Although a real time system can provide a valuable service, skilled staff are needed to run it, and it is expensive to install and maintain. Therefore, in order for a real time system to be efficient, it is important, first, that the appropriate skills are available in the workforce, and second, that the potential savings that can be made are greater than its cost of operation.

2 Cover the paragraph, and, using the notes, try to rewrite it exactly as it is.

3 Using the notes below, write a similar paragraph about training programmes. These words may help you: **although, therefore, first, second.**

— in-company training programmes can help improve efficiency of company/upgrade present knowledge and skills of staff/teach new skills
— training programmes can provide valuable service/skilled trainers required to run them/expensive to operate
— in order for training programmes to be efficient, important that qualified trainers available on staff/important that savings that result from training programmes greater than cost of operation

Unit 9 Productivity

SECTION A Reading

Read this article from the magazine *Business Eye.*

Rand leads the way

Market analysts have been following the progress of US electricals giant Rand International with interest over the past few years. Last week company president Laurence Essing announced another year of record output and profit. According to Essing: 'One of the critical aspects of any organization's environment is the state of technology which affects it. Rand has its plans ready for any change that might take place in the market.'

But Rand International has not always been one of the market leaders. Four years ago, company performance was at an all-time low and there was a lot of talk about a take-over from US rival Standard Electronics. David Kennedy, of the Wall Street firm of Trueman and Katz, suggests two reasons for this change-around: 'While it's true that technological development and high investment have had a strong impact on performance, this is not the whole story. In my opinion, the arrival of new executive vice-president Peter Freingel three years ago was very significant for the company, especially for the influence he has had on productivity.'

Business Eye spoke with Peter Freingel to get his view on the matter: 'In this industry, unless you invest in ideas and equipment, then you have little chance of success. In fact, as part of our new expansion programme, we will be investing 2.5 million dollars in our California components factory next year. But I think the major factor in our growth has been our ability to get all sections of the company operating efficiently.'

An important part of Freingel's policy has been the special emphasis placed on industrial engineering and O&M. A great deal of work on methods improvement and value analysis has led to greater efficiency of materials management, and of production and process methods. This, in turn, has meant better utilization of manpower, plant and equipment. On the administrative side, procedures have been greatly improved with the design of new data processing systems. Figure 1 illustrates the rise in productivity at Rand.

Had the change-around at Rand been difficult to achieve? Peter Freingel again: 'It would have been difficult, unless we had persuaded all personnel that the company had a future. We gave them the right incentives to believe that it had.'

It seems as if Peter Freingel has got it right. Rand will be expanding into Europe soon when the acquisition of the Dutch company, Speers, is finalized, and it is possible that the new C7 video unit will be ready for sale by the end of the year. Investors might do worse than put some money into Rand shares now. 35

Fig 1 Rand International Output per man hour 1971-81 (1971 = 100)

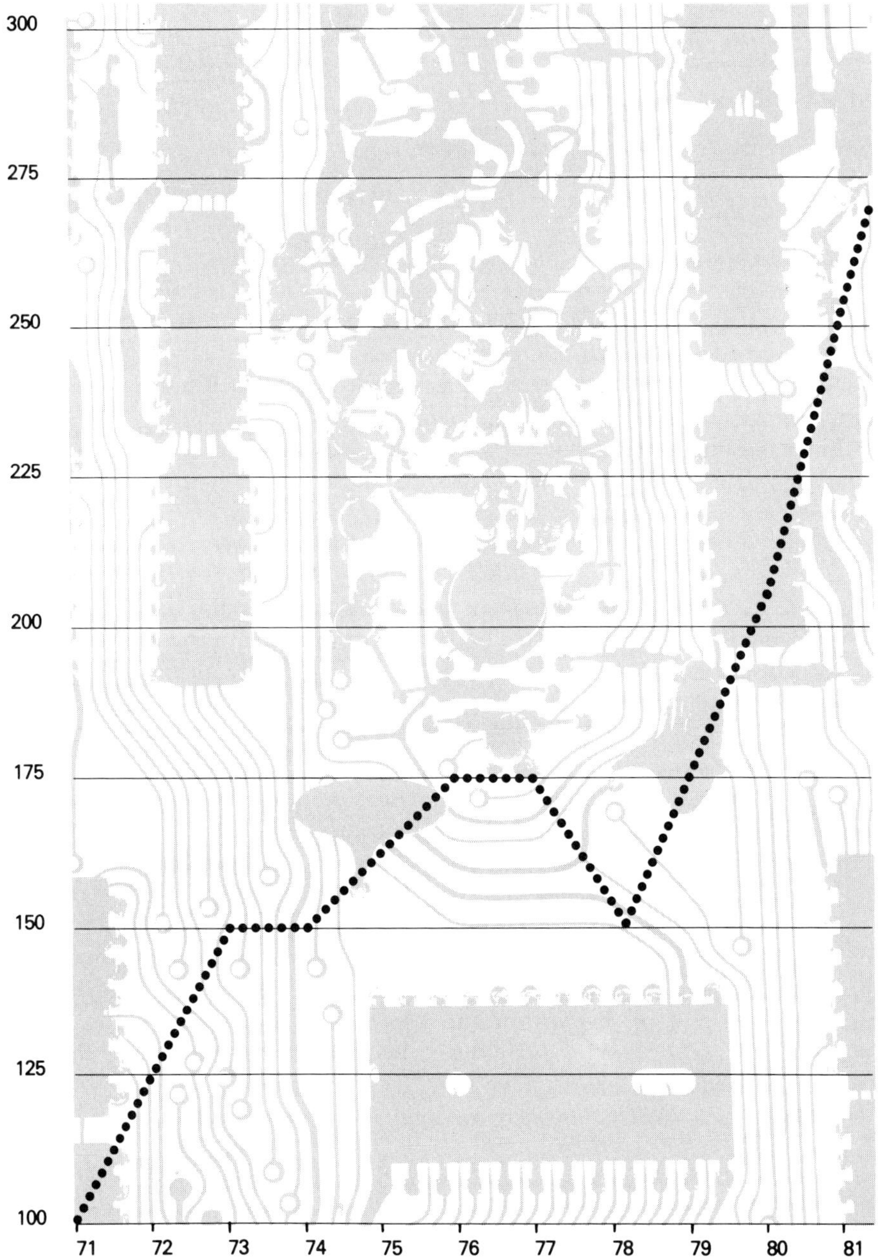

Word Study

leads *l.1* directs the course of; is at the head of.
giant *l.2* person or thing of very great size.
announced *l.4* gave notice of; gave out the information that.
critical *l.5* This is the adjective from *crisis,* which is a decisive turning-point in the course of anything. What is the meaning of *critical* in the expression *critical path analysis* (Unit 8)?
environment *l.6* all the surrounding conditions which *affect* (see the definition below) function and development. How do dirty, smoky factories affect the environment?
state *l.6* condition; way of existence as determined by surrounding conditions. *The machine parts were left outside and are now in a very bad state.* What is wrong with the parts? What must be done to them? What is meant by *an employee's state of health?*
affects *l.6* has an effect on; produces a change in. How does a dirty environment at work affect efficiency?
take-over *l.10* one company getting control of another.
rival *l.10* person, company, organization, etc. that competes with another.
change-around *l.12* change in course or path in the opposite direction.
impact *l.13* effect.
significant *l.15* important; full of meaning. The verb *signify* means 'be a sign or indication of'. On a factory floor, what do the symbols below signify?

influence *l.15* power to affect others; power to produce effects. The verb is also *influence.* How did Henry Ford influence production methods?
chance *l.18* possibility; opportunity (= 'good time for the purpose').
emphasis *l.23* attention or importance given to something. The verb *emphasize* means 'give special force or importance to'. How are *do/does/did* used for emphasis?
O&M *l.24* Organization & Methods (abbreviation).

utilization *l.27* getting profit or benefit from, by making better use of; putting into practical or profitable use.
persuaded *l.32* caused ('all personnel') to believe by suggestion, reason or argument. What do product advertisements attempt to persuade consumers to do? Why must good salesmen be persuasive?
acquisition *l.36* process of getting possession of. How is experience *acquired?*
shares *l.38* equal parts into which total worth of a corporation is divided. Describe the relative movements of the shares in the table below.

Company	*Friday's close*	*Change on week*	*1981 high*	*1981 low*
Canpan	80	+12	88	60
Royal Group	420	+27	420	230
AVG Oil	110	−18	164	12

(The symbols − and + are read as minus and plus.)

Comprehension

1 Complete the table.

Reasons given for Rand's good performance			
Essing	Kennedy	Freingel	Business Eye
. . .	. . .	. . .	. . .
etc.	etc.	etc.	etc.

2 Say what the words in **bold face** refer to.
a. '. . . for **this change-around** . . .' *(l.11)*
b. '. . . **this** is not the whole **story**.' *(l.13)*
c. '. . . his view on **the matter** . . . *(l.17)*
d. 'In **this industry** . . .' *(l.17)*
e. '**This**, in turn, . . . *(l.26)*
f. 'On the administrative **side** . . .' *(l.28)*
g. '**It** would have been difficult . . .' *(l.32)*

3 What has happened to Rand in the last four years?

4 Describe man hour output performance at Rand for the 1971-81 period. What is the relation between productivity and man hour output performance?

5 What advice is given to investors in the article?

6 What is the relation between Rand's expansion and Speers? How soon will the expansion begin?

SECTION B Listening

Cassette 2, side 1. While you are listening to the conversation between Mr. Deeds, a Training Officer, and two of his trainee managers, Sandra Fulton and Terry Weir, do the exercise below.
On the tape, Mr. Deeds explains to the trainees the method of value analysis used at Universal. They discuss a number of factors that are necessary to consider in order to achieve maximum product value. List as many of these factors as possible.

Deeds Good morning, Sandra. Morning, Terry. Everything all right so far this week? How's it going?
Fulton Very well, Mr. Deeds.
Deeds Any problems, Terry?
Weir Can't say there are. Everything's fine.
Deeds That's what I like to hear. Great. Okay, then, today I'd like to talk about the method of value analysis we use here at Universal Motors. Okay? Right. Let me start by giving you a definition. As we see it, value analysis is an organized approach which aims at maintaining product performance while reducing the costs of production; ie, cut costs, but don't cut down on quality. So, in order to maximize product value, we should have a systematic assessment made of every product we manufacture.
Fulton Every product? Wouldn't that be too time-consuming? To have it done for every product in our range, I mean.
Deeds It would, sure. That's why, in practice, we try to decide which products might offer the greatest savings potential before we go on to having them analysed.
Weir Is there a set procedure for having the analysis done?
Deeds Not exactly. But we've got what I call our 'twenty keys to value'.
Fulton Keys?
Deeds I'll explain. We've got a list of twenty factors that we feel we need to consider in order to achieve maximum product value, although we don't approach them in any fixed order of importance. As part of our training programme we'll be considering these different factors—or 'keys', as I call them—we'll be considering them in detail, and later we'll be examining a case study in order to show how the analysis works in practice. Maybe we could begin by discussing what you think these, um, keys might be. Sandra? Any ideas?
Fulton What about standardized processes? Shouldn't they always be used, unless there are very good reasons for not using them?
Deeds Good point.
Weir Doesn't that apply to the use of standard components, too?
Deeds Right, Terry. Anybody who wants to give up the benefits of standardization should examine his ideas very carefully. Very, very carefully.
Fulton And what about the question of information?
Deeds What about it, Sandra?
Fulton Well, um, I don't think our information always comes from the best people, or from the best places. And it seems to me that we often fail to bring new information into the areas that are being considered.
Deeds Yes, we don't seem to make the best use of the ideas and the experience of staff.
Weir Okay, but that's not so easy to do. I mean, people are usually very busy, and they haven't always got the time to answer a lot of detailed questions.
Deeds Sure, but you must be prepared to search out the answers you want. And this is an interesting point, you see, because another one of our keys to value is the emphasis we place on improving communications within the company by our own good example. And remember: deal with the easy things first, and keep it simple.
Weir So what about costs, then? Aren't they one of the factors?
Deeds Absolutely. Unless we've got the necessary costings data, we can't even begin to analyse the advantages of alternative methods.
Fulton Our own alternatives should be costed.
Deeds Of course. We say two things at Universal. First, have a value put on every idea you come up with. And second, spend the company's money like you spend your own. Right? That's of course if, um, you're good with your own money. Okay? Now, can you think of any other important factors we need to consider? No? All right, let's make a summary of what we've discussed so far, and then see if there are any points we can add . . .

☐ In your opinion, are there any other important factors to consider?

SECTION C Language Study

1 Nations and Nationalities

Use your dictionary to find out which nations these nationalities refer to: Finnish, Swedish, French, Greek, Turkish, British, Norwegian, Saudi Arabian, Egyptian, Swiss, Italian, Spanish, Portuguese, Icelandic, Argentinian.

Now find out the nationalities for the following nations: China, Thailand, Mexico, Japan, Germany, Senegal, Somalia, Denmark, Poland, Scotland, Wales, Belgium, Cuba, USSR, India, Ireland, Canada.

2 Definitions

Examples:
Wall Street firm
▷ a firm which is located in Wall Street

programme evaluation technique
▷ a technique which evaluates programmes

Now explain what is meant by each of the following.

a. California components factory

b. man hour output performance

c. company president Laurence Essing

d. Business Eye market analysis article

e. production programme status report

f. quality control assessment data

g. EDP stock control system

h. Standard Electronics network planning technique

3 Sequencing Past Events

Examples:
(1) Business Eye spoke to David Kennedy. (2) The magazine asked for Peter Freingel's view on the matter. (**after**)
▷ **After** Business Eye **had spoken** to David Kennedy, the magazine asked for Peter Freingel's view on the matter.

Notice how the Past Perfect is used to describe the action which takes place first. Now use the Past Perfect in linking the following pairs of sentences.

a. (1) The Board studied the report. (2) They made their recommendation. (when)

b. (1) He worked in the London Office for three years. (2) He was transferred to Paris. (before)

c. (1) They closed the meeting. (2) They reached agreement on the new pay structure. (after)

d. (1) The company used mechanical stock control techniques. (2) They introduced a computerized stock control system. (before)

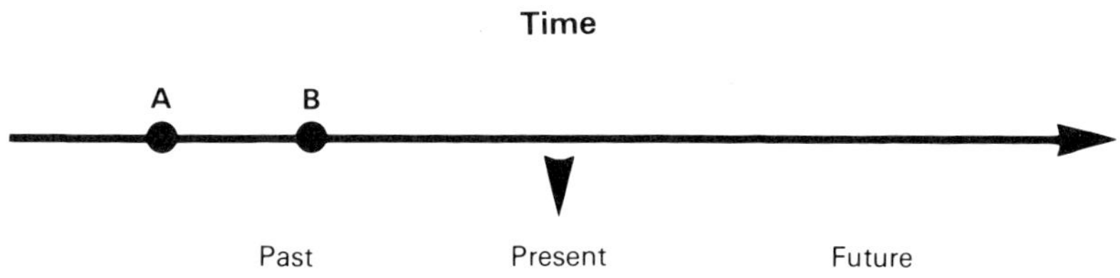

A and **B** are symbols for actions in the past. Which of the two is expressed in Past Perfect? In the exercise above, which actions are **A**s and which are **B**s?

SECTION D Listening

Cassette 2, side 1. While you are listening to tape, complete the table below.

Subject:	*Organisation of paperwork*	*Costing of administrative & clerical time*
Ways of improving	**a.** . . .	**d.** . . .
Suggested by	**b.** Mr . . .	**e.** Mr . . .
	c. Title . . .	**f.** Title . . .

☐ Why does Mr. Kohn think there will be a problem in providing costings for clerical work?

SECTION E Using Information in Different Ways

1 The manufacture of individual components is analysed by critical examination in order to find ways of improving production methods. Here are eighteen questions that it might be necessary to ask in an examination of this kind.

a. Can any limits be lowered to make manufacture easier?

b. Can the finished component be replaced by a standard part?

c. Is any function unnecessary?

d. Can suppliers suggest a means of reducing the cost of materials?

e. Can any assembly operation be reduced?

f. Can the finished components be produced by different processes?

g. Is the part oversized in comparison to competitors' products?

h. Can any other material be used?

i. Can another component incorporate this function?

j. Can items bought outside be more cheaply produced in-company?

k. Can any labour operation be reduced by a method or design change?

l. Can any limits be lowered to allow for alternative methods of manufacture?

m. Can the materials be standardized?

n. Can the materials be produced through different processes?

o. Can a change of manufacturing method reduce the amount of material which is wasted (= 'left over after use and thrown away')?

p. Is the part oversized in comparison to associated parts?

q. Can the amount of wasted material be reduced by design changes?

r. Can any other specification of the same material be used?

In the critical examination sheet on the opposite page, classify questions **a-r** according to the subjects to which they refer.

SECTION F Discussion

1 'There is a serious need to look critically at administrative and clerical costs in industry and commerce.' Do you agree? What are your reasons? How can the costs of administration be reduced?

2 What techniques can management utilize in order to improve the efficiency of a manufacturing organization?

3 What is the relation between productivity and investment?

Function	What functions are performed?	a. . . . b. . . .
Material Specification	What is the material specification	a. . . . b. . . .
Material Content	How much material is used in the component?	a. . . . b. . . .
Material Value	What % of basic material is not used?	a. . . . b. . . .
Limits	Which limits are critical?	a. . . . b. . . .
Process of Manufacture	Is this the best process?	a. . . . b. . . .
Standardization	Is the finished component standard?	a. . . . b. . . .
Labour Costs	What are the direct labour costs?	a. . . . b. . . .
Material Costs	What is the cost of materials and components?	a. . . . b. . . .

SECTION G Writing

1 Read these two related paragraphs on productivity.

Investment is an important factor in the successful development of modern industry. **Unless** there is a high level of investment in ideas, men and machinery, a company can not stay competitive. **However,** high investment by itself does not automatically mean the efficient utilization of skills and resources. Productivity is affected by such factors as company organization, leadership, training, and the way in which products are manufactured.

In order to improve manufacturing methods, companies can call on the services of the industrial engineer and the O&M expert. **First,** the use of industrial engineering techniques should lead to a greater efficiency in production methods and a better utilization of manpower, plant and equipment. **Secondly,** on the O&M side, the improvement of office procedures and data processing systems will also ensure that resources are efficiently used.

2 Now put the statements below into a suitable order.

a. A job description should give details of the performance that is required for a specific job.

b. Successful training depends on such factors as the quality of the staff under training, the quality of the trainers, and the suitability of the training specification employed.

c. Training is an important factor in the successful performance of a modern business.

d. In terms of job specification, there should be information about the behaviour, knowledge and skills of an employee for the performance of a specific job.

e. If a training programme does not exist, personnel can not develop the appropriate skills for the job.

f. In order to define a training specification, the Training Department uses a job description and a job specification.

g. A large training programme by itself does not necessarily mean the efficient training of staff.

3 Build the sentences up into two related paragraphs.

Unit 10 Distribution

SECTION A Reading

Here is another example of the descriptive English which is used in business textbooks.

The function of distribution is to move goods from the producer to the final consumer or user, and it applies to both industrial and consumer goods or services. There are a number of channels open to the producer for this purpose. He can deal directly with the consumer or with middlemen such as retailers, wholesalers or agents.

Channels of Distribution

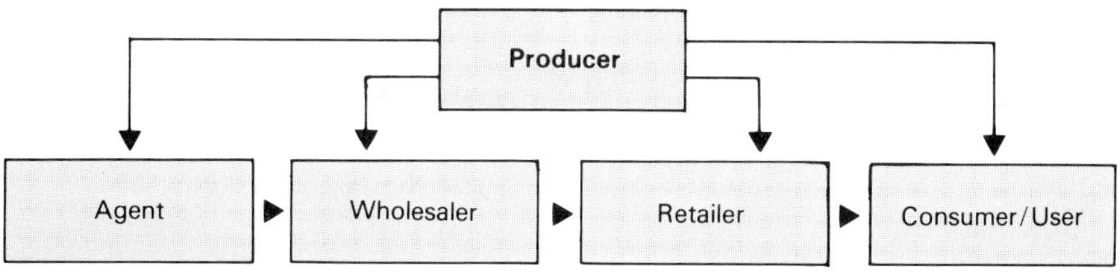

The choice of distribution channel, or combination of channels, is linked to financial, technical, and market considerations. For example, in the case of a product which is technically complex, it should be more efficient for the manufacturer to deal directly with the user, but a cigarette manufacturer, say, with a product that must be made available to a large number of potential customers, should find that dealing with a wide range of wholesalers is the best answer.

Circumstances are always changing, however, and this fact influences channel decisions. In 1963, for instance, J Lyons and Company, a British firm, was using the services of one thousand wholesalers when it decided to change its policy and to deliver its food products directly to its retail customers. Seven years later, the company was employing the services of middlemen again due to a further change in policy.

From the manufacturer's point of view, it is the total cost of distribution which is significant and not the costs of individual activities such as warehousing, order processing, or transport. For example, a company that reduced the cost of warehousing could find that the cost of transport was increased, with the net result that the total cost of distribution was also increased. On the other hand, there are examples where a high cost that had been incurred in one area resulted in a total net saving owing to cost reductions that had been made possible in related areas.

This last point is particularly important regarding transport policy. A company must decide whether it uses its own transport or employs the services of an outside company. If it decides on the former, it is faced with complex questions about the suitability of different types of transport and the routing choices in freight movement. These decisions will have an effect on, and must be related to, the overall distribution policy.

Word Study

channels *l.3* paths or courses through which something moves or passes.
middlemen *l.4* operators between the producer and the consumer.
retailers *l.5* those who sell goods individually or in small quantities directly to the consumer. The opposite of *retail* is 'wholesale', ie, the selling of goods in relatively large quantities, mostly to retailers.
wholesalers *l.5* See the explanation above.
agents *l.5* persons, firms, etc. with the power to act for others. The noun is *agency*. In the usual course of goods in business, where does an agency come in? Is it possible to have an agency for services? How?
combination *l.6* bringing together of two or more things so that they form a union.
say *l.10* imagine for example.
circumstances *l.13* conditions which surround and affect a person or persons.
deliver *l.16* transfer or hand over. Delivery is the last act in any distribution process.
due to *l.18* caused by; owing to.
transport *l.21* carrying from one place to another, especially over long distances. What are the means of transport by road, rail, air and sea?
net result *l.23* result after everything else has been considered; final result. Businessmen speak of gross and net profits, which are profits *before* and *after* all expenses have been subtracted.
incurred *l.25* met with. The verb incur is often used with reference to something undesirable (= 'not wanted or wished for'); eg, unnecessary expenses, very high costs, serious losses etc, *are* all *incurred*.
regarding *l.27* with reference to; relative to.
the former *l.29* the first one of the preceding group of *two* persons or things. Corby and McMillan will retire at the end of the month; *the former* is 65, *the latter* is 62. Who is the younger?
routing *l.31* tranwporting by a specified course. A *route* is a way, course or road which is travelled in going from one place to another. Describe the route you usually take in going to work.
freight *l.31* large goods or quantities of goods transported by land, sea or air.
overall *l.32* total; including everything.

Comprehension

1 List some distribution channels. What does the choice of distribution channel depend on?

2 Say what the words in **bold face** refer to.

a. '. . . **it** applies . . .' *(l.2)*
b. '. . . for **this purpose** . . .' *(l.3)*
c. '. . . **the best answer** . . .' *(l.12)*
d. '. . . **this fact** . . .' *(l.13)*
e. '. . . **its policy** . . .' *(l.16)*
f. '**This last point** . . .' *(l.27)*
g. '**The former** . . .' *(l.29)*

3 Complete the table.

Period	*J. Lyons Distribution Channels*
Pre- 1963	Producer ▷
1963-70	Producer ▷
1970 onwards	Producer ▷

4 What problems does a company face when it decides to use its own transport?

5 Does a high cost in one area necessarily mean a high cost overall? Why?

6 Why must the choice between in-company and outside transport services be related to overall distribution policy?

7 Complete the following table.

verb	*noun*	*verb*	*noun*
deliver	. . .	suit	. . .
distribute	. . .	. . .	consumption
transport	. . .	consider	. . .
. . .	subtraction	. . .	influence
. . .	route	. . .	significance

8 True or False?

a. Cigarette manufacturers generally deal directly with retailers.
b. A reduction in transport costs will automatically provide a total net saving in distribution.
c. If the 1963 channel decision at Lyons had not been taken, there would have been no basis for a policy change-around later.
d. In 1970 Lyons suddenly decided to employ the services of middlemen again.
e. Producers often use more than one type of distribution channel.

SECTION B Listening

Cassette 2, side 1. While you are listening to the conversation between Max Lumet, a Regional Sales Manager, and Larry Barth, a Marketing Director, complete the diagram below.

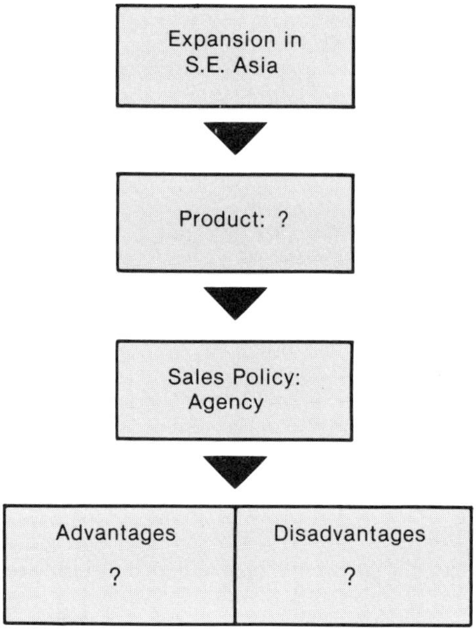

Barth Hello, Max. How are things?

Lumet They could be better.

Barth I saw your figures for last quarter yesterday. They were pretty good.

Lumet Yes, not too bad. So what's new, Larry?

Barth I was talking to Holmes, the executive vice-president, two days ago, and he, um, mentioned that our plans for Indonesia should go ahead.

Lumet That's a little strange, that the Board have decided already. I thought they were only discussing the alternatives.

Barth So did I, but it appears that they had already decided on expansion in South East Asia before we made our recommendations.

Lumet So? Where do we go from here?

Barth Well, for starters, I think you and I should discuss some of the details associated with the project.

Lumet Detail number one for me is the question of selling our farm machinery out there.

Barth Sure. For that we can do an analysis of, um, market conditions, right?

Lumet And get ourselves a good agent as soon as possible.

Barth You think that sales should be dealt with through an agency?

Lumet That has always been Landseer policy when moving into an unknown market.

Barth That doesn't mean to say that such a policy is the right one for this situation, Max.

Lumet I think there's a lot to be said for continuing the practice. We have very little experience in that market, for one thing, and for another we don't know a lot about the selling and distribution techniques they use.

Barth Come on, Max. Landseer was selling to Asia before you or I ever joined the company.

Lumet There are other considerations. Like, if we set up and maintained a sales organisation out there, I'm sure it would die from inefficiency. Look at our sales forecasts. There's no way we can maximize use of our salesmen.

Barth Maybe in the short run, but we are not talking about a Mickey Mouse manufacturer, Max, this is Landseer. We've got the know-how to achieve a large volume of sales in a very short time.

Lumet Know-how or not, the marketing problems are a question mark. Without the answers first, this large potential volume of sales you're talking about may never materialize.

Barth And what if we appoint the wrong sort of agent? What about the consequences there? Suppose we have little control of his activities and lose out on an expanding market in that way. Believe me, Max, if we don't make the sales, and make them fast, someone else will.

Lumet No. The market is too uncertain. Let's appoint an agent for a limited period, see how it goes, then make a decision about the future organization after, say, three years.

Barth We wait three years, we lose our chance.

Lumet Larry, why worry so much about the competition? At the present time the market is small, and we can cut potential losses by not incurring high costs at the very beginning.

Barth Look, Max, you want to know why we don't see eye-to-eye on this? I'll tell you. It's because I see a permanent set-up in Indonesia as central to the company's overall policy in South East Asia. We'll be expanding our operations in the Far East over the next few years, and the simple fact is that we need a strong base from which we can implement a policy of this kind.

Lumet Maybe so, but that's not really why you're against the agency idea for Indonesia. The reason for your position is the failure of our agency policy in South America.

Barth Okay, then, since you've mentioned it, you're right. If the establishment of an agency had worked in South America, I would probably regard it as a useful thing to try now.

Lumet But we've changed it in the light of circumstances, Larry. Take those problems we had in Brazil, for instance. We made mistakes, we learned from those mistakes, and we changed our policy accordingly.

Barth Not before we had lost a lot of money, Max.

Lumet Larry, Larry . . .

☐ What experience has made Barth feel that an agency policy would be wrong for S. E. Asia?

SECTION C Language Study

1 Probability

Notice how we can express the idea of probability.

Examples:

It is possible that the new warehouse will reduce distribution costs.
▷ The new warehouse **may** reduce distribution costs.

It is probable that the new warehouse will reduce distribution costs.
▷ The new warehouse **should** reduce distribution costs.

Write six sentences describing the jobs or activities that you **may** complete or you **should** complete this week.

2 Reference Numbers

The reference number 0-52/15(4) is read aloud as:
oh dash five two stroke one five brackets four close brackets
or *zero hyphen fifty-two oblique fifteen parentheses four close parentheses*
or any combination of the preceding two examples.

Read these reference numbers aloud:

a. PB/344/72/046
b. AO/TS-346-81
c. 22-34/Y/V-8388
d. AR/MLS/9(101)/005
e. WC2B 4PH
f. AE/72/CJ/3
g. IA/2EC/B32

3 Dates

The following dates are read aloud as follows.
31/5/79 = *the thirty first of May nineteen seventy-nine*
2/11/80 = *the second of November nineteen eighty*
13/3/64 = *the thirteenth of March nineteen sixty-four*

Now read these dates aloud:

a. 31/5/79 **d.** 11-2-81
b. 28-6-82 **e.** 18/7/69
c. 23/1/85

4 Combining Sentences

Notice how the following sentences are built up.

Examples:
The channel **through which** goods are distributed depends on financial, technical, and market considerations.
⊳ (1) Goods are distributed **through** a channel. (2) This channel depends on financial, technical, and market considerations.

The central point **on which** Barth and Lumet disagree is the failure of the agency policy in South America.
⊳ (1) Barth and Lumet disagree **on** a central point. (2) This point is the failure of the agency policy in South America.

In a similar way, show how the following sentences are built up.

a. The number of the tool to which we refer in our letter of the 21st September is FC-3266.

b. The highly undesirable conditions under which the machine-tool operators are working have been reported to the Union.

c. The list from which the applicants were selected had been prepared by the Personnel Manager.

d. The Safety Officer has a book in which he enters a daily report.

e. The marketing problems with which Landseer will have to deal are complex.

The sentences **a-e** above can be expressed in four different ways, as in the examples below. Some English speakers feel that (1) is more formal than (2), that (3) is less formal than (2), and that (4) is the least formal of them all. According to some English speakers, therefore, which of these examples would be more appropriate in formal business correspondence and in conversation?

(1) The channel **through which** goods are distributed depends on financial, technical, and marketing considerations.
(2) The channel **which** goods are distributed **through** depends on financial, technical, and marketing considerations.
(3) The channel **that** goods are distributed **through** depends on financial, technical, and marketing considerations.

(4) The channel goods are distributed **through** depends on financial, technical, and marketing considerations.

It should be noted that the modern trend in business English, especially in the USA, Canada and Australia, is towards less formal expressions overall.

SECTION D Listening

Cassette 2, side 1. While you are listening to the telephone conversation between a Product Manager and a Distribution Manager, note down the answers to the questions below.

1 What is Mr. Harvey's Job?

2 What is Mr. Harvey's telephone extension number?

3 What did Kranz of Hamburg order from Ocean Chemicals?

4 What was the reference number for the Kranz order?

5 When should Kranz receive their order?

6 What is the reference number for Roget's order?

7 When was Roget's order received?

8 When should Mr. Lamb know about the availability of Roget's order?

SECTION E Using Information in Different Ways

1 Study this description of the movements of a truck from Bristol, UK, to Lyons, France.

The truck had been timed to leave the factory in Bristol at 9.00am, but owing to the failure of the Dispatch Department to have all the necessary paperwork ready, it left ninety minutes late. However, the easy traffic conditions enabled the driver to make up most of the time on the run to Southampton where he arrived only fifteen minutes behind schedule.

The 6.00pm ferry was thirty minutes late in leaving due to rough weather conditions which also slowed the boat during the crossing with the result that it reached Le Havre an hour behind time. Being first in line at Customs made it possible for the driver to make up half an hour leaving Le Havre. Then, at Ivry, a stop was made for the regulation one hour before departure for Gien. The truck was scheduled to arrive in Gien at 6.00pm for its stop-over for the night, but owing to mechanical problems en route it got in three and a quarter hours late.

The truck left as scheduled the following morning, but it was an hour off its arrival time for the lunch-hour stop at Moulins because traffic had been held up by an accident at Cosne. The driver cut short his break by thirty minutes in order to make up time, and light traffic conditions made it possible for him to get to Lyons thirty minutes ahead of schedule.

2 Using the information in the previous passage, complete the transport schedule with timings and causes of deviations where they are required.

Transport Schedule

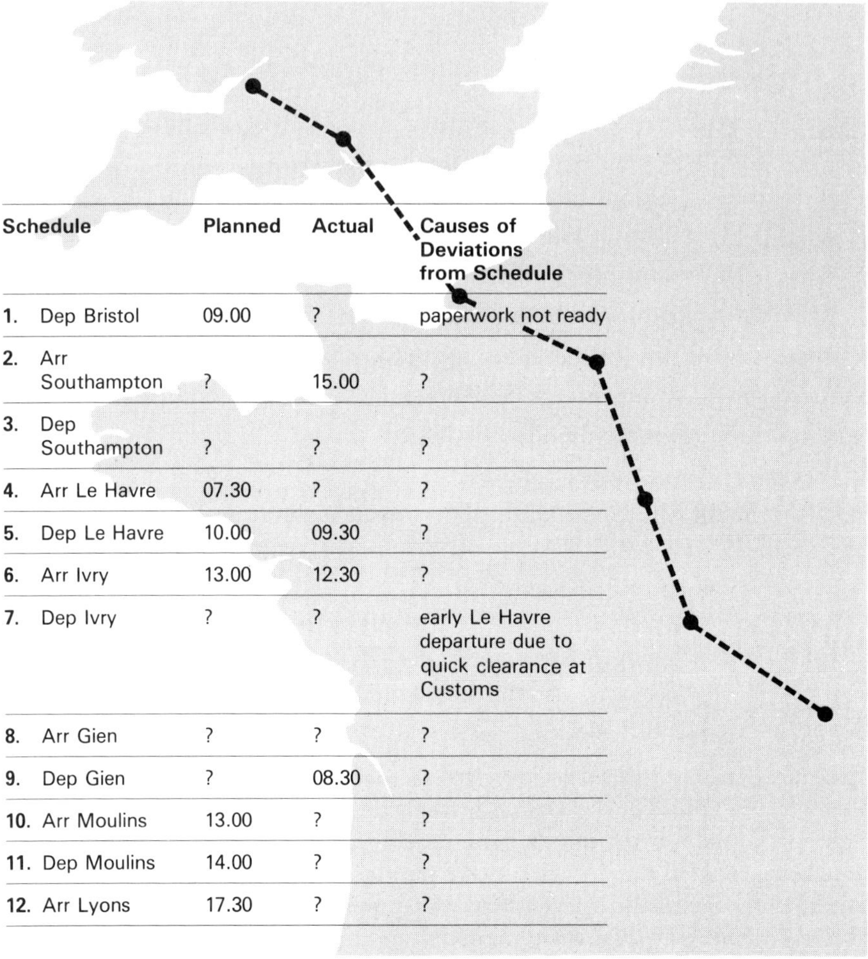

Schedule	Planned	Actual	Causes of Deviations from Schedule
1. Dep Bristol	09.00	?	paperwork not ready
2. Arr Southampton	?	15.00	?
3. Dep Southampton	?	?	?
4. Arr Le Havre	07.30	?	?
5. Dep Le Havre	10.00	09.30	?
6. Arr Ivry	13.00	12.30	?
7. Dep Ivry	?	?	early Le Havre departure due to quick clearance at Customs
8. Arr Gien	?	?	?
9. Dep Gien	?	08.30	?
10. Arr Moulins	13.00	?	?
11. Dep Moulins	14.00	?	?
12. Arr Lyons	17.30	?	?

SECTION F Discussion

1 What factors may influence the choice of distribution channel?

2 'In this period of high competition, marketing considerations should be the most important of all in designing an organization structure. This means basing departments on markets and channels by which they are reached, not on technical production factors.' Do you agree? Why?

3 In what circumstances might a company use the services of an agent for overseas distribution?

SECTION G Writing

1 Notice how the paragraph below uses information both from Figure 1, a bar chart illustrating the scheduled production at Canpan in 1981, and from Figure 2, a table which shows the actual production for this period and the reasons for deviations from schedule.

The Canpan factory had been scheduled to produce 30,000 units in January; but, because of a strike at a components supplier, it was able to produce a total of only 10,000 units. In February, the number of units produced amounted to 30,000; ie, 10,000 fewer than scheduled. This was due to a number of technical problems connected with the power supply to the factory. In the third month, production totalled 45,000 units, which was 5,000 more than the figure which had been planned. This was owing to the overtime which had been worked for the purpose of building up stocks.

Fig. 1 Scheduled Production at Canpan 1981

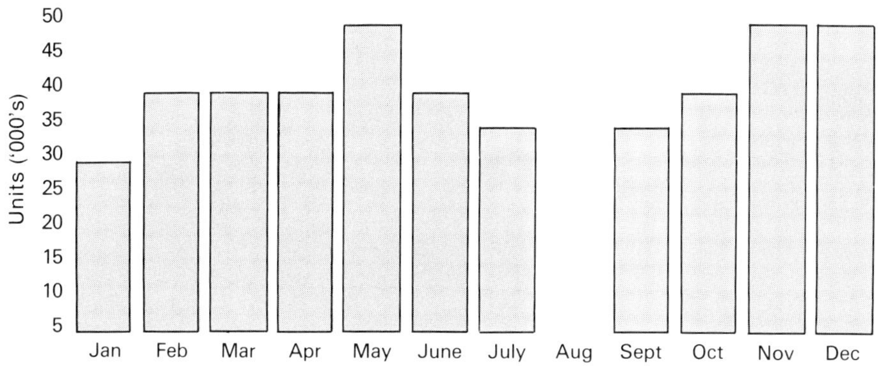

Fig. 2 Actual Production at Canpan 1981

Month	Actual Unit Production	Reasons for Deviations from Scheduled Production
Jan	10,000	Strike at components supplier
Feb	30,000	Technical problems over factory power supply
Mar	45,000	Overtime worked for stock building
Apr	45,000	Same as above
May	40,000	Production reduced owing to demand fall
June	33,000	Strike in toolroom
July	34,000	Strike by truck drivers
Aug	zero	Holiday shutdown
Sept	50,000	Overtime worked to meet demand
Oct	30,000	Number of machine breakdowns
Nov	45,000	Fire in warehouse
Dec	60,000	Overtime worked for stockbuilding

2 Now write a similar paragraph describing the situation from April to December. These words may help you: **because of, owing to, due to.**

Review Unit 2 Problem Solving

This unit is designed to help you to review the grammar and special vocabulary that you have learned from Units 6-10. There are no new words or structures in this unit.

1 Read the following passage.

Problem Solving

Types of Problems	
Improvement Problem	Improve the performance of a product, process, system or employee.
Deviation Problem	Set new objectives owing to the failure of the present system.
Potential Problem	Define what may go wrong and assess the possible effects of failing to meet planned performance.
Evaluation Problem	Select a method of operation from a number of specified alternatives.
Design Problem	Define the problems of producing a new product, work environment, or system.

All aspects of business activity are associated with uncertainty, the major reasons for which are the difficulties which businessmen experience in (1) trying to influence the future course of events, (2) determining the differences between the causes and the effects operating in any given situation, (3) making a viable choice between various courses of action that may be open to them, and (4) ensuring that those who are employed in the decision-making process are in receipt of full information.

The existence of uncertainty and the necessity of making decisions affect all the five central types of business problems. Decisions that are taken in order to improve the performance of a product or service, to produce a new product or to select a new method of operation can not be sure of success in terms of achieving stated company objectives. As a means of reducing uncertainty in business to reasonable limits, many companies seek to improve the efficiency of the decision-making process through problem-solving procedures.

Steps in Problem Solving

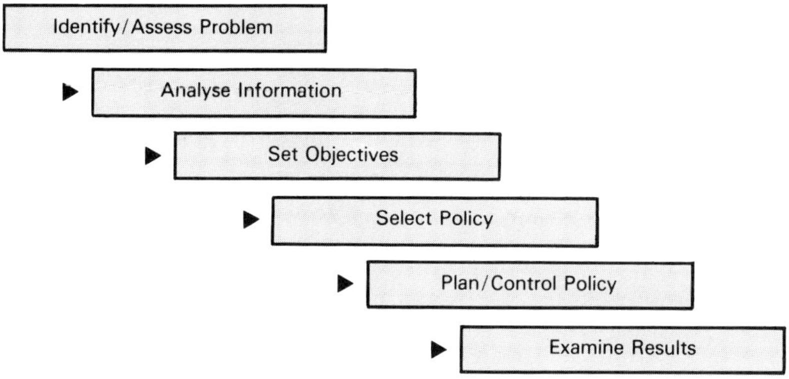

The ability to identify and assess a particular problem is related to the quantity and quality of the information available, and to how well it is analysed. After that, the setting of objectives and the selection of a particular policy are determined, on the one hand, by the ability of management to forecast events, and, on the other hand, by the capacity of management for identifying the possibilities and potentialities in a given or expected situation. Finally, planning and control of policy are linked to the distribution of limited resources between particular methods of operation which have been chosen from a number of other alternatives. They are also related to the evaluation of actual performance as compared to planned performance.

If, at the end of this sequence of steps, the problem is still unsolved, then the process must begin again in the hope of coming closer to a final solution. As part of this process, information must be re-assessed and the conclusions which were reached at the start must be critically re-examined in order to determine a new line of approach.

2 Now do these exercises based on the passage.

a. Say what the words in **bold face** refer to.

'. . . major reasons for **which** . . .' *(l.3)*
'. . . may be open to **them** . . .' *(l.7)*
'. . . **the five central types** . . .' *(l.10)*
'. . . **it** is analysed . . .' *(l.18)*
'After **that**, . . .' *(l.19)*
'. . . **this sequence of steps** . . .' *(l.28)*
'. . . **the process** . . .' *(l.29)*
'. . . at **the start** . . .' *(l.31)*

b. What are the major causes of the uncertainty associated with business activity? Explain the reasons for the uncertainty in each case.

c. Define (1) improvement problem, (2) deviation problem, (3) potential problem, (4) evaluation problem, (5) design problem.

d. Do you agree with the sequence of the six steps in the problem-solving process as it is illustrated above? Why?

e. Why do companies attempt to make decision-making more efficient? How?

f. What must be done before objectives have been set? Why?

g. What are the identification and assessment of problems connected with?

h. On what do the setting of objectives and the selection of policy depend?

i. What is the difference between *actual* and *planned* performance? How may this difference be caused?

j. When and why is a new line of approach required in problem solving?

3 Complete the following table.

verb	*noun*	*verb*	*noun*
. . .	pressure	. . .	delivery
influence	. . .	consume	. . .
offer	. . .	. . .	deviation
. . .	location	compete	. . .
improve	. . .	install	. . .
signify	. . .	subtract	. . .
indentify	. . .	justify	. . .
transfer	. . .	suggest	. . .
. . .	consideration	. . .	instruction
. . .	expansion	implement	. . .

4 Choose the correct word to complete the following sentences.

a. The Business Consultant's report reached a number of critical . . . . (considerations/summaries/conclusions/influences)

b. The new warehouse had the . . . of reducing overall distribution costs. (affect/effect/impact)

c. The . . . cost of the new plant amounted to £24 million. (sum/total/combination)

d. They intend to . . . the new computerized stock system at the end of the month. (implement/invest/incur)

e. The company is looking for a . . . alternative to its London site. (decisive/viable/significant)

f. A reduction in demand was the . . . given for the large number of redundancies. (result/reason/purpose)

g. MicroTech Ltd. has been . . . by International Electrics. (consumed/changed over/acquired)

h. The Production Manager was asked to . . . the heavy expenditure on the new presses. (identify/justify/suggest)

5 Read the following aloud.

a. The reference numbers you asked for are 0-63/28(9)-595 and, according to our GOW files, HM/KDB/4(202)/017-C.

b. On 3-4-81 a meeting was held to discuss redundancies.

c. All toolroom staff are requested to return the completed forms by 0930 on the 16/5/82. (What is the figure for *noon*?)

d. The production figures for May and June are 21,056 and 47,398. These represent an increase of about 125%, which is ⅓ more than actually planned. (What was the actual planned production?)

e. If you are phoning from outside London, the number to ring is 01-242 6789. Ask for Mrs. Pearson on extension 2386 or 2387. (Why do you need two or three different numbers to get through to Mrs. Pearson? What is the meaning of *extension* here?)

6 Explain what these abbreviations stand for: UK, USA, F, Co, C, Ltd, K, Arr, Dep, Dec, cm, spec, ie, USSR, EEC, etc, Est, PERT, £2.5m, Mar, O&M, cc, eg, R&D, 000s.

7 Who is speaking to who in each of the following? Decide on whether the words are being spoken by (1) a managing director to a manager, (2) one manager to another, (3) a manager to a secretary, or (4) a secretary to a manager. Give reasons for your choice of speaker in each case.

a. 'Please make sure that nobody disturbs us for the next half hour.'

b. 'I'm sorry but I just can't agree, Brian. You see, in my opinion we need more flexibility in our marketing approach—not less, as you seem to think. So I go along with what we've been told from upstairs.'

c. 'Will it be all right if I have next Tuesday off, Mrs. Leonard?'

d. 'Come in, Smith. Don't bother to sit down, this will only take a moment. I'd like to know about your department's transport policy recommendations. I must have them by tomorrow, as you know.'

e. 'Thank you. That will be all until after lunch. Take an extra half hour all right? You've done a very good job this morning.'

f. 'I welcome this opportunity to tell you how well the Board think of your dealings with Atchinson's.'

g. 'No, you've pressed the wrong keys again. Watch now, and I'll show you once more.'

h. 'I understand. I'll have them distributed this morning.'

i. 'Something must be done to improve productivity in your department, Mr. Jones. We're unhappy with the way things are going there.'

j. 'I'd like her a lot more if she didn't expect me to spend my weekends and half my holidays thinking about policy decisions.'

8 Use appropriate forms of these phrasal verbs to complete the sentences below: **go ahead with, change over, hand over, hold up, point out, break down, look around for, take over, build up, put through.**

a. It . . . in the report that the production processes down in B department were inefficient.

b. At fifty-one years of age, Raymond Stack had to begin . . . for a new job.

c. He had to wait almost a quarter of an hour before the operator . . . his call . . . to Bangkok.

d. Charles Bond . . . soon . . . his present responsibilities to his assistant.

e. Canpan has decided . . . its plans to acquire a Canadian manufacturing base.

f. The delivery was delayed because the truck . . . at Le Havre.

g. In 1979, Canpan . . . Addison Engineering for £13 million.

h. In 1980, Canpan . . . from a process system to a flow system.

i. It has taken us many years . . . our highly-skilled labour force into an effective production team.

j. Deliveries . . . last week owing to the drivers' strike.

9 Complete the following paragraphs using suitable prepositions.

It is usual to classify types . . . production as job production, batch production and flow production. . . . job production, products are supplied . . . the special requirements . . . a customer, and the whole project is undertaken as one operation which is completed . . . passing . . . . . . the next. A good example . . . this kind . . . work is shipbuilding. . . . job production a single item is produced . . . a time, whereas . . . batch production a number of similar items are produced . . . order . . . meet a continuing sales demand. Batch sizes vary, but the quantity which is produced amounts . . . more than immediate requirements, and the surplus production is stored. Finally, . . . flow production, the manufacture . . . a product proceeds . . . one operation . . . another . . . at planned rate . . . output.

It is argued that the type . . . production method which is employed depends . . . the development . . . an individual company. That is . . . say, many factories begin manufacturing . . . a job production basis and proceed, as the volume . . . production increases, . . . batch and flow production methods. This is not always the case, however, since the type . . . production is not necessarily determined . . . the product volume which is aimed . . . . fact, . . . the car industry, tools are produced . . . jobbing methods, components are produced . . . batch methods, and the final product is assembled . . . flow methods.

10 If a speaker uses the expression 'In my view . . .', then it is clear that an opinion will follow. In the examples below, link the expressions on the left with what will probably follow on the right. For example, **d.** Let's . . . could be followed by (1) a suggestion.

Expression		Followed by	
a.	I am saying that . . .	(1)	a suggestion
b.	Don't you think . . .	(2)	an opinion
c.	It seems to me that . . .	(3)	an explanation
d.	Let's . . .	(4)	an excuse
e.	. . . so that's why . . .	(5)	a reason
f.	We've found that . . .	(6)	a purpose
g.	Why don't we . . .	(7)	a clarification
h.	Thanks anyway, but . . .		
i.	. . . so that we can . . .		

11 Choose from the following to complete the sentences below: **because, if, although, unless, owing to.**

a. The driver lost three hours . . . heavy traffic conditions.

b. The driver lost three hours . . . traffic conditions were heavy.

c. . . . the driver lost three hours between Southampton and Le Havre, he was able to make up time and deliver only 30 minutes late.

d. . . . circumstances beyond our control, the driver will be about three hours late.

e. . . . the weather clears, the driver will be late departing by ship from Southampton.

f. . . . the driver had followed instructions, he wouldn't have arrived so far behind schedule.

g. . . . the weather stays fine, the driver will be on time departing by ship from Southampton.

h. The driver was late . . . he failed to follow instructions.

i. The driver was late . . . his failure to follow instructions.

j. The driver was late . . . his instructions were clear and there was no difficulties en route.

12 Read this advertisement and answer the questions which follow it.

Purchasing Management & Systems Development in the oil industry

AVG OIL

Nigeria
Owing to expansion AVG announce the following two appointments which require a degree and related job experience.

Purchasers (managerial status)
You will assist in implementing company purchasing policy of utilizing local sources by managing existing suppliers and evaluating potential suppliers. Close co-operation with local businessmen will be called for to familiarize them with all aspects of the buying and selling process from first order to final delivery. Your experience should be at least five years in purchasing with a wide knowledge of business practice, excellent communications and good organizational skills. *Ref: VOG/043A*

Systems Designers
Working with the AVG Purchasing Department, you will be working on one or more of the following projects:

- Implementing computer-based management systems.
- Designing, preparing and reviewing written purchasing procedures.
- Training departmental staff. *Ref: VOG/043B*

Excellent salaries and renewable (single status) contracts will be offered. AVG provides low-cost, air-conditioned accommodation, free medical care, fine sports facilities, and there are 40-day holiday provisions including company-paid return air fares to the UK.

Please send full details, quoting the appropriate reference, to:

Norman MacIntyre, The Personnel Division, AVG Oil Company, 44 Laan van Meerdevoort, 2751 AG The Hague, The Netherlands.

a. What must applicants for each position have before applying? Why?
b. What will selected applicants for each position be expected to do?
c. What rewards can selected applicants expect?
d. Why are the numbers VOG/043A and VOG/043B given?
e. Where are the jobs?
f. Where should applications be sent?
g. What is the reason for the differences between **e** and **f** above?

Unit 11 Marketing Research

SECTION A Reading

Read the following report.

Countryfresh Soups Marketing Research Report

Analysis

The results of our most recent surveys of the market potentials of our existing products and comparability tests on our competitors' products have revealed a situation which must be a cause for concern. Despite the fact that our ex-factory sales figures had suggested a good performance for Countryfresh, in reality these figures concealed the true picture. Our latest total market surveys show to what extent Markham's Soups have penetrated the market since their new product launch in January of last year. Figure 1 below provides an analysis of the market.

Fig. 1 Market Analysis

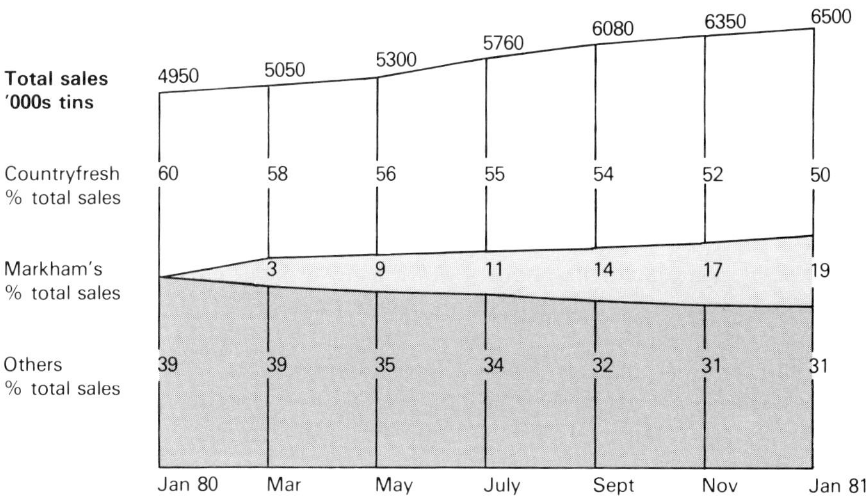

It can be seen from the above that, in spite of the fact that our brand has achieved a point of sales rise of 18%, our share of the market has dropped from a peak of 60% to an equal 50% compared to all of the competitors. The entry of Markham's Soups must have made a serious impact, since it now appears that we are dealing with a much larger market than before.

If these present trends continue, Markham's will have increased its market share to over 28% by the end of the year, and we will have been reduced to 40% of the market. It is difficult to predict the overall behaviour of the market, but it is more than likely—in fact it is highly probable—that on present trends our own sales will soon begin to fall.

From the marketing point of view, much more work should have been done on investigating the characteristics of our product, of the user market, and of the sales operation as a whole.

Recommendations

In order to re-establish ourselves in a dominant market position, it is recommended that we launch a new sales campaign. For this purpose we need to examine the completeness of our product range and carry out related tests on packaging to assess factors such as design and product identification. User research is required to define purchasing and usage habits together with user characteristics in terms of age, regional location, and social class. Other facts are needed on changes and trends within the market concerning quality and price. When all this information has been collected and analysed, we will be in a position to assess our advertising and promotional policies.

Word Study

surveys *l.3* general studies; overall views.
revealed *l.5* made known; shown.
concern *l.5* worry.
despite the fact that *l.5* although; even though. An expression of similar meaning is 'in spite of the fact that'.
concealed *l.7* hidden; kept from view.
extent *l.8* amount, degree or size. To what extent does the economy of your country depend on tourism? To what extent does it depend on industry?
penetrated *l.9* forced a way into.
launch *l.9* A *product launch* refers to a company's first marketing and sales operations for a new product.
brand *l.11* manufacturer's name or mark of identification on merchandise (= 'goods; things bought and sold'). Name three brands of cigarettes.
point of sales *l.12* retail.
peak *l.13* highest point (on a graph, for example).
predict *l.18* This verb is very close in meaning to 'forecast'. A *prediction* is generally based more on facts and statistical calculations.
characteristics *l.22* identifiable qualities; features.
dominant *l.25* ruling; controlling; having the greatest effect.
campaign *l.26* number of related actions which are planned and organized to achieve a particular objective. The aim of a sales campaign is the winning of new sales, customers or markets.

packaging *l.28* putting merchandise into the boxes, cans, paper, plastic wrapping, etc., in which it is sold. The word can also refer to the actual boxes, cases, cans, etc., *in which* merchandise is sold.
habits *l.30* usual ways of doing things. A habit is also an act which has been repeated so often that it has become automatic. Habits are often expressed in Present Simple; eg, Tony *smokes* 25-30 cigarettes a day.
concerning *l.32* with reference to; related to.
promotional policies *l.34* policies designed to develop interest in a new product. *Promotion* also refers to raising or moving a person forward to a higher or better position; eg, Tony *was promoted* from Area Sales Manager to Marketing Manager.

Comprehension

1 By how much has Countryfresh's share of the market dropped in the period under review?

2 Say what the words in **bold face** refer to.
a. '. . . **these figures** . . .' *(l.7)*
b. '. . . since **their** new product launch . . .' *(l.9)*
c. 'It can be seen from **the above** . . .' *(l.11)*
d. '. . . than **before**.' *(l.15)*
e. 'For **this purpose** . . .' *(l.26)*
f. 'When all **this information** . . .' *(l.32)*
g. '. . . **we** will be in a position . . .' *(l.33)*

3 How is it possible to achieve a point of sales rise and still have a reduced share of the market?

4 In what way did Markham's entry probably change the soup market?

5 In terms of sales, explain what happened to Markham's Soups for each of the quarters (= 'periods of three months') between January 1980 and January 1981.

6 How many tins did Countryfresh sell in the third quarter of 1980? What about Countryfresh's other competitors in the same period?

7 If the trend on the graph continues, what will happen to the competitors' sales?

8 What action do you think that Countryfresh should have taken in 1980? Why do you think they failed to take it?

9 What is the relation between (1) packaging and (2) design and product identification?

10 Explain the relation between (1) marketing and (2) user characteristics in terms of age, regional location, and social class.

11 Explain what is meant by (1) comparability tests, (2) the true picture, (3) the user market, (4) a cause for concern.

SECTION B Listening

In the Listening sections of Units 11-15, certain new words are introduced. The meanings of these words can be determined by referring to the diagrams and illustrations in the exercises for each section.

Cassette 2, side 1. While you are listening to the conversation between Mr. Ted Radley, a Marketing Manager, and Mr. Mitch Pilger, a Marketing Research Manager, answer questions 1 and 2 below.

1 Complete the graph below to show the member of staff responsible for each of the predictions.

Sales Data & Forecasts – Tinned Soup

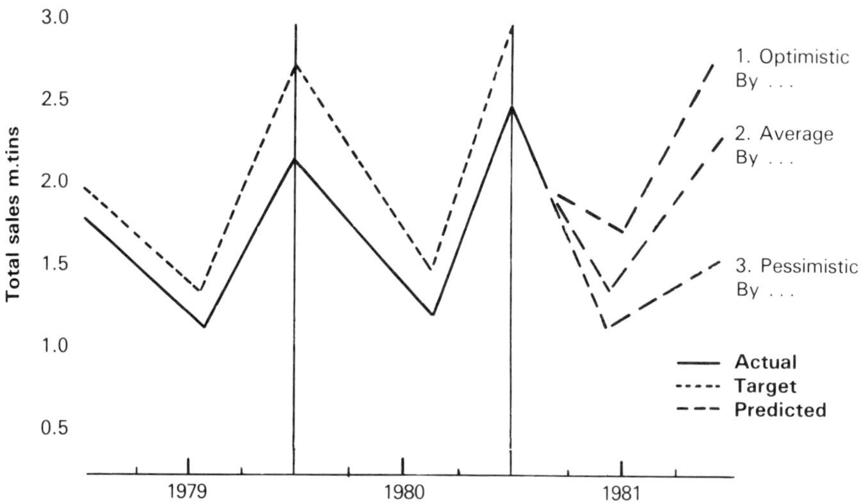

2 What reason is suggested for the failure of actual sales of tinned soup to reach the target for 1980?

Pilger Good to see you again, Ted.
Radley Mitch.
Pilger How was the Belgium trip?
Radley From the point of view of marketing, fine. On the social side, terrible. I was so busy I hardly managed to get out of the hotel.
Pilger I've heard that story before.
Radley It's true.
Pilger Okay, I believe you.
Radley How are things in market research?
Pilger Same as usual. We provide your people with the facts, and they don't take any notice of them.
Radley Come on, Mitch, you know how much we value your statistics.
Pilger I'll give you a few more, then. Here are some details about our tinned soup sales.
Radley What have you got?
Pilger This graph. The solid line represents our actual sales, the dotted line is target sales, and the broken line is for predictions.
Radley Shows the quarterly sales fluctuations well, this.
Pilger The swings are quite big, as you can see. And here's the 1980 peak, at $2\frac{1}{2}$m tins.
Radley According to our target, we should have sold $2\frac{3}{4}$ million.
Pilger That must have been the result of Markham's entry into the market.
Radley How well are they doing?
Pilger On present performance it looks like they will have overtaken us, in terms of market share, by the middle of next year.
Radley I don't think that's very likely with our new sales campaign starting up soon.

Pilger I'm not so sure. Our market surveys show that Markham's will probably continue to increase their share.

Radley What about these predictions, Mitch?

Pilger Prediction one is based on the figures that you prepared. It's the most optimistic, as you can see.

Radley Why optimistic? I don't think it's optimistic at all. We based our calculations on a careful assessment of the market position and on sales forecasts from my people on the ground.

Pilger Despite Markham's performance?

Radley Our new sales campaign is going to alter the picture, Mitch.

Pilger Let's hope so.

Radley I suppose the pessimistic prediction is yours.

Pilger No. As a matter of fact, it's Dan Sloane's.

Radley The new Marketing Director?

Pilger The new Marketing Director.

Radley Does he really think that sales will be that bad?

Pilger I'm afraid so. He's worried about the competition.

Radley So prediction two here, that must be yours then.

Pilger Yes. And we think it's realistic.

Radley Are you sure that you're not playing it too safe?

Pilger No, I don't think so. It looks like a good average to me.

Radley You should have made a higher estimate of sales than this, Mitch.

Pilger An under-estimate is better than an over-estimate, Ted.

Radley In my experience, predictions like these have a habit of coming true. It all has to do with the psychology of our sales people, Mitch.

□ 1 What reason does Mr. Radley give for prefering an over-estimate of sales to an under-estimate?

2 Who are Radley's 'people on the ground'?

SECTION C Language Study

1 Future Time

Notice how the Future Perfect is used to describe the completion of an action in the future.

Markham's **will have increased** its market share to over 28% by the end of the year, and we **will have been reduced** to 40% of the market.

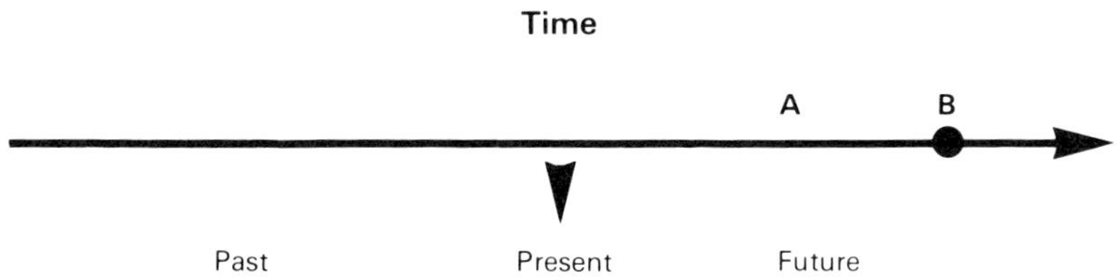

In the diagram, both Markham's increase and Countryfresh's reduction can be represented by the symbol **A**. Symbol **B** can stand for the expression 'by the end of the year'.

a. Find other examples of the use of the Future Perfect in this unit and, in each case, say what information can be represented by **A** and **B** in the diagram above.

b. Look again at the graph of Countryfresh's sales data and forecasts. Say what **will have happened** or what **will have been done** if each prediction comes true.

2 Probability

Example:
It is highly probable that the entry of Markham's Soups *made* a serious impact, since it now appears that we are dealing with a much larger market than before.
▷ The entry of Markham's Soups **must have made** a serious impact, since it now appears that we are dealing with a much larger market than before.

Use the same form of **must** to express probability in the following.

a. *It is highly probable* that Markham's *knew* that the soup market was ready for expansion.

b. *It is highly probable* that Countryfresh *underestimated* Markham's ability to penetrate the market.

c. *It is very likely* that Countryfresh's target sales for '79 and '80 *were* too optimistic.

d. *It is highly probable* that Radley's marketing trip to Belgium *was* a busy one, since he hardly managed to get out of the hotel.

e. *It is highly probable* that Dan Sloane *had* an excellent record of sales, if they promoted him to Marketing Director.

3 Referring to Mistakes or Failure

Notice the different ways in which we can emphasize that an action was not performed in a correct or acceptable way.

Examples:
The goods were packaged in a light container. This was a bad idea.
▷ The goods **should have been packaged** in a stronger container.

The fire doors were locked. This is not allowed.
▷ The fire doors **should not have been locked.**

Now change the following sentences in a similar way.

a. The report under-estimated Markham's ability to penetrate the market. This was a mistake.

b. Work was not done on investigating the characteristics of Countryfresh's product. This was an error.

c. The operator did not wear safety glasses when working. This is not permitted.

d. A low estimate of our competitor's sales were made. This was wrong.

e. The stock list was not checked at the end of the month. This was a serious failure.

SECTION D Listening

Cassette 2, side 1. While you are listening to the conversation between Mrs. Dilley, a Market Research interviewer, and Mrs. Saunders, a housewife, complete 1, 2 and 3 below.

1 Label thc illustration.

Refrigerator

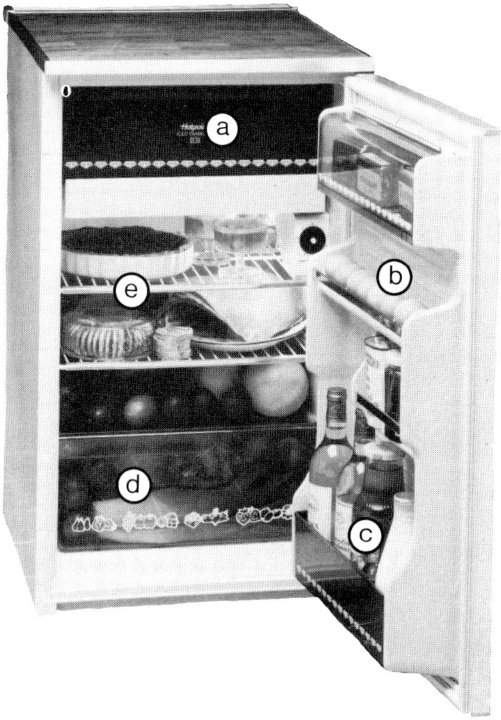

2 Complete the table below to show what Mrs. Saunders does not like about the Imperial.

a. Freezer compartment	Too small
b. Shelves	. . .
c. Egg rack	. . .
d. Bottle rack	. . .

3 Complete the table below to show what Mrs. Saunders considers important qualities expected of a refrigerator.

Qualities of good refrigerator
a. . . .
b. . . .
c. Functional design

SECTION E Using Information in Different Ways

Here are nineteen questions which might be asked for the purposes of marketing research. Read through them.

1 What trends are developing in the market?

2 Do we provide the right incentives for our workforce?

3 Is the packaging of our products right for the market?

4 Is our sales organization set up efficiently?

5 Do we maintain a good after-sales service?

6 Can the product be simplified in any way?

7 Are we aware of general social and political developments?

8 Are our sales statistics up to date?

9 Is our product range as complete as possible?

10 Is sales information reaching the right people?

11 Are the prices of our products right?

12 What is the size of the market?

13 What are the different 'shares of the market'?

14 Are we aware of general business trends and forecasts?

15 Do we make good use of different advertising channels?

16 Is our salesforce doing a good job?

17 Are the most appropriate distribution channels being used?

18 What are the user characteristics in this market?

19 Is our advertising successful?

Now classify questions 1-19 in the table below according to the areas of marketing research to which they refer.

Types of Marketing Research	
1. Product Research	a. ?
	b. ?
	c. ?
	d. ?
2. User Market Research	a. ?
	b. ?
	c. ?
	d. ?
3. Sales Operations Research	a. ?
	b. ?
	c. ?
	d. ?
	e. ?
	f. ?
4. Communications Research	a. ?
	b. ?
	c. ?
5. Economics and Business Research	a. ?
	b. ?

SECTION F Discussion

1 'Consumer market research and industrial market research require different approaches.' Do you agree? Why?

2 What information would a market research investigator seek in order to assess the demand for a new product?

3 'The trouble with market researchers is that they believe too strongly in statistics.' What do you think is meant by this statement? Do you agree with it? Why?

SECTION G Writing

1 Read this paragraph.

A company frequently needs to reassess its marketing plans to ensure that its basic objectives, in terms of consumer services, are met by the existing range of products. In a competitive economy, competitors will always be seeking to provide better products and services. Products which were right five years ago, or five months ago, will not necessarily be right today. Therefore, continuing research is needed into the way products are used, the state of competitors' products, and new ways of meeting consumer needs. Information on such subjects can be provided by marketing research into product usage, user behaviour, and sales operations. The results of this research must be measured in relation to the company's own efficiency and to that of other companies working in the same field. Indexes* of profitability, for example, can provide the means of such measurement.

*Some English speakers use the plural form 'indices'.

2 Now notice how the paragraph above has been re-written without altering the *central* ideas expressed in it.

A company frequently needs to reassess its marketing plans to ensure that its basic objectives, in terms of consumer services, are met by the existing range of products. In a competitive economy, competitors will always be seeking to provide better products and services. Therefore, continuing research is needed into the way products are used, the state of competitors' products, and new ways of meeting consumer needs. The results of this research must be measured in relation to the company's own efficiency and to that of other companies working in the same field.

3 Re-write the following paragraph in the same way, ensuring that the *central* ideas are not affected.

Manufacturing companies need to make frequent assessments of their production methods and processes in order to maintain the competitive value of their products. This can be achieved by such methods as value analysis and method study. In a developing technical world, techniques and methods are often changing as the state of knowledge improves. Many machine operations, for example, have become standardized and, consequently, much cheaper to perform. As a result, some manufacturers may have benefited from the introduction of more efficient methods, tools and equipment. Therefore, they will be able to show a competitive advantage over other producers in the market. Comparisons of productivity and price, for example, will reveal the extent of that advantage.

Unit 12 Advertising and Promotion

SECTION A Reading

Read these minutes.

Minutes of Marketing Meeting

1 A meeting was held on the 22/3/82 to evaluate the advertising strategy for the new range of Alpine soap which the company is to launch in November of this year.

2 Present: Mr. Arnott, Marketing Manager; Mr. Stanton, Product Manager; Mr. Mayer, Account Executive (Lambert Associates Ltd).

3 The meeting began with a discussion of the budget proposals for the product launch. Mr. Mayer was of the opinion that the proposed allocation was too low. He pointed out that, with high turnover goods such as soap, it was necessary to spend a high percentage of anticipated sales revenue on advertising. Mr. Arnott supported this view and also thought that they should be prepared to consider a situation where first year sales revenue was not sufficient to cover costs. Mr. Stanton, however, disagreed with these arguments because he considered the budget figures were based on a highly realistic estimate of a ten per cent market share for Alpine.

4 After further discussion, Mr. Stanton agreed to accept an increase in the budget figure of twelve and a half per cent.

5 Next, an assessment was made of the intended media strategy. It was Mr. Arnott's opinion that Alpine needed to make a reasonable compromise between three important factors, namely: impact, frequency, and coverage. It was obvious, Mr. Arnott went on to say, that they could not achieve an ideal combination of all three. Mr. Mayer suggested that it was much better to restrict spending geographically, given the constraints of the budget. He explained that a full advertising campaign against half the market would be more effective than half a job against the whole market. Both Mr. Stanton and Mr. Arnott agreed with this approach.

6 Mr. Mayer expressed the view that in order to begin work on the design of the advertisements, more details of what needed to be said and to whom were required. In reply, Mr. Stanton said that by the end of the following week he would provide facts and figures so that Mr. Mayer could define his campaign.

7 Finally, various aspects of promotional policy were considered. Mr. Stanton pointed out that the company used to favour coupons as a means of encouraging sales, but Mr. Mayer was not at all in favour of using this method. The latter said that he preferred a combination of price cuts, trade discounts, and consumer special offers. Mr. Arnott's feelings on the matter were that it would be better to use the available resources on packaging, design and display. Owing to the lack of agreement on this last subject, a decision on promotion methods would be put forward to the next meeting.

8 Mr. Arnott is to arrange a futher meeting as soon as possible.

Word Study

minutes *l.1* written record or report of what was said and done at a meeting, conference, etc.

strategy *l.2* plans for the overall operations in a campaign.

budget *l.7* plan for controlling *expenses* during a certain period relative to *estimated profit or income* for the same period.

proposals *l.7* plans put forward for acceptance or rejection (rejection = opposite of 'acceptance'). The verb is *propose.*

allocation *l.9* fixed amount allowed for a specific purpose.

turnover *l.9* sales and the replacement of stock. Turnover also refers to the total amount of money received from sales.

anticipated *l.10* looked forward to; expected.

revenue *l.11* return (of money) from investment; income.

media *l.19* This is the plural of *medium.* It refers to the means or agency by which something is done, achieved, realized, etc.; eg, radio is a *medium* of communication. **The media** = radio, TV, film, newspapers and magazines.

compromise *l.21* agreement or settlement in which each side gives up some demands. *In view of the company's predicted poor performance over the next six months, the staff have decided to compromise on their salary demands.* What have the staff agreed to accept?

coverage *l.22* amount of space (in newspapers and magazines) or time (on radio, TV and film). To *cover* an item for the media = 'to report it'.

ideal *l.23* exactly as desired; perfect.

restrict *l.24* hold down; keep within certain limits.

constraints *l.25* factors which force something into specific channels.

favour *l.35* like; approve of; prefer; desire.

coupons *l.35* certificates which can be used to buy a product at reduced price.

encouraging *l.36* giving help or support to.

trade discounts *l.38* special price cuts to retailers.

lack *l.40* absence; condition of not having any.

Comprehension

1 Complete this table.

Person	*Alpine budget*	*Promotional policy*
Arnott	**a.** . . .	**c.** . . .
Stanton	**b.** . . .	Coupons
Mayer	Too low	**d.** . . .

2 Say what the words in **bold face** refer to.

a. '. . . **the company** . . .' *(l.3)*
b. '. . . **this view** . . .' *(l.11)*
c. '. . . **these arguments** . . .' *(l.14)*
d. '. . . **all three** . . .' *(l.23)*
e. '. . . **a job** . . .' *(l.26)*
f. '. . . **this approach** . . .' *(l.27)*
g. '. . . **this method** . . .' *(l.37)*
h. '**The latter** . . .' *(l.37)*
i. '. . . **the matter** . . .' *(l.39)*
j. '. . . **this last subject** . . .' *(l.41)*

3 What sort of Company is Lambert Associates Limited?

4 For what reason should a company consider not making a profit during the first year of a new product's sales?

5 In advertising terms, explain what is meant by a compromise between impact, frequency and coverage.

6 How is it suggested and agreed that Alpine should compromise on their advertising coverage?

7 What facts does Mr. Mayer require before he can begin working on the ads? Who will supply the information? When?

8 When will a decision on promotional policy be taken?

9 True or False?

a. Mr. Mayer is an employee of Alpine.

b. Mr. Arnott thought that 10% was a realistic estimate of Alpine's market share.

c. The restricted budget would result in a geographically restricted campaign.

d. Mayer favours coupons as a means of encouraging sales.

e. The three men have completely different ideas about promotional policy.

SECTION B Listening

Cassette 2, side 1. While you are listening to the conversation between Mrs. Boone, an Account Executive with an advertising agency, and Mr. Ferrara, a Product Liaison Manager, answer questions 1, 2 and 3 below.

(a) handlebars (c) mudguards (e) dynamo

(b) gears (d) frame (f) saddle

1 What is special about the Solent frame and gears?

2 What is the proposed price of the Solent?

3 Explain Mrs. Boone's strategy for selling the Solent.

Boone Nice to see you again, Mr. Ferrara.

Ferrara Mrs. Boone, hello. I've been expecting you.

Boone How is the new model launch coming along?

Ferrara We've been having some minor problems on the production line, but we're used to that. We'll sort them out.

Boone When do you think you'll get the Solent into the shops?

Ferrara Mid-October at the latest. We want to catch the build-up for the Christmas trade.

Boone And overseas?

Ferrara That may be a little late. Jim McIntyre told me yesterday that he couldn't promise anything before April.

Boone Did he say why?

Ferrara No, but he told me he would send me a full report as soon as he had all the information.

Boone I see. Well, shall we knock a few ideas around now about the advertising campaign?

Ferrara Splendid.

Boone Let's start with the national newspaper campaign. You know, I think the Solent is ideal for the general market, and that's the main line I want to take in the ads. The bike is really what I'd call a multi-purpose machine, so I'd like the campaign to aim at all sections of the market. At those who want a touring bike, say, and at those who want a bike for going to the shops, or whatever.

Ferrara Are you sure that's wise? With a strategy like that we might end up without any defined market group, and find that we miss everyone.

Boone Not necessarily, although I do agree that we will have to be careful how we put the idea across.

Ferrara You have something in mind?

Boone I want to promote the bike on its strongest points of general interest, and use those to catch the specialist buyer.

Ferrara So you'd build on such things as our new lightweight frame, for instance.

Boone Exactly. The frame is one of the Solent's biggest advantages. And then there are the gears. Machet six-speed gearing is not usually offered on a bike designed to sell at under a hundred pounds.

Ferrara We had Machet gears on some of our previous models.

Boone But they didn't have the new frame.

Ferrara I'm still not certain that we can take the chance of selling to all sections of the market.

Boone Suppose we were able to offer a number of variations of the basic bike.

Ferrara Hold on a moment, Mrs. Boone. We're nearly into full production.

Boone I don't mean anything that would affect the standard design, Mr. Ferrara. I'm proposing that we offer choices on minor pieces of equipment.

Ferrara For example?

Boone For example the saddle, the handlebars, the gears, the lights, the dynamo, anything. We could offer the racing saddle or the touring saddle, standard or heavy-duty mudguards—

Ferrara Not bad, Mrs. Boone. Not bad at all.

Boone And perhaps the Solent with or without Machet gears.

Ferrara That would certainly give us the opportunity to extend our price range—

Boone —and it would help to sell the Solent to a very much wider market, I feel.

☐ 1 What disadvantage does Mr. Ferrara see in Mrs. Boone's strategy?

2 What does he like about her strategy?

SECTION C Language Study

1 Habits

Examples:

Although coupons were part of company practice at one time, the company does not favour them now.

▹ The company **used to** favour coupons.

Universal often experiences production line problems in its London factory.

▹ Universal **is used to** production line problems in its London factory.

Notice how the first example indicates the practice of doing something in the past, whereas the second example refers to a present habit.

Explain what is indicated by **used to** or **am/are/is used to** in these statements:

a. Ferrara's company used to have problems with their training programme.

b. Alpine are not used to strong competition.

c. Mrs. Boone is used to working with the media.

d. I enjoy my work in New York, although I'm not used to doing so much business by telephone.

e. The company head office used to be in London.

2 Reporting Statements

Examples:
'I can't promise anything before April,' McIntyre said to Ferrara yesterday.
▷ McIntyre said to Ferrara yesterday that he couldn't promise anything before April.

'I'll send you a full report as soon as I have all the information,' McIntyre told Ferrara.
▷ McIntyre told Ferrara that he would send him a full report as soon as he had all the information.

Study this table which shows some of the changes necessary when we report.

Speech	*Report*
I/we/you	he/she/they (as appropriate)
live/have lived/lived	lived/had lived/had lived
can/will	could/would
must/should	must/should
this/now/tomorrow etc.	that/the next day/then

Write a *single* paragraph to report the following discussion.

a. 'I think that the proposed allocation is too low,' Mr. Mayer said. 'With high turnover goods such as soap, it's necessary to spend a high percentage of anticipated sales revenue on advertising.'

b. 'I agree,' Mr. Arnott said. 'And I also think that we should be prepared to consider a situation where first year sales revenue is not sufficient to cover costs.'

c. 'I'm afraid I can't go along with that,' Mr. Stanton said. 'The budget figures are based on a highly realistic estimate of a ten per cent market share for Alpine.'

d. 'I don't agree at all,' Mr. Mayer said. 'If this campaign is going to be a success, we must have a considerable increase now.'

e. 'Absolutely,' said Mr. Arnott. 'We should be talking about an increase of at least twenty per cent.'

3 Suggesting

Study these different ways of making a suggestion.

Problem	*Suggestion*
Costs have doubled	Shall we increase the budget by 10%?
No American sales organization	Why don't we appoint an agent?
No experience of computers	What about using a consultant?

Note that 'Shall we' and the singular 'Shall I' are used only for the purpose of suggesting or asking for instructions. 'Shall I make an appointment for you?' but *not* 'Will I make an appointment for you?'

Use the forms in the table to make suggestions in response to the following:

a. Many trainees are failing the course.

b. We need to discuss this matter again.

c. The sales of our product are falling.

d. We know very little about the changes and trends within the market.

e. It's been a very long and tiring meeting.

SECTION D Listening

Cassette 2, side 1. While you are listening to the conversation between Mr. Steiner, a Marketing Director, and Mr. Prince, a Regional Sales Manager, complete 1 and 2 below.

1 Label the graph to indicate the number of each Region and the type of selling support used.

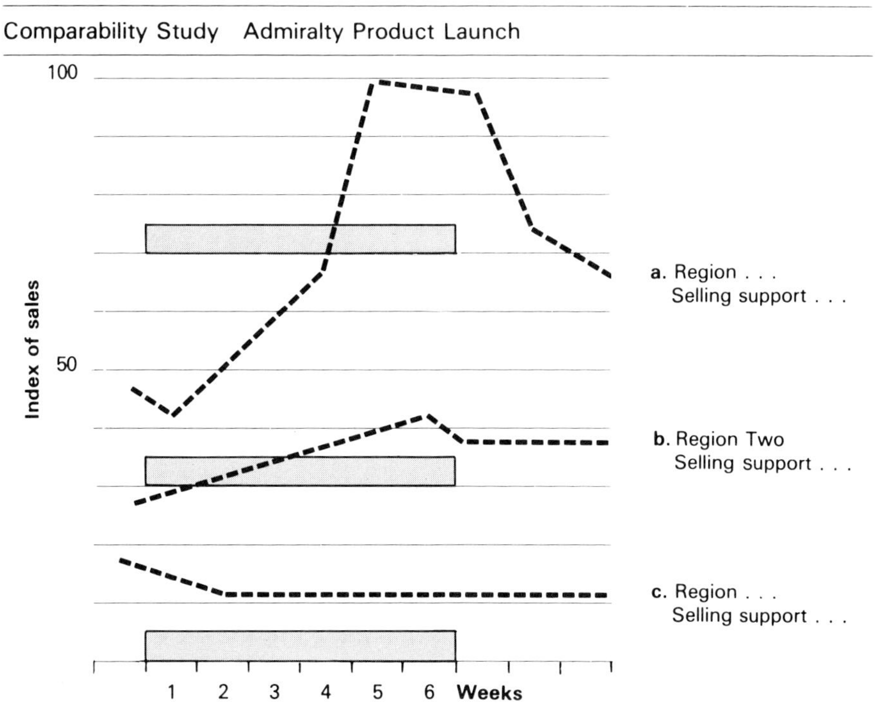

2 As a result of the comparability test, what is the intention for the Admiralty range?

☐ Steiner advises care in deciding the media strategy for those regions where the Admiralty range is already launched. Why?

SECTION E Using Information in Different Ways

1 Read this description of budgeting.

In 1976, Pearl Soaps were launched onto the market with a total advertising and promotional budget of £1 million. This figure was divided among four areas of expenditure: television advertising, newspaper advertising, magazine advertising, and promotional activities such as coupons and special cash discounts.

The major part of the budget (exactly half) was spent on television advertising. Half as much as this was allocated to newspaper advertising. Magazine advertising accounted for 10% of the total budget, and the remainder was spent on sales promotion.

2 Complete the following pie diagram.

Total Expenditure on Advertising & Promotion £1 million

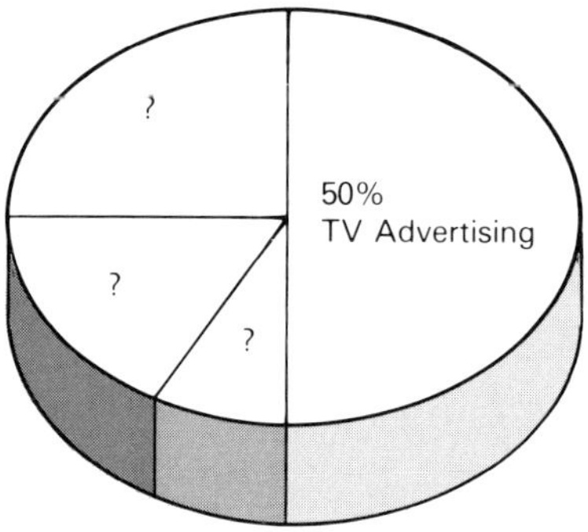

3 The table below shows the percentage change in advertising and promotional expenditure for Pearl Soaps compared to 1976. In 1977, for example, the amount spent on TV advertising was 10% less than in 1976, but in 1979 the amount was 20% more. Complete the table.

Percentage Changes in Advertising & Promotional Expenditure Base Year 1976

	TV	Newspapers	Magazines	Promotion	Total £s
1977	−10	+10	−10	−20	a. . . .
1978	+10	+20	0	−10	b. . . .
1979	+20	−10	+10	+10	c. . . .
1980	+30	+20	+20	+20	d. . . .
1981	+50	+30	+20	+25	e. . . .

4 Enter a line on the graph for each of these: (i) TV advertising, (ii) newspaper advertising, (iii) magazine advertising, (iv) sales promotion.

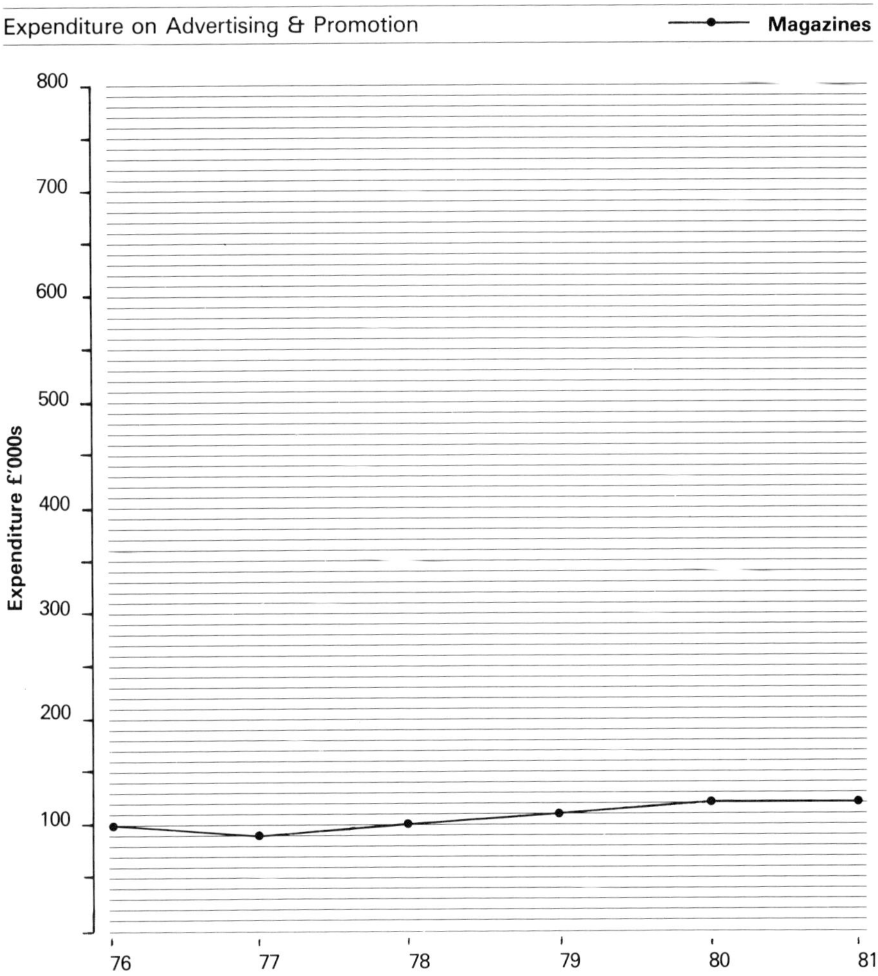

SECTION F Discussion

1 'Sales can be increased either by price reductions or by advertising and promotion.' Do you agree? Why?

2 How would selling techniques differ between heavy industrial machinery and toothpaste?

3 'Television advertising is a necessity for high turnover consumer goods.' Do you agree? Why?

4 'Advertisements must never be translated directly from one language to another in any campaign.' Do you agree? Why?

SECTION G Writing

1 Join each of the following groups of notes into one sentence, using the words or expressions in parentheses. Make any changes that may be necessary. The first group has been done for you.

a autumn of 1979, company ran limited sales training course/course lasted two weeks/purpose was to introduce part of salesforce to appropriate selling techniques for new product called Ace (**which, in order to**)
▷ In the autumn of 1979, the company ran a limited sales training course, which lasted two weeks, in order to introduce part of the salesforce to the appropriate selling techniques for a new product called Ace.

b. training programmes introduced/all salespeople had to complete training programmes (**which**)

c. completely satisfactory results not achieved from test areas/decision taken to go ahead with national launch (**although**)

d. national advertising campaign launched/campaign based on television and national newspapers/campaign aimed at maximum coverage of market (**that, and which**)

e. restricted production of new product begun/new product test marketed in two selected areas (**which**)

f. existing production lines altered/altered production lines could be used for new product/full production of new product begun (**so that, and**)

2 Now re-arrange the six completed sentences so that they form a paragraph about the schedule for the new product launch. Words such as **next, then,** and **finally** will help you to link the sentences smoothly.

Unit 13 Sales

SECTION A Reading

Read this letter.

Pierre Rouen & Cie. 78 Rue Des Fleurs Paris 75015
Tel: 924 62 23
Telex: 89323 PIRO F

Ref: JR/CB/AD
23 May 1980

Mr Clive Bellamy
Export Manager
Simpson Ltd
24 Shipton Street
London W1N 3LT
England

Dear Mr Bellamy

I am now in a position to provide you with more details of our plans for the Saint Tropez Shampoo campaign which is to be launched in July. This would have been done sooner if the results of our market analyses had been prepared on time. I am sorry for the delay.

1. *Distribution*
We have persuaded all but one of our wholesalers to keep the article number for Saint Tropez on their computer sheets. Carrols have not yet decided their position but we feel that we may still be able to get a favourable response from them.

2. *Advertising*
At the moment, as you are aware, we are running a UK television campaign for Rouen soaps. This is going to continue until the end of June and will act as a natural lead-in for our TV campaign for the shampoo launch in July. The theme for the campaign is going to be 'Never So Natural'. Further advertising support is scheduled for the end of July with ads in magazines and the national press.

3. *Salesforce*
The salesforce are to begin their campaign in week 20, and from then until week 24 they are going to make calls on about 8,000 retailers. After that, they will spend two to three weeks introducing the new display material.

4 *Display Material/Promotion*

In your last letter, you asked if dump bins could be provided in the retail outlets. As you may remember from our February meeting, I explained that we had tried a similar method of promotion two years before when we had launched Rouen bath salts and it had not been a success. In our opinion, dump bins would be bad for the up-market image that we wish to create for Saint Tropez. Therefore, we have decided to limit display material to specially prepared stands and counter dispensers.

In the letter to which I have already referred, you also wanted to know if we would consider presenting a banded offer of Rouen soap together with the new shampoo. It is felt that this approach would fail to establish Saint Tropez as an individual product and that the extra cost of banding and printing would not be worthwhile.

5 *Public Relations*

At present we are considering the preparation of a special PR pack which will contain a sample of the shampoo together with an insert on our promotional and advertising activities, and a sales letter. The distribution of this pack has not been decided yet but it will certainly include fashion editors and selected prime prospects.

I hope this campaign layout meets with your approval and that it reflects the discussions we have already had on the matter.

Our Managing Director, M. Delmas, has asked when and where it would be convenient for us to hold a pre-launch meeting. I would be pleased if you would suggest a selection of dates and a venue.

I am enclosing a copy of the proposed sales budget.

Your sincerely

Jean Renoir
Sales Manager

enc. Sales Budget

Word Study

shampoo *l.3* soap for washing the hair.
article number *l.7* business reference number for particular goods.
on . . . computer sheets *l.8* in a computer's store or records.
response *l.10* something that is said or done in answer to something else. The verb is *respond*. Find the same verb in the word *correspondence* and explain why it is there.
theme *l.15* (in advertising) short, easily-remembered expression which helps to develop the basic idea of a campaign.
dump bins *l.23* See the illustration below.
outlets *l.24* places where customers can buy. So, retail outlet = 'shop' or 'store'.
up-market *l.27* where goods are most expensive and customers richest.

image *l.27* picture in the mind.
to create *l.27* to produce; to bring into existence; to originate.
stands and **counter dispensers** *l.29* See the illustration below.

dump bins

stand

counter dispenser

banded offer *l.31* two related items tied together and sold at a single special price.
sample *l.37* small quantity to demonstrate quality.
insert *l.37* printed information put inside a pack, box, etc.
fashion editors *l.39* people who control what is printed in magazines and newspapers about the newest things being worn, bought, tried out, etc.
prime prospects *l.40* most important potential buyers.
layout *l.41* overall design.
approval *l.41* favourable opinion.
reflects *l.41* reproduces; corresponds to.
convenient *l.44* easy and suitable with regard to time, place, etc.
venue *l.45* place.

Comprehension

1 Why has Renoir's letter been delayed?

2 Say what the words in **bold face** refer to.
a. **Ref: JR/CB/AD** . . .'
b. '**This** would have been done sooner . . .' *(l.3)*
c. '**Carrols** have not yet decided . . .' *(l.8)*
d. '**This** is going to continue . . .' *(l.13)*
e. 'After **that**, . . .' *(l.20)*
f. '. . . **it** had not been a success.' *(l.26)*
g. '. . . **this approach** . . .' *(l.32)*
h. '. . . **the matter**.' *(l.42)*
i. '. . . **a selection of dates and a venue**.' *(l.45)*
j. '**enc.** Sales Budget' *(l.50)*

3 Why do Rouen want their wholesalers to keep the article number for Saint Tropez on their computer sheets?

4 At the start, how many calls per week will the salesforce make on average?

5 Complete the table.

Renoir against	*Reasons*
Dump bins	**a.** . . .
b. . . .	c. 1 No individuality 2 . . .

6 What is the purpose of the PR pack?

7 Why will the distribution of the sample pack certainly include fashion editors?

8 What do you think is the relation between Simpson Ltd. and Pierre Rouen & Cie?

9 What further meeting between the two companies will be arranged?

10 Give your own advertising theme for an up-market hair shampoo.

SECTION B Listening

Cassette 2, side 2. While you are listening to the conversation between Ms* Inger Brunsberg, a Marketing Manager, and Mr. Otto Muller, a Managing Director, answer 1 and 2 below.

*Some women use the title Ms rather than Miss or Mrs.

1 Complete the table below.

Subject	*Muller*	*Brunsberg*
Price rise last year	Supported large increase	**a.** . . .
Response to falling sales	**b.** . . .	**c.** . . .

2 What important details about the sales figures are not revealed by the graph?

Muller Inger, I've just received our first-quarter sales figures on our venetian blind range, and they don't make good reading.
Brunsberg How bad are they?
Muller See for yourself. Sales have slumped badly this year. Look. A drop in sales for three months consecutively. We're running over twenty per cent below target, and if this keeps up we're going to face a loss position in the very near future.
Brunsberg I'm not really surprised. You know that I was against the large price rise that was hurried through at the back end of last year. I asked you at the time if you would consider a much smaller increase.
Muller I remember that. And what do you think our strategy should be now?
Brunsberg It's obvious, isn't it? Our

Lowry Venetian Blind

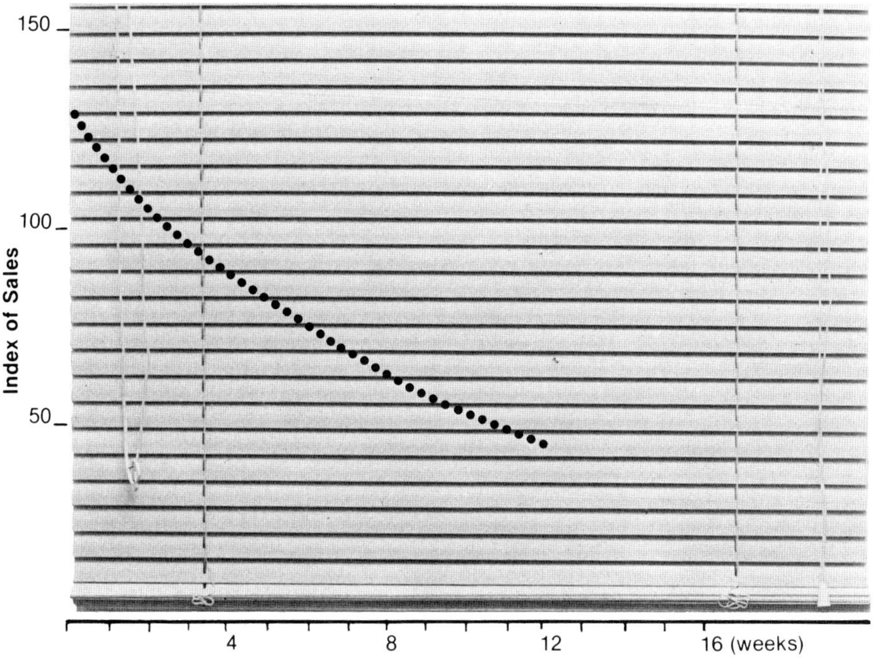

Lowry First-Quarter Sales Figures 1982

response must be to reduce our prices quickly or provide some kind of special discount for the retailer. I don't understand why we've left it so late. It could have been done months ago.

Muller You don't think that's going to solve the problem now, do you? A price reduction would do nothing at all to encourage a higher volume demand and increase our total revenue.

Brunsberg But surely, Otto, in the present economic climate, that's the very thing that should be done. A drop in price and an extra push on the advertising and promotion side are certain to increase our market share.

Muller You don't understand the situation, Inger. Demand is falling and all our costs are on the increase. Salaries, distribution costs, production costs—they're all sky high.

Brunsberg Surely some savings can be made on production.

Muller What can we do? We have already made some quality reductions on the slats and cords. And according to the production department, the amount of money saved was minimal. Remember there's the quality of our competitors' products to think about. No. My recommendation is for our prices to be increased again. It's the only way.

Brunsberg Are you being serious? That would only make the situation worse.

Muller I'm being perfectly serious, and let me say that I think your own assessment is wrong. There's another important factor which must be considered, you see, which is not revealed by the overall sales figures. When the figures are broken down territory by territory, we see a different picture. In the larger cities, sales have remained pretty stable. It's in the country districts and smaller towns where there has been a sharp decline in sales.

Brunsberg It was my policy to promote Lowry Blinds on a national basis with full TV and magazine support. I wouldn't have been given the go-ahead by the Board if they hadn't thought I was right.

Muller Circumstances have changed, Inger. In my view we must make economies and plan a holding operation in the short run.

Brunsberg How short?

Muller Until the market takes an upward turn. Until that happens we should put all our efforts into marketing in the city areas where our consumers seem least affected by price considerations.

Brunsberg That would mean wasting most of the work that has gone into promoting our blinds nation-wide.
Muller It's our only chance this year to keep a viable operation running.
Brunsberg And how would all this affect the size of our sales operation?
Muller It will certainly mean cutting down on our salesforce—possibly maintaining some limited representation in some of the less important regions, or completely reorganizing our operations to combine existing functions into fewer offices.
Brunsberg I can only say that if a policy like this is followed, it will be a big mistake. It takes no account of the alternative strategy that I've put forward.

☐ Complete the diagram below describing Mr. Muller's approach to Lowry's problems.

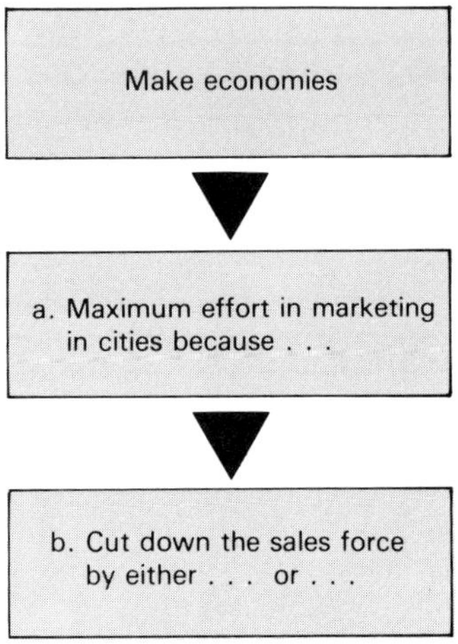

SECTION C Language Study

1 Reporting Questions

Example:
'Can dump bins be provided in the retail outlets?' Mr. Bellamy asked.
▷ Mr. Bellamy asked if dump bins could be provided in the retail outlets.

Notice that the auxiliary verb has moved from the question-position to the statement-position, so the reported form does not end in a question mark. Look for this and other changes in the following examples.

'Are you being serious?' Mr Muller asked Ms Brunsberg.
▷ Mr Muller asked Ms Brunsberg if she was being serious.

'How bad are our first-quarter sales figures?' Ms Brunsberg asked.
▷ Ms Brunsberg wanted to know how bad their first-quarter sales figures were.

Report the following questions.

a. 'Will it be possible to offer a banded pack?' Bellamy enquired.

b. 'May I give out the details of the advertising theme?' Mr Renoir's assistant wanted to know.

c. 'Can we be sure that Simpson Ltd will approve of our layout?' Renoir asked.

d. 'Is your advertising support going to continue after week 30?' M. Delmas asked his Sales Manager.

e. 'Have you received anything yet from Bellamy on the pre-launch meeting you're planning?' one of Renoir's salespeople asked.

Now notice how auxiliary **do/does/did** *disappear* in reported questions.
'**Do** you **realize** how serious the consequences may be?' Mr Muller asked Ms Brunsberg.
▷ Mr Muller asked Ms Brunsberg if she **realized** how serious the consequences might be.

'**Does** this idea of yours **mean** that the size of our sales operation will be affected?' Ms Brunsberg asked Mr Muller.
▷ Ms Brunsberg asked Mr Muller if this (or 'that') idea of his **meant** that the size of their sales operation would be affected.

'**Did** Renoir **say** when the meeting would take place?' Bellamy's boss wanted to know.
▷ Bellamy's boss wanted to know if Renoir **had said** when the meeting would take place.

Report these **do/does/did** questions.

f. 'Do Simpson want us to enclose the sales budget?' Renoir's secretary asked.

g. 'Does the PR pack include an insert?' he asked.

h. 'Did the truck leave Wilhelmshaven on schedule?' he wanted to know.

i. 'Why did the truck wait so long at Wilhelmshaven?' he wanted to know.

j. 'Where did the truck stop after Wilhelmshaven?' he wanted to know.

2 Future Time

Notice how we can speak formally or officially about the future. A meeting of the Board **is to be held** on Monday./The Managing Director **is to hold** a Board meeting on Monday./A meeting of the Board **will be** held on Monday./The MD **will hold** a Board meeting on Monday. Any one of these sentences can be used to describe the arrangement for Monday in the Managing Director's appointment book below.

Monday	*Board Meeting*
Tuesday	*Discussions on Expansion Plans*
Wednesday	*Consideration of Senior Management Appointments*
Thursday	*Investigation of Declining Overseas Sales*
Friday	*Evaluation of Relocation Plans*

Write sentences to describe the arrangements for Tuesday-Friday.

3 Comparing

Lamb and Beef Prices 1978 – 81

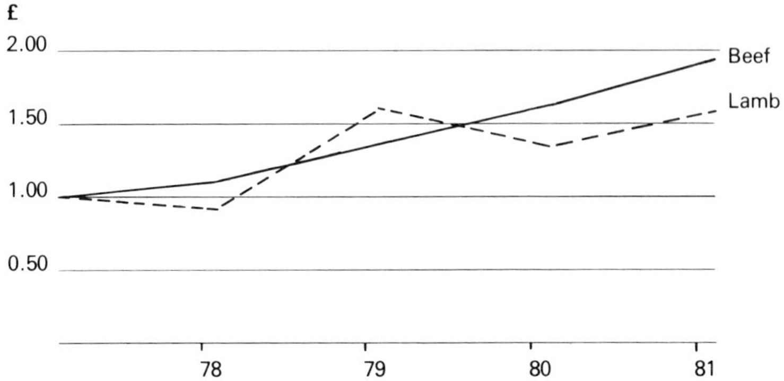

Study these questions concerning information on the graph.

a. When were beef prices **the lowest**?/When were beef prices **the least expensive**?

b. Was beef **less expensive than** lamb in 1979?/Was beef **cheaper than** lamb in 1979?

c. When was lamb **the cheapest**?/When was lamb **the least expensive**?

d. Why was beef **more expensive than** lamb in 1978?/Why was lamb **cheaper than** beef in 1978?

Notice that with words of more than one syllable we generally use **more** and **most** to express comparison and not **-er, -est.**

Now construct eight similar questions about the graph using types a, b, c, d. However, notice the pattern of adjectives ending in -ly, -y, -er: early, earlier, earliest; heavy, heavier, heaviest; clever, cleverer, cleverest.

SECTION D Listening

Cassette 2, side 2. While you are listening to the conversation between a Regional Sales Manager and a Senior Salesman, do 1 and 2 below.

1 Complete the following assessment form.

Sales Personnel Assessment Form

Name . . .	**1**	**2**	**3**	**4**	**5**
. . .	✓				
Persuasiveness		✓			
. . .				✓	
. . .	✓				
Initiative					
Co-operation		✓			

Key

1 Outstanding
2 Excellent
3 Above average
4 Average
5 Unsatisfactory

2 What level of performance is needed in order to qualify for the District Sales Manager's Training Course?

☐ 1 In what way has the Senior Salesman shown initiative about improving his performance?

2 *Ambition* is the desire to do well and become successful. How ambitious is the Senior Salesman? Give your reasons.

SECTION E Using Information in Different Ways

1 Listed below are a number of subjects to be covered on a sales managers' training course and the titles of the individual papers that will be given on these subjects. Read both lists carefully.

Subjects

(1) The Sales Manager's Role as Leader
(2) Leadership Styles
(3) Effective Communications
(4) Action Session
(5) Meeting Strategy
(6) Time Management
(7) Sales Activity
(8) Responsibilities of Management
(9) Leadership Practice
(10) Development of Operational Plan

Papers

(a) 'A review of the responsibility of management is using personnel to their fullest potential.'
(b) 'Group discussions on the practical applications of points from the course.'
(c) 'Discussion of the film *'Meetings, Meetings, Meetings'*.'
(d) 'Establishing and communicating objectives.'
(e) 'Discusion based on the film *'Time to Manage'*.'
(f) 'Developing a checklist of leaders' actions.'
(g) 'Ensuring that what needs to be communicated is understood and acted upon.'
(h) 'Practical leadership exercise.'
(i) 'Meetings cost money.'
(j) 'The effectiveness of teams and a definition of leadership.'
(k) 'Planning, organizing and controlling sales.'
(l) 'What a leader should do to increase effectiveness in achieving results through people.'
(m) 'How to make the best use of the time available.'
(n) 'Identification of leadership styles.'
(o) 'How to utilize available skills and resources.'
(p) 'The appropriateness of different management styles to effective decision-making.'

2 Arrange the subjects in a suitable order for a training course of this kind.

3 Classify the various papers according to the subjects to which they refer.

SECTION F Discussion

1 'The best method of payment is payment by results.' Do you agree? Why?

2 Describe how selling methods must differ in various types of industry.

3 'Successful salesmen are always the same kind of person.' Do you agree? Why?

4 Find ten advertising themes and assess their merits.

SECTION G Writing

1 Join each of the following groups of notes into one sentence, using the words or expressions in parentheses. Make any changes that may be necessary.

a. experience will enable everybody to take full part in discussions and decision-making/everybody must show interest and capacity (**who**)

b. we need new sales manager/new sales manager must be able to build effective salesforce/salesforce must re-establish our position in home market/we dominated home market until last year (**who, in order to, which**)

c. sales manager's first objective must be to produce sales team/sales team must utilize skills of all members (**which**)

d. effectiveness of decisions and performance will depend on new sales manager's ability to establish and maintain close co-operation between all members of team/effectiveness of decisions and performance will depend on quality of individual skills and knowledge of team members/recruitment of team members responsibility of sales manager (**both . . . and, whose**)

e. all individuals within team must be encouraged to express own opinions and ideas/each person must be encouraged to contribute to framing of proposals (**not only . . . but also**)

2 Now re-arrange the five completed sentences to make a paragraph about the function of a new sales manager. You may use additional words to link the sentences if you think they are necessary.

Unit 14 Finance

SECTION A Reading

Read this statement.

Chairman's annual statement

1981 was a satisfactory year for MacGregor's with sales rising by 15% compared to the previous twelve months. The profit before tax increased by 22% and the after-tax profit showed an increase of 31%. The disparity between the pre-tax and after-tax figures was due to the increase in the proportion of our profits earned overseas. These profits generally attract a lower rate of tax than the rate charged in the UK.

Engineering Division

The performance was good not only in relation to previous years but also in comparison with other British engineering companies. The return on capital increased by 31% and the Division, even after capital expenditure of over £2 million, generated in excess of £3 million in cash for the Group. We intend to implement expansion plans for the Division which include investment in new manufacturing facilities and a major overhaul of some existing equipment.

Plastics Division

Despite the difficulties in the home market, trading levels were maintained as a result of our successful concentration on export markets. Our Belgian subsidiary, however, experienced such a low volume of orders that it was unable to do more than contain its losses. This is a company which, it should be noted, has a high break-even point.

Finance

The company's liquidity is so strong that our net borrowings are less than 25% of our total share capital and reserves. As a result, we have a borrowing capacity of several million pounds. If we require higher investment as a consequence of an improvement in trade, we intend to obtain funds by bank borrowing which, despite high interest rates, would be the cheapest way of raising money. Should additional cash be required for an acquisition, the board will consider the possibility of raising more capital.

Earnings

The net worth of your ordinary shares is 154p compared with a market price of half that figure. The earnings are 15.8p per share and the total dividend for the year amounts to 5.2p.

There is every reason to be optimistic about the company's prospects in the current year. The higher the inflation rate, however, the more difficult it will be to maintain our profit position. Last year, I asked you to be realistic in your expectations and to remember the difficult trading conditions. This year I repeat that advice in view of the world economic recession.

Word Study

satisfactory *l.2* meeting all requirements, wishes, needs, etc.
disparity *l.4* difference in amount.
proportion *l.6* comparative relation between parts. This can be expressed, for example, as 2 to 1 or 2:1.
attract *l.6* incur.
capital *l.11* money invested in the stock of goods used in production.
generated *l.12* produced.
in excess of *l.12* more than.
implement *l.13* put into operation.
overhaul *l.14* repairs or replacement of parts to bring machinery, motors, equipment, etc. into good working order again.
concentration on *l.18* collecting and directing efforts toward a common centre.
subsidiary *l.19* company controlled by another company which owns most of the former's shares.
contain *l.20* keep within reasonable limits.
break-even point *l.21* point at which income equals expenditure.
liquidity *l.23* ability to convert company property into cash or to use it in paying money that is owed.
reserves *l.24* cash, or things which can be turned into cash, kept out of use in order to meet expected or unexpected demands.
obtain funds *l.27* get money.
interest rates *l.27* *Interest* is money which is paid for the use of money. An interest rate is expressed as a percentage per unit of time, eg, 12½% p.a. (= per annum = per year).
raising money *l.28* getting cash.
ordinary shares *l.32* shares which allow the holders to take a percentage of distributed profits after fixed-interest lenders have been paid.
dividend *l.34* an individual's share of a sum of money to be divided among stockholders.

prospects *l.35* chances for success.
inflation *l.36* process of rising prices, resulting in a fall in the value of money.
recession *l.40* period in which business activity drops and unemployment rises.

Comprehension

1 Say what the words in **bold face** refer to.
a. '**These** profits . . .' *(l.6)*
b. '. . . **the Division,** . . .' *(l.11)*
c. '. . . **the Group.**' *(l.12)*
d. '**This** is a company . . .' *(l.20)*
e. '. . . **your** ordinary shares . . .' *(l.32)*
f. '. . . half **that figure.**' *(l.33)*
g. '. . . **your expectations** . . .' *(l.38)*
h. '. . . **that advice** . . .' *(l.39)*

2 What is the relation between a rising inflation rate and holding on to MacGregor's profit position?

3 How are 154p, 15.8p and 5.2p related?

4 If you owned 1,000 ordinary shares in MacGregor, what would your dividend be? How much could you sell your shares for?

5 What is the disparity between MacGregor's pre-tax and after-tax profit? What is the reason for it?

6 How did other British engineering companies perform in 1981 in relation to MacGregor?

7 Describe the expansion plans for the Engineering Division.

8 How did MacGregor manage to maintain trading levels in the Plastics Division?

9 What happened in 1981 at the Belgian subsidiary?

10 Explain 'high break-even point'.

11 Explain the relation between MacGregor's liquidity and the company's borrowing capacity.

12 What is the relation between the world economic recession and the Chairman's advice this year?

13 What may cause higher investment at MacGregor's?

SECTION B Listening

Cassette 2, side 2. While you are listening to the conversation between Mr. Tyler, a Personnel Director, Mr. Curry, a Financial Director, and Mr. Brown and Mr. Scott, both Trade Union Representatives, do 1, 2, 3 and 4 below.

1 Complete the graph.

Hamilton Automotive – Profit Position 1972–81

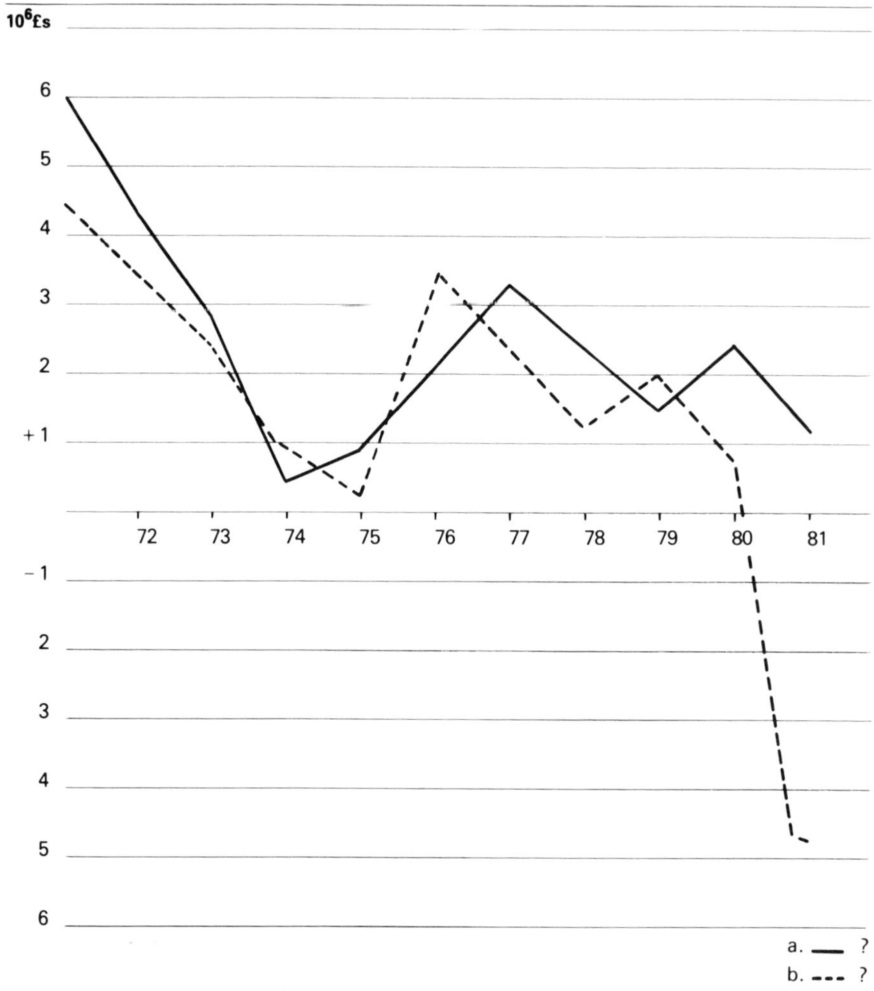

2 What two reasons are given for the substantial losses in 1980?

3 Why can't the government increase its shareholding in Hamilton's at the moment?

4 What action is favoured by some of the shareholders?

Tyler This meeting has been called, gentlemen, because of the serious financial situation in which Hamilton's now finds itself. I'm sure this comes as no surprise. We have been told by the Board, in short, to reduce costs.

Brown This isn't going to be another call for more redundancies, is it, Mr. Tyler?

Tyler I'm not asking for anything at all at this stage, Mr. Brown. I merely want to explain the position clearly to you so that you can inform your members. We need a full and open discussion on the matter.

Scott I'm glad to hear that. At our last meeting, when Mr. Brown here explained that our Union wanted more information on all financial matters, you told him to let the managers do the managing. Now it seems that a 'full and open discussion' is convenient from management's point of view. So, perhaps Mr. Curry will now fill us in on some of the financial details.

Curry I have the latest figures here with me, Mr. Scott. They are the worst in the company's long history—even worse than the trough we experienced in 1975. In point of fact, a trading profit of just over one million pounds was turned into an overall loss of substantially more than four million pounds.

Brown And what do you say was the cause of that?

Curry Amongst other things, an overseas tax charge of five million pounds, and an unusual cost of ten million pounds which was incurred after we had been advised to close down our unprofitable Asian operation.

Brown That's all behind us now. It's this current year we should be worrying about.

Curry Worry is the right word to use, Mr. Brown. We calculate that with the fall in world demand, we will be working at only three-quarters capacity next year.

Brown So we are talking about redundancies.

Tyler Mr. Brown, please. We are also talking about finding ways of making the company more competitive, surely. That means finding about 90 million pounds to invest in new plant and equipment.

Scott And where is the 90 million pounds going to come from?

Tyler Well, for example, we could ask the government if they would be prepared to support an increase in our bank borrowing. After all, our exports are worth over fifty million pounds to the country.

Scott And there are the hundred and fifty thousand people who work for this company all over the UK, and the thousands of other workers employed by our components suppliers.

Tyler We haven't forgotten that, Mr. Scott. I said at the beginning of this meeting that things were very serious. However, the government is considering its policy very carefully at the moment.

Brown What? Is the government going to increase its shareholding in Hamilton's?

Tyler We have been asked to find out if there is any way in which the government could take up more shares in the company. The advice we've received on the matter, however, is that at the moment such a move would be against regulations. We are working on that problem now.

Curry In the meantime, our shareholders are far from happy about recent developments. There is talk of an extraordinary meeting of the shareholders and a number of them have said that the company should be sold.

Brown Hamilton's would go to a foreign company, then.

Scott Yes, and if history is any guide, they would sell off the most profitable parts of Hamilton's, and our members would face even—

Tyler Let us talk more realistically, gentlemen. Although some of our shareholders may want to make a sale of this kind, I'm sure the government would not allow it.

Curry And, indeed, should the government decide to take up a large number of shares, they may very well consider selling them to Hamilton's employees at an attractive rate.

Scott Ah, Mr. Curry, I think we are getting to the point of this meeting at last. But before you start introducing plans like that, remember that our members are looking for immediate improvements in their wages.

Tyler Mr. Scott, do you know that over half of the present shareholders have holdings that are worth little more, on average, than twenty pounds?

Scott Meaning?

Tyler Meaning that it is quite common to have a small investment in a company. Surely—Mr. Scott, Mr. Brown—surely, the greater our employees' share in the company, the better the incentive to make the company profitable.

☐ What does Mr. Scott think is the real purpose of the meeting?

SECTION C Language Study

1 Comparing

Study the table below.

As this increases/decreases:	*This also increases/decreases:*
a. Employee's share in company	Incentive to make the company profitable
b. Inflation rate	Ability to maintain profits
c. Speed of working	The number of mistakes made
d. Production costs	The selling price
e. Earnings	Expenditure
f. The rate of technological change	The reduction in people employed in manufacturing

Examples:

a. **The greater** an employee's share in a company, **the better** the incentive to make the company profitable.
or
The smaller an employee's share in a company, **the lower** the incentive to make the company profitable.

Use similar sentences to compare **c-f**.

2 Anticipated Response

Example:
If it happens that additional cash is required for an acquisition, the Board will consider the possibility of raising more capital.
▷ **Should** additional capital be required for an acquisition, the Board will consider the possibility of raising more capital.

Now re-write the following without 'if'.

a. If it happens that the government decide to take up a large number of shares, they may very well consider selling them to Hamilton's employees at an attractive rate.

b. If it is decided that the government take up a large number of shares, they may very well consider selling them to Hamilton's employees at an attractive rate.

c. If you ever need assistance, call on me.

d. If a recession takes place in the UK market, we will concentrate on overseas sales.

e. If you require additional information, please contact the sales office.

3 Degree

Study the following table.

Situation	*Result*
a. Heavy demand for metals	Prices very high
b. High number of cars sold	Record profits for manufacturers
c. Large number of imported cars	Domestic manufacturers facing losses
d. Heavy pressure on plant facilities	Necessary to acquire new land for extensions
e. Heavy losses in the Asian market	Company closed down the operation
f. High dependence on short-term loans	Company future not secure

Examples:

a. The demand for metals is **so heavy** | **that** prices are very high.
There is **so much** demand for metals |

b. The number of cars sold was **so high** | **that** manufacturers made record profits.
There were **so many** cars sold |

Remember that **much** is used for the things we can not count, eg, demand, and **many** is used for things we can count, eg, cars.

Now write similar sentences using **so . . . that** for the rest of the table.

SECTION D Listening

Cassette 2, side 2. While you are listening to the presentation by Mr. Spellman, Chairman of Associated Metals, complete tables 1 and 2 below.

1

Subject	*Information*
a. Production	Increase in UK and Overseas
b. Plant Utilization	. . .
c. World Metal Prices	. . .
d. Group Profit	. . .

2

Final Dividend	*Undistributed profits 1980*
a. 1979 . . .	c. . . .
b. 1980 . . .	

□ **1.** Complete the table below.

Associated Metals – Sources of Profit 1980			
Products	%	**Geographical**	%
Metals	32.6	Europe: UK	. . .
		Other	17.1
Chemicals	?	Australasia	?
?	20.3	Asia	8.2
Wallpaper	15.8	North & South America	4.9

2. Describe the prospects for growth in the current year.

SECTION E Using Information in Different Ways

1 Read the following description of how a Capital Tax is calculated. Notice particularly the difference between tax which is **charged** and tax which is **allowed.**

If the selling price is greater than the market value and the market value is greater than the cost price, then tax is charged on the selling price less market value and less expenses. If, however, the cost price is greater than the market value, and the selling price is greater than the cost price, then tax is charged on the selling price less the cost price and less expenses. If the selling price is not greater than the cost price, no tax is charged.

If, on the other hand, the selling price is not greater than the market value and the market value is not greater than the cost price, then tax is allowed on the market value less the selling price plus expenses. If, however, the market value is greater than the cost price, and the cost price is greater than the selling price, then tax is allowed on the cost price less the selling price plus expenses. If the selling price is greater than the cost price, no tax is allowed.

2 Using the information in No. 1, complete the flow chart below.

Flow Chart for Capital Tax

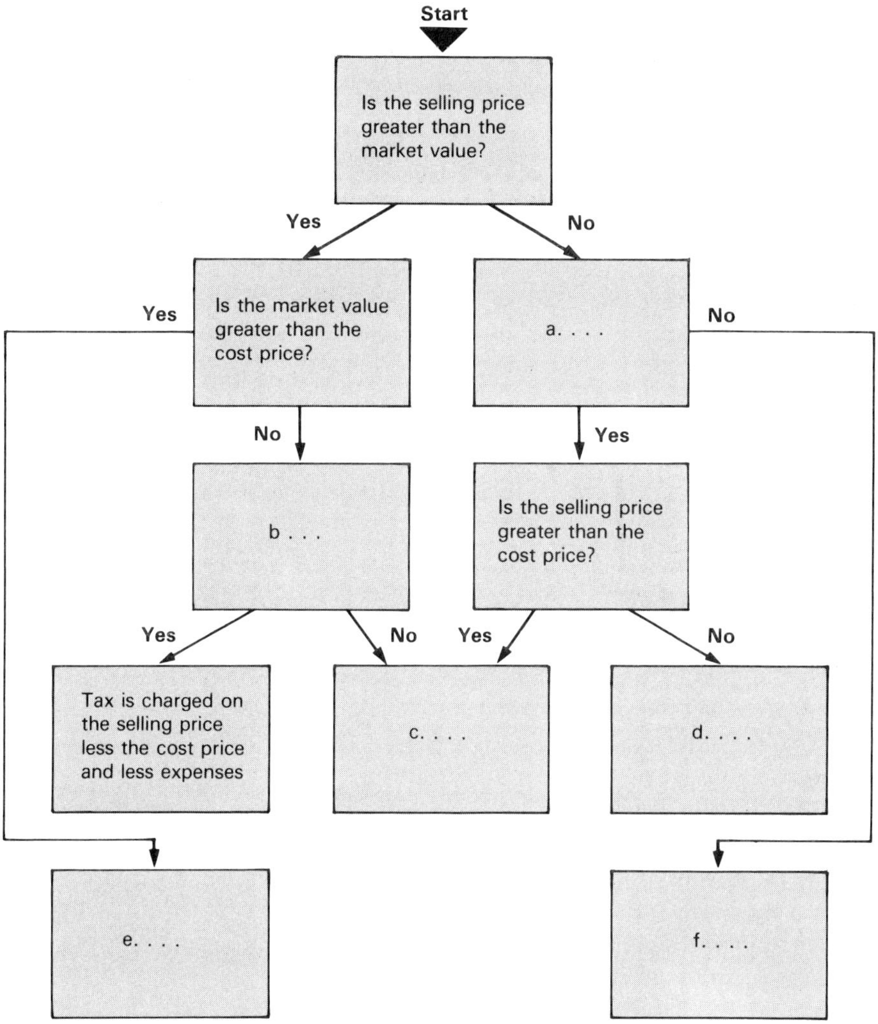

SECTION F Discussion

1 'The best method of financing is to use the company's own profits.' Do you agree? Why?

2 What different methods can a company use in order to raise finance?

3 'There are good financial reasons for appointing top financial executives from outside the company.' What might some of these reasons be?

4 In a period of inflation, what do you think the government should do about the money supply?

SECTION G Writing

1 These three sentences have been removed from the paragraph below:

a. This balance is known as the 'capital gearing'.

b. They are often given this right, for example, when the preference dividends have not been paid.

c. This may mean very high rewards for the ordinary shareholders in a good year but no dividends in a bad one.

One of the functions of financial management is to ensure that the correct balance exists between the value of a company's ordinary shares and the value of its preference shares. If a company has a small proportion of ordinary share capital then its structure is said to be 'highly geared'. In the case of extreme financial difficulties, the preference shareholders have the power to take over the control of a company from the ordinary shareholders.

Write out the paragraph above with the insertion of the three missing sentences.

2 In the same way, insert the three missing sentences in the paragraph below.

a. Supply conditions can change as materials become more expensive or wage costs increase.

b. This excess demand can then be satisfied in monetary terms only by a rise in the general price level.

c. The fact that prices are rising means that expenditure is greater than the value of output.

The general level of prices in the economy depends on the relation between spending and the volume of goods and services which the production processes make available. The pressure on prices can come either from the supply or from the demand side. As a result, prices may be increased as firms try to recover their higher costs from consumers. On the other hand, the amount which people plan to consume and invest may add up to more than the output coming on to the market.

Unit 15 Accounting

SECTION A Reading

Here is another article from *Business Eye*.

Balancing the Books

Although accounting has been moving towards a common standard of comparability in company reporting, experienced company watchers know that for a full understanding of a profit and loss account or of a balance sheet, careful interpretation may be required. At the moment, it seems that this question of standards has divided the profession.

I asked Henry Lovett, who is about to retire from his job as Managing Director of the international auditing firm of Henshaw's, why his company were in favour of the flexible approach: 'Having studied the problem closely, Henshaw's decided that in special circumstances we were justified in not using a common standard. My own view, based on over thirty years' experience, is that all creditors are sufficiently protected, provided that there are proper explanations in the notes to the accounts.' However, according to Samuel Wright of Denham, Coutts and Partners: 'We want to see an end to the present flexibility in company reporting and a system of penalties for those who do not follow regulations.'

Of course, if accounting policies were completely voluntary, all kinds of methods might be employed by companies intent on presenting themselves in the best possible way. A good example of this are the voluntary guidelines in relation to inflation accounting. For a variety of reasons, many companies have avoided publishing inflation adjusted figures.

Problems of avoidance such as this should be solved when current cost accounting becomes compulsory. Yet there are other areas of accounting where discretion is allowed. Take the old case of extraordinary items which are often treated in different ways. Extraordinary costs incurred for such items as plant overhaul and redundancies have in the past been charged differently by different accountants. Nor is it difficult to find discrepancies in the way that assets are valued and depreciated, for it appears that some companies have been recommended not to carry balance sheet assets at their present value but at some anticipated value. Tyne Oil is a good example. Having acquired a new tanker, they valued it at an optimum disposal price.

The problem centres on the question of flexibility. The system of accounting in the UK is neither at historical cost, as in the US, nor at current cost. It is a system favoured by companies because they can revalue their assets at convenient times, such as when their liabilities are heavy. Then a short qualification is made in the auditor's report pointing out the difficulty of making an accurate evaluation of assets, and that is all.

Word Study

profit and loss account *l.4* statement of the revenues and expenses of a firm. The expression *income statement* is also used.
balance sheet *l.4* statement of a firm's financial position.
interpretation *l.5* bringing out the full meaning; making understandable.
auditing firm *l.8* firm that performs a critical examination and analysis of a company's accounts.
creditors *l.12* persons to whom money is owed. A person who owes money to another or others is called a *debtor.*
provided that *l.12* on the condition or understanding that; if.
protected *l.12* kept safe from danger, loss, injury, etc.
penalties *l.16* fines or other punishment.
voluntary *l.17* freely chosen; done by one's own free choice. The opposite is *compulsory* (= 'obligatory or required').
guidelines *l.20* standards or principles of operation.
avoided *l.21* escaped from; kept clear of.
adjusted *l.21* altered so as to make suitable, appropriate, fit, etc.
compulsory *l.23* See *voluntary* above.
discretion *l.24* freedom to make choices and decisions.
treated *l.25* dealt with; handled.
discrepancies *l.27* differences and disagreements.
assets *l.28* all the entries on a balance sheet which show all of a company's property and resources; eg, cash, equipment, accounts receivable, etc. The opposite is *liabilities* (= 'all debts; eg, accounts payable, losses, capital stock, etc.').
depreciated *l.28* lessened in value; given an allowance for a decrease in value due to age, wear, etc.
optimum *l.31* best or most favourable.
disposal *l.31* transferring, selling or throwing away.
liabilities *l.35* See *assets* above.
qualification *l.36* statement limiting full approval.

Comprehension

1 Say what the words in **bold face** refer to.
a. '. . . **this question of standards** . . .' *(l.6)*
b. '. . . **the profession.**' *(l.6)*
c. '. . . **the flexible approach** . . .' *(l.9)*
d. '. . . **the problem** . . .' *(l.9)*
e. 'A good example of **this** . . .' *(l.19)*
f. 'Tyne Oil is **a good example.**' *(l.30)*

g. 'It is a system . . .' *(l.34)*
h. '. . . and **that** is **all.**' *(l.37)*

2 Why is the article entitled *Balancing the Books*?

3 In Henshaw's view, how are creditors protected in company reporting?

4 State in as few words as possible the difference between Lovett's and Wright's view of company reporting.

5 What one reason is suggested for companies not publishing current cost figures?

6 What does the writer think will probably happen when voluntary current cost accounting comes to an end?

7 Give examples of how accounting practices are still left to the discretion of individual companies.

8 When did Tyne Oil value their new tanker? Why did they value it at an optimum disposal price?

9 In what circumstances might an auditor enter a qualification in his report?

10 What three methods of accounting are mentioned in the article?

SECTION B Listening

Cassette 2, side 2. While you are listening to the conversation between Mr. Bob Royston, a Financial Manager, and Mr. Harry Klyne, a Financial Accountant, answer questions 1, 2 and 3.

1 Why do Barlow and Peters consider themselves qualified to carry out a management audit?

2 Why does the MD favour a management audit?

3 Who has linked a high rate of management turnover to periods of poor performance in the market?

Morgan International

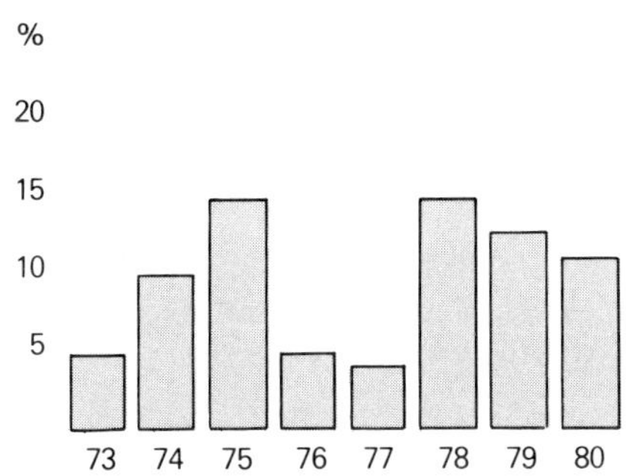

Management Turnover 1973-80

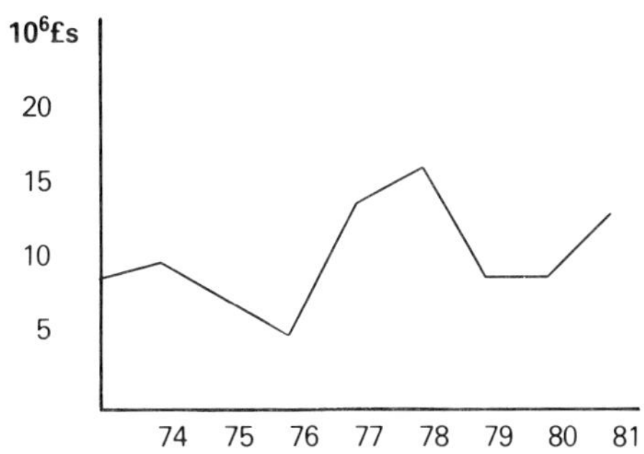

Profit Record 1974 – 81

Royston Can I get you anything before we start, Harry? Coffee? Tea? Something stronger?

Klyne No thanks, Bob.

Royston Okay, then, our meeting with the Managing Director tomorrow.

Klyne You know more about it than I do, Bob. What's it all about?

Royston The MD gave me this report to study after the management meeting yesterday. It's the result of a proposal from our outside accounting audit firm, Barlow and Peters. It seems they're about to extend their activities into the field of management auditing and consultancy. They've suggested to the board that they carry out a management audit here at Morgan's.

Klyne What exactly do they mean by that?

Royston Basically, an assessment of the quality of all our management personnel.

Klyne By Barlow and Peters? What makes them think that they have the qualified people or the experience to make a proper assessment? They should concentrate on balance sheets and profit and loss accounts.

Royston They argue that their extensive financial experience of Morgan's puts them in an ideal position to analyse the problems and performance of our management team.

Klyne How can an accounting firm be responsible for a company's accounts and give advice on the running of the company?

Royston They say they would organize their work into two divisions so as to avoid problems of identity.

Klyne You should be able to guess what I think about that one. What I want to know is why the MD is taking it so seriously.

Royston I think I can tell you. It seems that the Board has been pressuring him for some time to take action over our recent poor performance. He has been told to find a solution quickly.

Klyne And they're going to make management responsible.

Royston Maybe. It appears that a number of the larger investors are concerned about their assets. They have linked our periods of poor performance in the market to the rate of management turnover, for one thing.

Klyne The connection isn't at all clear to me.

Royston It checks with these graphs. See? High management turnover closely followed by falling profits. Low turnover, then considerably better performance.

Klyne This is far too simplistic, Bob. There are a hundred and one reasons why profits have fluctuated, and as many more to explain the high turnover-rate in personnel.

Royston I agree, of course, but the decision about a management audit is serious.

Klyne It looks to me like the MD is trying to take pressure off himself with this.

Royston You may be right, but I've been told not to treat the audit lightly. We need to prepare ourselves properly for tomorrow's meeting.

Klyne Very well, then, let's look at it in practical terms. First, the comparison between profit and loss and management turnover just doesn't stand up. It shouldn't be difficult to point that out. Secondly, if we do accept that there are some managerial weaknesses, then we need to argue that a management audit is not the best method of handling them.

Royston Yes. I think there are two good reasons why your second point is true. For one thing, I would question the experience of Barlow and Peters to carry out an audit like this even if they are about to bring in new men. And for another, it would be a long and costly job. Our management structure would have to be understood as an entire system, not just as a financial accounting problem.

Klyne Agreed.

☐ Complete the following:

a. Comparison of management turnover and profit	Not realistic because . . .
b. Managerial weakness	Not solved by management audit because . . .

SECTION C Language Study

1 Past Time

Example:
First, the MD discussed Barlow & Peters's proposal with the Board. Following that, he wrote a report on the matter for Morgan's management team.
▷ **Having discussed** Barlow & Peters's proposal with the Board, the MD wrote a report on the matter for Morgan's management team.

Use the same structure to join the pairs below.

a. First, Tyne Oil acquired a new tanker. As soon as they had done that, they valued it at an optimum disposal price.

b. First, the investors compared the graph on the company's management turnover to the graph on its profit record. As a direct result of that, they concluded that personnel turnover was related to the company's overall performance.

c. First, the Board decided in favour of Barlow & Peters's proposal. Immediately after that, they prepared a special statement for distribution to Morgan's investors.

d. First, Royston and Klyne agreed on their approach to the Board. When they had done that, they asked to meet with the MD to tell him what they intended to say.

e. First, the MD heard what Royston and Klyne intended to say to the Board. Then, he tried to persuade them to change their minds.

2 Reporting Orders

Examples:
'Please be realistic in your expectations and remember the difficult trading conditions,' the Chairman said.
▷ The Chairman told the shareholders **to be realistic** in their expectations and to remember the difficult trading conditions.
or The Chairman advised the shareholders to be realistic . . .
'Don't treat the audit lightly,' the MD said to Royston.
▷ The MD told Royston **not to treat** the audit lightly.

Report the following.

a. 'Don't forget about tomorrow's meeting,' Royston said to Klyne.

b. 'Let the managers do the managing,' Mr. Tyler said to Mr. Brown.

c. 'Report back to me as soon as you've reached a decision,' he said.

d. 'Don't let anyone disturb us for the next few hours,' he said.

e. 'Tell us where the 150 million pounds is going to come from,' he said.

f. 'Do not for one moment think that the Board is not serious about this proposal,' Bob advised Harry.

g. 'Be reasonable, Mr. Scott. Try to see the situation from management's point of view,' he said.

3 **Immediate Future and Past Time**

Notice how we can express the immediate future and the immediate past.

Examples:

He is going to retire from his job as MD very soon.
▷ He **is about to retire** from his job as MD.

The Sales Manager arrived five minutes ago.
▷ The Sales Manager **has just arrived.**

Use the 'about to' form or Present Perfect with 'just' to change the following sentences.

a. The MD finished reading the report a short while ago.

b. The machine was repaired a few minutes before you arrived.

c. In a few days, the company will open their new factory extension.

d. The management trainees completed the course yesterday.

e. The train is leaving in five minutes time.

SECTION D Listening

Cassette 2, side 2. While you are listening to the conversation between Mr. Ambrose, a Bank Manager, and Mr. Pierce, a Company Director, answer questions 1, 2 and 3 below.

gas furnace

1 Why is Mr. Pierce very pleased with his company's progress?

2 How does Mr. Pierce think he has avoided many potential problems?

3 What information does Mr. Ambrose require in order to make a decision about a loan?

☐ 1 Complete the table.

a. Reason for visit	To borrow money
b. Amount	. . .
c. For what purpose	. . .
d. Reasons for purchase	. . .

2 What important advice does Mr. Ambrose give Mr. Pierce concerning the financial principles of business?

SECTION E Using Information in Different Ways

Below, the Balance Sheet for R. Leger Limited has been set out incompletely in two different ways. The information on each can be used to fill in the other. Complete both balance sheets.

a. Balance Sheet	R Leger Ltd			at 31 December 1980	
	(£)1980	(£)1979		(£)1980	(£)1979
Share Capital	62,189	. . .	. . .	59,068	26,115
. . .	30,202	. . .	Plant	5,070	. . .
Undistributed Profits	32,140	. . .	Investments	11,450	3,119
. . .	39,000	12,150	. . .	7,291	. . .
. . .	2,658	1,918	Cash	3,060	1,090
Proposed Dividend	. . .	1,760	. . .	. . .	35,112
Creditors	98,000		Debtors	79,082	45,976
	. . .	. . .		. . .	117,990

b. Balance Sheet	R Leger Ltd		at 31 December 1980	
		(£)1980		(£)1979
Fixed Assets				
Land & Building		. . .		. . .
. . .		5,070		. . .
Investments		. . .		3,119
Research		. . .		2,460
		82,879		35,812
Current Assets				
. . .	. . .		. . .	
Stock	102,018		35,112	
Debtors	79,082	184,160	45,976	82,178
		267,039		. . .
Share Capital & Reserves				
. . .		. . .		38,341
Reserves (Capital)		. . .		9,615
		. . .		15,190
		124,531		63,146
Loan Capital				
Loans		. . .		. . .
Current Liabilities				
Taxation	. . .		1,918	
. . .	2,658		. . .	
. . .	98,000	103,508	39,016	42,694
		. . .		. . .

SECTION F Discussion

1 'We should aim to make accounting practices universal.' Do you agree? Why?

2 'Accountants know figures but not business.' What do you think is meant by this statement? Do you agree? Why?

3 'Managers should be open to an independent audit of their management quality.' Do you agree? Why?

SECTION G Writing

Write out the paragraph below with the insertion of the following:

a. These objectives place a heavy responsibility on top management.

b. Secondly, they must maintain sufficient working capital and be able to repay their debts without unreasonable delay.

c. The aim of business managers is to make the maximum profit without subtracting from the stability and future interest of the company.

d. This process of planning, recording, reporting and taking action, together with special studies showing the probable financial results of alternative courses of action, is known as management accounting.

e. It is also important to record and measure actual events against the forecast at frequent intervals.

Management Accounting

There are basically three things that business managers must try to do. First, they must obtain an acceptable return on investment. Thirdly, they must pay proper attention to the image of the company, and show reasonable consideration for the interests of the shareholders, fixed-interest lenders and customers. In a large company, the managing director must recruit key personnel of the right experience to help him to optimize company profits. For the management team, there are three effective ways of ensuring that objectives are achieved. To begin with, it is important to forecast sales and production activity. Finally, corrective action must be taken during the year in order to ensure that there is as little deviation as possible from the forecast.

Review Unit 3 Executive Effectiveness

This unit is designed to help you to review the grammar and special vocabulary that you have learned from Units 11-15.

1 The following passage is from *Management—Principles and Practices,* Dalton E McFarland, Collier Macmillan Publishers, New York, 1974 (adapted).

The subject of the executive's job in business organizations is one of great complexity, which is reflected in the range and weight of executive responsibility. In the performance of his work, the executive faces situations which often require difficult or even critical decisions. However, the results for which he is accountable are not achieved through his own direct effort. The weight of his responsibilities can produce pressures that test his health as well as the quality of his managerial skills.

The executive has many resources to employ that help to reduce the difficulties and to minimize the possibility of making mistakes. In addition, both his own training and experience and the history and organization of his company should act as valuable guides in determining the correct method of approach to his job. He will also find that other employees respond to him not so much as an individual executive, but as one who is acting in ways that are expected of him. They, in turn, act in ways which they know are expected of them. To some degree, an organization continues to function automatically, unless the executive moves too far or too suddenly from his defined position.

The executive's most important responsibility is administrative leadership. He learns to think analytically in order to identify and solve problems. He must be personally effective in managing his own life and in relating to the needs of his organization. He requires skills in dealing with people and the ability to select a team with the appropriate background and knowledge for the job.

There are considerable differences in current definitions of managerial effectiveness. Reddin defines it as the extent to which a manager achieves the output requirements of his position—by what he achieves and not what he does. Drucker, however, defines it as a habit and a complex of practices that lead to getting the right things done. Both these definitions contain key elements: results, organizational objectives, and managerial action. The basic difference of opinion lies in what the manager does and what the manager produces. Yet, whether measuring results or the determinants of results, it seems clear that effectiveness is not entirely within the control of the manager himself, nor is it restricted to a particular type of manager. Such factors as the environment, the organization structure, and the reward system combine with the manager's personal characteristics in determining final results.

Relationships among Executive Functions, Executive Actions, and Results

Organization Environment

Executive Functions		**Executive Actions**		**Results**
Planning Organizing Assembling Resources Co-ordinating Representing Deciding Evaluating Leading Etc.	▶	Speaking Writing Reading Travelling Telephoning Interviewing Attending meetings Calling meetings Etc.	▶	Efficiency Productivity Plans Procedures Schedules Processes Organization structure Policies Objectives Ideas Criticism Etc.

Organization Environment

2 Now do these exercises based on the passage.

a. Which factors demonstrate the complexity of the executive's job?

b. What is the difference between '*difficult* or even *critical* decisions' *(l.4)*?

c. What is the relation between (i) the executive's accountability for the actions of others and (ii) his health?

d. Discuss some of the resources which the executive can employ to reduce difficulties and minimize mistakes.

e. How do other employees respond to the executive?

f. How can an organization function automatically? When may it not function this way? Why?

g. Why must an executive be personally effective in managing his own life?

h. Who are Reddin and Drucker? What do their definitions share?

i. Give examples of 'determinants' of results.

j. Why isn't effectiveness entirely within the control of the manager himself?

3 Complete the following table.

verb	*noun*	*verb*	*noun*
. . .	promotion	exceed	. . .
. . .	restriction	concentrate	. . .
. . .	penetration	interpret	. . .
allocate	. . .	penalize	. . .
cover	. . .	. . .	adjustment
constrain	. . .	. . .	depreciation
lack	. . .	respond	. . .
approve	. . .		

4 Example: method of accounting used in the UK⊳UK accounting method
Use nouns as adjectives to express the following in shorter forms.

a. loan made by a bank for a period of five years
b. profit of the Group after tax has been paid
c. report on research into the marketing of the soups made by Countryfresh
d. share of the market amounting to ten per cent
e. campaign of advertising run in the UK on television
f. pack containing Rouen's material for establishing good relations with the public
g. figures for the sales made by Ford in the first quarter of the year
h. form used for assessment of personnel working in sales
i. plans for the expansion of the division responsible for engineering
j. prices obtained for metal in the UK

5 Describe the total sales and total production of Lalle red wine for the eleven years represented on the graph below.

Total Production and Total Sales of Lalle Red Wine 1971 – 81

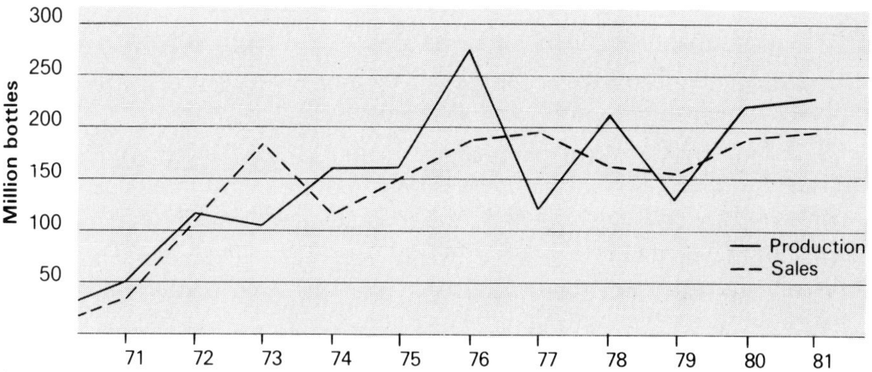

6 Classify the words below under these five subjects:

Graphs and statistics

Finance

Advertising and promotion

Production

Personnel

vacancy	furnace	launch	incentive
dividend	peak	audit	level off
grading	stable	liquidity	liability
negotiations	plant	media	trend
packaging	debtor	bonus	process
discounts	share	survey	decline
award	output	sample	component
depreciation	fluctuations	recruit	batch
image	trough	merchandise	reserves
coupons	interest	lathe	

Review Unit 3
Executive Effectiveness
170

7 Choose from the following Passive form expressions to complete the sentences below: **have been reported, is believed, are grouped, had been taken over, can be provided, were offered, has been negotiated, is expected, could not be measured, is being criticized, will be asked, were removed, have been supplied, will not be affected.**

a. When several workshops . . . together, various facilities . . . for the common use of all employees.

b. Early retirement without penalties . . . for a wide range of jobs in the UK and the list is growing.

c. The Governor of the Bank of England . . . in Downing Street for the failure to control the money supply.

d. Richardson told the government that if exchange controls . . . , this would create possibilities for avoidance of a kind that . . . .

e. It . . . that the company's liabilities are in excess of £3.8m.

f. Most small export firms . . . by the proposed regulations.

g. If Canpan fails, unemployment in the area . . . to reach 30%.

h. Shareholders in Peter Baker (Soaps) . . . tomorrow to approve a five-point plan for reducing company expenditure.

i. CTM and Dan Copy, the photocopier giants, . . . to the Department of Trade for opening rival retail outlets only doors away from independent copy shops who . . . with new CTM and Dan Copy machines.

j. As soon as Mitchell's . . . by the Swedish international, Andersson, several of the former's top executives . . . an attractive relocation scheme for Andersson's chemicals division at Kalmar.

8 Read the following letter and answer the questions which follow it.

'Dear Sir—In response to the nation's call for small businessmen to help reduce the number of unemployed, I recently decided I would take on my first employee. I informed the Inland Revenue of my intention and they sent me the following forms concerning income tax for the young lady who would soon be employed by me: one P24, one P24N, one P34, one P34, one P7X, one P45, one P46, one P47, two P11s, one P7, one NP18, one CF427A, one CF391, one P8, one Tables 'A', and one Tables 'B' to 'D'.

'My heart sank like a stone as I realized that life might be more difficult with an employee rather than easier, and that some of the time she would save me by sharing my current workload would in fact be spent administering her own social benefits rather than increasing productivity.

'It seems that all these forms are designed to be understandable only by specialists employed at great expense by large national companies. No account seems to be taken of the small employer with only limited resources for dealing with all this paperwork. In fact none of the forms actually says in simple language what it is supposed to be about.

'Until someone starts reducing and simplifying governmental paperwork at a day-to-day level, the unemployed are going to remain unemployed and small businesses small.

Yours faithfully,
Daniel Lawrie.'

a. Who do you think this letter was addressed to? What makes you think so?

b. Why did Mr. Lawrie decide to take on this employee? What did he do after taking this decision? What happened immediately after that?

c. Why does he feel that life may be more difficult with an employee than without one? What does he believe his new employee will be doing instead of helping him?

d. How would Lawrie like to see the situation improved?

e. What does Lawrie believe will happen if the situation is not improved?

9 Explain what is meant by (1) campaign lead-in, (2) extra push on advertising, (3) low break-even point, (4) down-market image, and (5) healthy balance sheet.

10 Complete the following sentences using suitable prepositions.

a. The company disposed . . . . . . excess . . . three million pounds worth . . . assets due . . . the unfavourable trading conditions . . . Europe.

b. Alec Murphy retired . . . his position . . . Managing Director . . . Southern Industries . . . thirty years . . . service . . . the company.

c. A combination . . . low demand and inflated prices contributed . . . the decline . . . the company.

d. The trainees adjusted . . . their new positions . . . a very short time.

e. The most important source . . . company profits was sales . . . chemical products . . . the company's own subsidiaries . . . South America.

f. . . . increasing the price . . . one pound . . . one pound fifty pence, profits were ten per cent higher compared . . . the year . . . .

g. The Chairman was . . . favour . . . concentrating . . . the export market . . . a period . . . at least two years.

h. The extent . . . the recession makes it certain that the company will not increase its staff . . . more than 5% . . . the next eighteen months.

11 Complete the following sentences using ideas of your own.

a. The recession must be coming to an end, seeing that . . .

b. If we had not expanded so quickly into Scotland, . . .

c. Having listened carefully to the arguements on both sides, the Chairman . . .

d. Canpan used to be very interested in Southeast Asia, but now . . .

e. Provided that market demand remains steady, . . .

f. We will not have improved our market position by next summer if, in the meantime, . . .

g. If you really wanted to avoid those problems with the Union you should . . .

h. It's very likely that . . . , since . . .

i. It's highly unlikely that . . . , seeing that . . .

j. Expenditure is in excess of . . . , owing to . . .

12 Here are three speakers' descriptions of the performance of two companies. Each speaker has his facts right but does not provide the complete picture. Use the information given by each speaker to complete the graph and provide it with a title.

Speaker A

In general, we can be pleased with the performance of Harcourt over the last five years. There has, after all, been an upward trend in sales leading to the present 1980 peak of £50 million. This 25% increase in 1980 compared to the previous year does more than re-establish the growth record of the company. A £30 million increase in sales over a five year period is very good progress indeed even allowing for the rate of inflation and the uncharacteristic fluctuations in sales.

Speaker B

Although Mathews did well to recover last year from the disastrous slump in sales in 1978 (when sales totalled only a bare £10 million), this year's total of only double the 1978 figure is very disappointing. One need only consider the £50 million sales of 1976 to realize that overall the company is experiencing a period of decline, only slightly interrupted by the improvements made last year.

Speaker C

Analysts have certainly noticed a reversal in fortunes between the machine tool firms of Mathews Ltd. and Harcourt International. It is interesting to note that in 1977 Harcourt could only manage half the Mathews sales total of £42 million, whereas in 1978 Mathews achieved four times the Mathews sales, admittedly in an unusual year. In the following year, both companies had almost the same level of sales, but in 1980 Harcourt's sales were two and a half times more than those of Mathews.

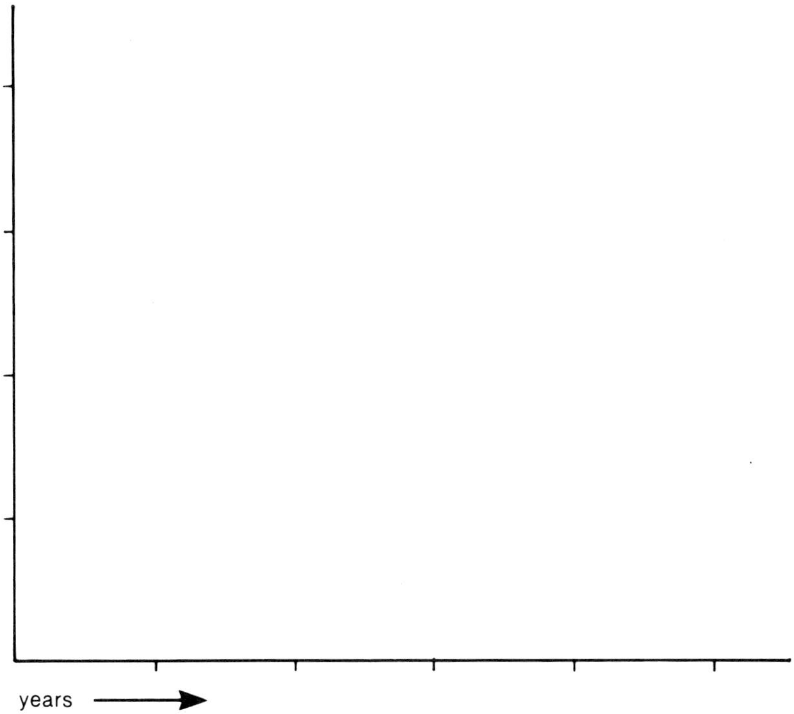

Key

In the following Key, the symbol Δ has been used to show that this is a model answer; there are other possible answers.

Unit 1

A Reading Comprehension

1 **a.** 2. News bulletin; 3. Recommendations **b.** 1. Commercial and government employment offices; 2. Consultants; 3. Own advertisements **c.** Personnel specification **d.** References **e.** Interview assessment form
2 **a.** the introductory letters **b.** the interview panel **c.** knowing what information is needed from applicants **d.** an interview assessment form
3 a personnel specification
4 age, education, qualifications, work experience and references
5 *verbs:* assess, inform, decide, describe, manage *nouns:* qualification, reference, education, advertisement, specification, recruitment, selection

B Listening

Mr. Frame; Management Trainee; University/Business School; Business School Diploma; No work experience; Very Good; Football/Tennis; Personnel; 1. Mr. Lyle 2. Mr. Coates

C Language Study

1 Asking for Information
a. Is this your/her first interview? **b.** What do you mean? **c.** What subjects did you/he like the most at business school? **d.** Did you have a pleasant journey? **e.** Can you explain why you like working with people? **f.** May I see your letters of reference? **g.** Who is the Training Manager? **h.** What does the starting salary depend on? **i.** Why doesn't Frame have any experience? **j.** Where did you/he pass your/his diploma? **k.** When does the job start?

2 Nouns as Adjectives
c. notice boards **d.** application forms **e.** work experience **f.** personnel specification **g.** seven-point plan **h.** interview panel **i.** job description **j.** high school diploma

3 Ways of Doing Things
a. A company can find out about the past performance of an applicant by asking for references/by means of references. **b.** A company can . . . about job vacancies by using the staff bulletin/by means of the staff bulletin. **c.** A manager can . . . forms by working from a personnel specification/by means of a personnel specification. **d.** A manager can . . . interview by using an interview assessment form/by means of an interview assessment form. **e.** Applicants can describe themselves by giving their age, qualifications and experience/by means of their age, qualifications and experience.

4 Describing
(3) Letters are received from job applicants. (4) Application forms are sent to the job applicants. (5) The application forms are checked. (6) Letters are sent to all the applicants informing them about who is short-listed for interview. (7) Interviews are held for the short-listed applicants. (8) Assessment of the short-listed applicants is made during interviews. (9) Information is sent to the interviewees on the results of their interviews. Δ

D Listening

1 Management Trainee 2 Galaxy
3 £3,500-£4,500 4 Two years
5 Four weeks 6 Personnel Manager and Training Manager
☐ Tony thought that the interview went quite well. Δ

E Using Information in Different Ways

2 Application for the position of Assistant Personnel Manager.
1.2 Malcolm David **1.3** 23.2.52

1.4 Married **1.5** Address: 22, Norfolk Road, London W2
2. Education **2.1** Holton High School
2.2 1971-74
3. Qualifications **3.1** Diploma in Business Studies **3.2** Diploma in Personnel Management
4.1 Table Tennis **4.2** Badminton
5. Work Experience **5.1** Nathan; 1974-77
5.2 Pinewood Ltd; £4,400; Get more experience; 1977-79 **5.3** Litham; Personnel Officer; £5,280; — ; 1979 onwards

G Writing

Judy Shepherd–First Judy Shepherd worked for Lloyds Bank as a Clerk at £2,300 a year. She was with the company from 1972-74. Following that she joined Barclays Bank, at £2,750 a year, where she stayed until 1976 as a Typist. Now/at the moment she is working for Norwich Union as a Secretary at a salary of £3,000 a year. Δ

Unit 2

A Reading Comprehension

1 **a.** Based on a job description which gives information about the performance required for a specific job. **b.** Based on a job specification which gives information about the behaviour, knowledge and skills expected in a job. **c.** 1. What to teach. 2. What methods to use.
2 **a.** a specific job **b.** information about job descriptions and specifications **c.** a training specification **d.** training methods **e.** skills **f.** evaluation of operator and technician training
3 'Learning about skills' takes place in the classroom and 'training in using them' takes place on the job. Δ
4 For operators and technicians, a company can evaluate the manual work of those who have completed a training programme. For supervisors and managers, a company may examine such things as the number of staff who leave their employment and the number who stay away for health reasons. Δ
5 *verbs:* require, know, behave, evaluate, employ *nouns:* definition, analysis, weakness, performance, rotation, success

B Listening

Trainees did not like the course for reasons b, d, f, h.
☐ The most important problem is the method of job rotation.

C Language Study

1 Sentence Links

a. To evaluate something is not only to find what a thing is worth in money but also what it is worth in quality, time spent, importance to the company, etc. **b.** Companies must not only look at the number of management and supervisory staff who leave their employment but also at the number who are absent from work for reasons of health.
c. Wrights are in business not only to educate management trainees but also to make lifts.

2 Present and Past Time
a. Yes, he has. He assessed them last week.
b. Yes, I have. I received them last week.
c. Have you applied for the job of Training Officer? **d.** Have you sent the letters to the trainees? **e.** Yes, I have. I recruited him/her/one in week 34.

3 Completed Actions
The typewriter has been covered. The files have been moved to the shelf. The letters have been taken away. The calendar has been changed. The diary has been closed.
The chair has been turned round.
The desk lamp has been switched off. The desk drawers have been closed.
The desk key has been removed.

D Listening

They agree about b, c, d, e

E Using Information in Different Ways

1. Analyse behaviour, knowledge and skill of staff. 3. Look at present performance and performance required. 4. Make a training plan. 6. Decide who does the training.
7. Decide on training methods. 9. Collect course material. 11. Test trainees.
12. Evaluate the training programme.

G Writing

In order to fill a staff vacancy at Lawsons, a meeting is held first in the Personnel Department. Management decide either to recruit outside of the company by means of employment offices or newspaper advertisements or to recruit in-company by asking for recommendations or by using the staff bulletin. Next, the application forms are checked and the applicants are informed if they have been short-listed. Then interviews are held before the job is offered to an applicant. Δ

Unit 3

A Reading Comprehension

1 *Financial Incentives:* merit awards, bonuses, monetary schemes *Non-financial:*

pension schemes, sports clubs, housing, canteens
2 **a.** companies **b.** a firm **c.** the 'points' or 'factor' values **d.** the Hay System **e.** in administrative work **f.** the Personnel Department
3 An incentive offers employees more for producing more. A bonus is an additional payment to wages and salaries. A merit award is an increase in wages and salaries based on better job performance. Δ
4 By placing a value on the requirements of a job as specified in a job description.
5 By evaluating personnel on their knowledge of the job, responsibility, and their ability to solve problems.
6 A direct worker such as a machine operator makes the product. An indirect worker such as a canteen assistant does not make the end product. The wages and salaries of indirect workers are often more difficult to calculate because these workers do not always have a measurable output. Δ
7 Because of merit awards, for example. Δ
8 *verbs:* negotiate, solve, measure, agree *nouns:* negotiation, calculation, benefit, solution, pension, agreement

B Listening

1 Business Consultant 2 1976 3 750
4 800 5 3 weeks 6 A few years
☐ Many of the staff feel they are paid lower than others who do the same kind of work. Δ

C Language Study

1 Plans, Intentions, Possibilities
Tuesday – I am interviewing applicants for the job of Training Manager./I am going to send letters to the job applicants./I will check the progress of the job evaluation.
Wednesday – I am preparing the monthly report./I am going to visit the Safety Officer./I will meet Bob for lunch.
Thursday – I am visiting the Business Exhibition./I am going to telephone for references./I will prepare for the wage negotiations.
Friday – I am meeting the Personnel Director for lunch./I am going to evaluate the training course./I will write to the employment office.

2 Comparing
In 1977, the sales of Morgan Ltd. were worse than the sales of Wright's./In 1977, the sales of Wright Ltd. were better than Morgan's/In 1977, the sales of Morgan Ltd. were not so good as Wright's.

3 Prepositions
Check with paragraphs two and three in the Reading Passage.

D Listening

Unions feel that merit assessments are not based on performance.
Some managers feel it is impossible to decide on the difference in merit between one employer and another.

E Using Information in Different Ways

GRADE I Factory Workers, £2,950-£5,200
1. skilled, eg. machine operators; 2. unskilled, eg. labourers
GRADE II Indirect Workers, £2,200-£5,400
1. supervisory, eg. office supervisor; 2. non-supervisory, eg. typist, canteen assistants
GRADE III Management, £4,500-£12,500
a. eg. Personnel Assistant; d. eg. Production Manager

G Writing

Between 1931 and 1938, the company developed heavy lorries and farm machinery. Between 1939 and 1945, the years of the Second World War, tanks and aeroplane parts were produced. During these years both the number of staff and the production greatly increased. After the War, in 1947, Lind bought Airframe Ltd, manufacturers of light aeroplanes. During the next eight years, three new factories were built, one of them in France. In 1958 profits of the company reached £20 million. From 1960 to 1962, the export policy of the company was unsuccessful and in 1963 profits fell to only £8 million. In the following year Lind was bought by Runcorn Industries. Δ

Unit 4

A Reading Comprehension

1 **a.** service the information requirements of the company. **b.** ensure that office services run smoothly. **c.** contribute to business efficiency.
2 **a.** the office **b.** the information requirements **c.** clerical operations **d.** the large increase in clerical workers compared with the increase in total workforce
e. check, sort, copy and file correspondence and other paperwork **f.** a system
3 Check Word Study notes.
4 No. If, for example, the economy of a country is changing to a service industry base. Δ
5 The office manager must make sure that administrative work is performed efficiently. Δ
6 By using different data processing systems in different departments and by not making data available to all managers.
7 The size and resources of a company.
8 *verb:* mechanize, computerize, process,

service/serve *nouns:* communication, equipment, contribution, comprehension, administration, correspondence, balance
9 **c.** False. Efficiency is output divided by input. **d.** True. **e.** True.

B Listening

2 Reports and correspondence are typed.
4 Corrections and additions are made on screen. 6 End copy is typed out automatically.
☐ Typing efficiency has increased by 130%. Four fewer typists required. 75% of managerial typing now done. Δ

C Language Study

2 Short Forms

a. Mr., Inc., St., U.K., Ave., V.D.U. (Often written without full stops.)
b. advertisement, electronic data processing, carbon copy, etcetera, post meridiem – after noon, ante meridiem – before noon/morning, id est – that is

3 Phrasal Verbs

a. stands for **b.** call up **c.** changed over **d.** built up **e.** taken away/switched off

4 Expressing Sentences in Different Ways

a. The (operation of the) video typing system is smooth. **b.** John Masters, the new management trainee, works well. **c.** The Administration Manager's secretary is a quick and efficient typist. **d.** The Union Representative negotiates badly. **e.** Mrs. Cooper is a very careful office supervisor. **f.** The training programmes are evaluated regularly.

D Listening

1 The long journey to work./She would like a job nearer home./She does not want to move house./She gets very tired at the end of the day. Δ
2 Because Marie has one of the best secretarial positions./Marie has one of the best bosses./Because Marie is 'just having a bad week'. Δ

E Using Information in Different Ways

2 Recruitment: Adams, Watson Training: Cooper, Marlow, Trench Pay and Conditions: Francis, P., Johns, Underwood, West Health and Safety: Hines, Parks, Thomas Social: Francis, L., Spellman Δ
3 Dino Bertolucci, N. Brieger, D. F. Brown, D. J. Brown, Hilary Brown, Laura M. Bryce, Yousef Al Diwani, P. D'Youville, G. Frank Forbes-Eliot, Marie Goldscheider, S. Hetz, Kerstin Klasson, V. G. Mastorakis, Peter Mackechnie, Chuntana Metha, Harvey L. Meyer, K. Patel, Antonio Sanchez, M. T. M. Sidebottom, T. Siemens, Mark Xavier

G Writing

2 (1) An analysis of the performance of six typists working for Canpan Ltd gave some interesting results. The bar chart shows that Patricia Davidson has the highest output of the six typists, completing six hundred lines per day. The second most productive was Heather Murray who produced 450 lines a day. Judy Dyson produced twenty fewer lines than this. Next, Mary-Ellen Jacobsen completed 400 lines per day, fifty more than Jill Fox. Much slower than the others was Davlyn Smith who managed only 200 lines a day. The six typists completed a total of 2,430 lines at an average of 405 lines. Δ

Unit 5

A Reading Comprehension

1 **b.** Length of time to complete research
c. Makes full use of resources, development engineering and marketing capacity.
d. Provides steady growth in income and profits **e.** Has psychological importance, for management is assessed on this basis by those outside the company
2 **a.** the supply of projects and the selection of schemes **b.** making full use of resources, development engineering and market capacity **c.** new market winners **d.** people **e.** the company's **f.** products **g.** a specific need
3 Industrial products are often the result of laboratory work aimed at a general need. Consumer products are developed to meet a specific need.
4 When it does not meet customer needs, for example. Δ
5 Because to achieve results R&D must define the areas for investigation and the objectives that should be achieved in each area.
6 (1) projects with good potential (2) a supply of successful products (3) a product developed to meet a specific need
7 *verbs:* benefit, base on, define, apply, add, relate *nouns:* length, width, definition, application, specification, addition, relation *adjectives:* long, wide, specific
8 **a.** False. The area is one point four four square metres (1.44 sq.m.). **b.** True. **c.** True. **d.** False. Industrial products are often the result of work done in the laboratory aimed at a general need. **e.** False. It is aimed at specific needs.

B Listening

1 They have received much less for R&D expenditure and have fewer projects.
2 Spend more on R&D.
☐ In the 1970's, R&D spending in Britain fell by 11%. In Japan it increased by 29%, in West Germany it increased by 28%, and in France by 12%.

C Language Study

1 Advice and Possible Results
b. If it doesn't, the products may not meet consumer needs. **c.** If it isn't, staff may use information in the wrong way. **d.** If it isn't, the company may have fewer successful products. **e.** If it doesn't, the growth in income and products may slow down. **f.** If it doesn't, it may provide inefficient programmes. Δ

2 Supposition
a. If United Chemicals did the necessary research, their products would improve.
b. If there was a vacancy for a Training Manager, the company would advertise in the national press. **c.** If there was a need to reduce expenditure, the R&D Department would have to make cuts. **d.** If the training programme was not a success, the Training Manager would analyse and assess the training methods. **e.** If there was an accident in the factory, the Personnel Manager would inform the Safety Inspector.

3 Suggesting
a. If there was an increase in manufacturing costs, the company could raise its prices or it could improve efficiency or it could reduce staff. **b.** If young managers were leaving the company, it could improve the training programme or it could pay them more money or it could give them more responsibility.

D Listening

1 (a) Companies can make a quicker return on their money. (b) Companies would find it difficult to change their product range later.
2 They do not market new products as high-priced items in a limited market.
☐ Because the applications of new technology are seldom the same as the use for which the technology was developed.

E Using Information in Different Ways

1971 = 50; 1972 = 75; 1974 = 90; 1975 = 90; 1976 = 80; 1977 = 72; 1978 = 125

G Writing

1 White Cross spent £42½ million on R&D in 1960. In the following year, expenditure increased to £50 million, and in 1962 it reached £55 million. In 1963, there was a reduction in expenditure to £50 million. Expenditure stayed at this figure in the following year. In 1965, there was a very large increase to £90 million but then a downward trend began. In 1966, expenditure was £70 million. It was £10 million lower in the following year and a further £2½ million lower the year after that. In 1969, the expenditure was back to the 1960 level of £42½ million. Δ
4 If a country invests successfully in R&D, it will benefit in a number of ways. First, it will achieve an increase in profits, an increase in employment, and an increase in national income. Second, a flow of successful new products will cut down on the quantity of goods brought in from other countries. Finally, this can be important socially, for it is often on this basis that people outside the country assess industrial achievement. Δ

Review Unit 1

2 **a.** (*l.* 2) the present day (*l.* 4) the limited number of decisions that can be made by one person (*l.* 11) people that one person can manage directly (*l.* 12) various groups (*l.* 14) carefully defined (*l.* 20) maximisation of output against input (*l.* 27) the means for individuals to assess their relations with other employees
b. A non-technical world. **c.** Because of the complexities of decision-making. **d.** To achieve objectives that can not be reached individually. **e.** In order to achieve company policy in an efficient way. **f.** The right information will not reach the right people. **g.** There will be no individual job satisfaction. **h.** An efficient work system/a means of communication/satisfaction for company personnel. **i.** By ensuring that company organization functions smoothly.

3 **a.** False. The variations in performance were about the same. **b.** True. **c.** False. The trend was downwards. **d.** True. **e.** True. **f.** True. **g. True.** **h.** True. **i.** False. The graph is suitable for the information in it. **j.** True. But it would give a different picture.

4 Check with paragraphs three and four in the Reading Passage in Unit 2.

5 *verbs:* know, weaken, widen, calculate, benefit, solve, pension off, agree, lengthen, specify, relate to, base on, decide *nouns:* knowledge, width, definition, success, variation, negotiation, solution, measurement, agreement, length, application, specification, addition, basis, decision

adjectives: weak, definable, successful, variable, negotiable, calculable, beneficial, pensionable, measurable, applicable, additional, relative

6 have been analysed   is required   can be made   must be specified   must be decided   is done   must be used   must be collected   have been completed   are tested   should be evaluated

7 **a.** seven-point plan   **c.** training needs analysis   **d.** product development   **e.** pay negotiations   **f.** management training programme   **g.** development engineering   **h.** consumer products   **i.** application forms   **j.** notice board   **k.** work experience   **l.** data processing system   **m.** research laboratory   **n.** marketing capacity   **o.** computer programme   **p.** management decision-making   **q.** organisation structure   **r.** job satisfaction   **s.** company information flow   **t.** group activity

8 **a.** experience   **b.** evaluate   **c.** policy   **d.** staff   **e.** methods   **f.** selected   **g.** based on   **h.** rate

9 Number the left-hand column from a-j; and the right-hand column from 1-12.
a/in order to/4   b/because/6   c/in order to/5   d/in order to/9   e/in order to/2   f/in order to/1   g/because of/3   h/in order to/11   i/in order to/8 *or* i/because of/12   j/because of/7

10 **a.** Where does Dwight Stone work? **b.** Who has been made Director of Research? **c.** Why did you change over to a computerized system? **d.** By how much has production increased? **e.** Who is Sheila Wright going to work for? **f.** When does the plane for New York leave? **g.** Why was a consultant called in? **h.** How many additional marketing staff is Canpan recruiting? **i.** What sort of staff is Canpan recruiting? **j.** When did Canpan become a limited company? **k.** What is the average salary in management at Canpan? **l.** How long did the new computer system take to develop? **m.** Why does he take the Financial Times? **n.** When will he give us the details? **o.** How can complex objectives be achieved? **p.** Why did the trouble happen? **q.** Who first developed the process? **r.** How often are the machines cleaned and checked? **s.** Where have the vacancies been advertised? **t.** Whose idea is it for dividing responsibilities between two departments?

11 **b.** Tony thinks the interview was satisfactory. **c.** John is agreeing with Frank's idea. **d.** David is excusing himself. **e.** Godfrey is requesting more details. **f.** Paul is asking for reasons. **g.** Margot is recommending a course of action. **h.** Gareth is giving advice. **i.** Mary is giving her opinion. **j.** Peter is making a polite request. **k.** Cooper is asking for reasons. Δ

12 **a.** The cigarette should be put out. **b.** The bunsen burner should be turned off. **c.** The tap should be turned off. **d.** The window should be closed. **e.** The fire door should be closed. **f.** The liquid should be cleaned up. **g.** The cupboards should be closed. **h.** The wastebaskets should be emptied. **i.** The milk should be put in the fridge.

Unit 6

A Reading Comprehension

1 **a.** Large increase in output   **b.** Unable to purchase more land in Wembley   **c.** Majority of workforce redundant
2 **a.** From 1957 to the present day   **b.** the increase in output   **c.** Keynsworth (UK) Ltd.   **d.** the Board of Directors/purchase more land in Wembley   **e.** offering alternative employment   **f.** transferring to Peterhead
3 To keep their competitive position in the market.
4 The availability of skilled labour, transport, materials, and government grants.
5 To be redundant or move to Peterhead.
6 Check Word Study
7 *verbs:* offer, be situated, transfer   *nouns:* location, division, pressure, facility, competition, record, expansion, consideration, alternative
8 Location B. Highest points total of 182.

B Listening

a. Stack   **b.** Stack   **c.** Neither. Stack's wife has, ie, Stack's 'mother-in-law'   **d.** Hymes and Stack   **e.** Stack   **f.** Hymes   **g.** Hymes
☐ It is probable that Ray will move because he is young, because Forningsby is pleasant, and because he has a good chance of becoming a manager. Δ

C Language Study

1 Past Time

a. for   **b.** since   **c.** in   **d.** —   **e.** since   **f.** for   **g.** since   **h.** —   **i.** since

2 Past Intentions

a. If, however, we had been able to call in a consultant, the problem of the salary structure would have been solved. **b.** If we had been able to employ more staff, the training programmes would have been improved. **c.** If the company had been able to increase its production, the supply position would have been improved. **d.** If we had been able to introduce a computer system, the administration would have been efficient.

3 Adding Information
a. The Board of Directors, which includes the Managing Director of Keynsworth (UK) Ltd, is aware of the difficult situation.
b. Peterhead, which is a very pleasant town, has excellent housing, schools and sports facilities. **c.** The pay offer made by the Personnel Director, who leads the negotiating team, has not been accepted by the Union Representatives. **d.** The various redundancy payments, which can be seen on the notice board, were negotiated and agreed with the Unions in April.

D Listening
(a) Marie Pinet requires the form recording personal details for the Police Department and company records. (b) Charles Bond wants to know about his Paris house.
□ She thinks that Charles Bond will 'get to know Paris' and be in a better position to make a choice between the two houses.

E Using Information in Different Ways
2 k, a, i, f, b, c, h, d, g, e, j, Δ
3 1. Negotiate for land 2. i 3. Purchase land 4. f 5. b 6. c 7. h 8. Make roads & paths 9. g 10. e 11. j Δ

G Writing
2 b, a, c, d, e, f
Leemax Ltd. have requested . . . Bristol headquarters. Therefore, David and his wife . . . housing facilities. However, they found . . . with Birmingham. Consequently, David has been investigating . . . Birmingham area. As a result, he is undecided . . . job near home. However, he does . . . his mind. Δ

Unit 7

A Reading Comprehension
1 **a.** shipbuilding **b.** one project completed at a time **c.** car components **d.** product produced at a planned rate of output
e. flow **f.** flow **g.** process **h.** similar machines grouped in same section of factory
2 **a.** operation **b.** job production **c.** batch size **d.** the movement from job production, to batch production, to flow production
e. another part of the factory **f.** operations performed on the product
3 *Process:* high level of stocks needed/skilled workforce needed *Flow:* little flexibility/ little specialisation of machines and labour
4 Because different products can be efficiently produced by different production methods.
5 **a.** False **b.** False **c.** True **d.** False **e.** True

B Listening
1. Production processes inefficient 2. low level of stocks/smaller manufacturing area/lower degree of skill/production control easier 3. King 4. use skills and resources that exist at Renco/no problems with job grades, responsibilities and salaries
5. Cairns
□ Less degree of skill required by the employees in order to produce the product. It would be necessary when flow methods and more automated machinery were introduced. Δ

C Language Study
1 Impersonal Reporting
a. It is stated that . . . **b.** It has been said that . . . **c.** It was pointed out that . . . **d.** It was generally felt that . . . **e.** It is understood that . . . **f.** It was hoped that . . . **g.** It is generally believed that . . . **h.** It was thought that . . .

2 Comparing
a. She is tall, whereas he is short. **b.** The management team will be asked to relocate, while most other staff will be made redundant. **c.** In 1971, the index of industrial production was 100 in the UK, while in Germany it was two points higher. **d.** King agrees with the consultant's recommendations, whereas Cairns would like to see a regrouping of operations under the system as it is. **e.** At Renco last year investment in R&D was up by £2m over the year before, whereas this year it increased by £1.2m.

3 Defining
Number the left-hand column from a-g; and the right-hand column from 1-7.
a. a/which/3 b/which/4 c/who/7 d/who/6 e/which/2 f/which/1 g/who/5
b. In the first, 'who is fifty years old' can be removed from the sentence. In the second, 'who applies for a job' can not be removed from the sentence.

D Listening
a. 1. The parts arrived three days late from Leeds. 2. Half of the plates were not drilled to the correct specification. b. 1. Two machines were broken down for over a week. 2. Parts were sent to J Department for cleaning.

E Using Information in Different Ways
2 1971, UK = 100; Ger. = 102; Italy = 100
1973, UK = 110; Ger. = 113; Italy = 114
1974, UK = 106; Ger = 111; Italy = 120

1975, Italy = 108   1976, UK = 102; Ger. = 114; Italy = 122

G Writing

1 . . . with the figure for Japan at 127 and for the USSR at 123. The following year, the figure for Japan declined by three points to 124, whereas in the USSR it went up to 133. The trends continued in 1975 when the figure for Japan was down to 110, and the figure for the USSR went up to 143. In 1976, Japan showed an increase again at 125, and the USSR continued its upward trend with a figure of 150. Δ

Unit 8

A Reading Comprehension

1 Because of the failure of the real time computing facilities to improve the control of production.
2 **a.** established standards **b.** corrective programmes **c.** factory rejects **d.** the cost of collecting real time data **e.** the requirement of a control system to deal with potential problems
3 Five years.
4 It has provided good measurement data and identified deviations from standards. The development of corrective programmes has still been required.
5 A future-directed means of control. This will provide the quick implementation of corrective programmes.
7 That more use is made of network planning techniques.
8 *verbs:* identify, improve, install, suggest, justify *nouns:* deviation, implementation, consideration, instruction, summing up
9 **a.** True. **b.** False. A report on the system may have been required. **c.** True. **d.** False. This implementation has been slow. **e.** True.

B Listening

b. end-plates **c.** Too much pressure made by tool on side of plate
a. 764B 2. Time-consuming
☐ To check if he could be responsible for the bad work.

C Language Study

1 Getting Things Done

a. The foreman had the tooling altered slightly. **b.** The company had a report written by a Business Consultant. **c.** The Production Manager had the press repaired by an outside company. **d.** The Production Director had a new production control system introduced by management. **e.** The foreman had the job done again.

2 Sentence Links

a. Althogh the tooling has been changed twice, the end-plates are still not meeting specifications. **b.** Although the Production Manager instructed D Department to clean the components, the Foreman there did not remember to schedule the work. **c.** Although Raymond Stack was rather old, he was able to find a new job in Leeds.

3 Degree

a. very **b.** enough **c.** too **d.** very/enough **e.** enough **f.** too

D Listening

1 Mr Fanfoni: Production Director Mr Simms: Production Manager Mrs Barnett: Management Services Manager
2 Fanfoni–Barnett: neither friendly or unfriendly Fanfoni–Simms: neither friendly or unfriendly Barnett–Simms: unfriendly
3 To discuss the major problems in quality control and production control in order that corrective work can begin.
☐ The computing service provided by the Management Services Department.

E Using Information in Different Ways

2 **a.** sorts paperwork **b.** begins work **c.** Is secretary in? **d.** discusses programme for day with secretary **e.** Is it Tuesday? **f.** goes to production meeting **g.** Is production meeting long? **h.** works on administrative jobs in office
3 *Input:* **a.** stock control data **b.** working file **c.** stock file **d.** alterations to orders **e.** completed orders *Output:* **f.** updated working file **g.** layouts etc. **h.** programmes and schedules

G Writing

3 In-company training programmes can help to improve the efficiency of a company by upgrading the present knowledge and skills of the staff and by teaching new skills. Although training programmes can provide a valuable service, skilled trainers are required to run them, and the programmes are expensive to operate. Therefore, in order for training programmes to be efficient, it is important, first, that qualified trainers are available on the staff and, second, that the savings that result from the training programmes are greater than their cost of operation. Δ

Unit 9

A Reading Comprehension

1 Essing: Rand is prepared for market changes. Kennedy: Technological development/high investment/arrival of Peter Freingel. Freingel: Investment in ideas and equipment/efficient operations. Business Eye: Emphasis on industrial engineering and O&M.
2 **a.** moving from all-time low performance to position of market leader **b.** the impact of high investment and technological development as reasons for improvement in performance **c.** growth of Rand International **d.** electricals **e.** greater efficiency of materials management, and of production and process methods
f. organisation of the company
g. the change-around at Rand
3 There has been a move from an all-time low performance to a position of market leader.
4 From an index figure of 100 in 1971, output per man hour increased to 125 in the following year, and to 150 the year after that. In 1974, there was no change on the previous year but in 1975 . . . Δ
5 Invest in Rand shares.
6 Speers will soon be bought by Rand.

B Listening

a. standardized components **b.** standardized processes **c.** get information from the best people and the right places **d.** use new information **e.** make the best use of ideas and experience of staff **f.** improve communications by your own example **g.** deal with the easy things first **h.** keep it simple **i.** cost present methods **j.** cost alternative methods

C Language Study

1 Nations and Nationalities

Finland, Sweden, France, Greece, Turkey, Britain, Norway, Saudi Arabia, Egypt, Switzerland, Italy, Spain, Portugal, Iceland, Argentina
Chinese, Thai, Mexican, Japanese, German, Senegalese, Somali, Danish, Polish, Scots, Welsh, Belgian, Cuban, Russian, Indian, Irish, Canadian.

2 Definitions

a. a components factory which is located in California **b.** performance which is measured in output per man hour **c.** a company which has Laurence Essing as president **d.** an article in Business Eye which analyses the market **e.** a report which shows the status of production programmes **f.** data which assesses quality control **g.** an EDP system which controls stock **h.** a network planning technique which is used by Standard Electronics

3 Sequencing Past Events

a. When the Board had studied the report, they made their recommendations. **b.** He had worked in the London office for three years before he was transferred to Paris.
c. After they had reached agreement on the new pay structure, they closed the meeting.
d. The company had used mechanical stock control techniques before they introduced a computerized stock control system.

D Listening

a. standardization of forms and paperwork
b. Mr. Kohn **c.** Office Supervisor
d. staff self-assessment method in order to calculate standards of performance
e. Mr. Flint **f.** O&M Manager
□ This kind of work is difficult to measure and the staff might not like having their work quantified.

E Using Information in Different Ways

Function: c, i Material Specification: h, r
Material Content: g, p Material Value: o, q
Limits: a, l Process of Manufacture: f, n
Standardization: b, m Labour Costs: e, k
Material Costs: d, j

G Writing

2 c, e, g, b, f, a, d
3 Training is an important . . . a modern business. If a training . . . skills for the job. However, a large training programme . . . training of staff. Successful training depends on . . . employed.
In order to . . . specification. First, a job description . . . a specific job. Secondly, in terms of job specification . . . a specific job. Δ

Unit 10

A Reading Comprehension

1 producer to retailer; producer to wholesaler to retailer; producer to agent etc. It depends on financial, technical and market factors.
2 **a.** the function of distribution **b.** moving goods from the producer to the final consumer **c.** the most efficient way
d. changing circumstances **e.** using wholesalers **f.** total net savings after a high cost has been incurred **g.** to use its own transport
3 Pre-1963: wholesaler 1963-70: retailer 1970 onwards: wholesaler
4 Problems of suitability of transport and routing choices.
5 No. Total net savings can be made owing to cost reductions that are possible in related areas.

6 Because it is the total cost of distribution which is significant and not the costs of individual activities such as warehousing, order processing, or transport.
7 *verbs:* subtract, route, consume, influence, signify *nouns:* delivery, distribution, transport, suitability, consideration
8 **a.** False. **b.** False. **c.** True. **d.** True. **e.** True.

B Listening

Product: Farm Machinery
Advantages: past company policy/little experience of market/little knowledge of selling and distribution techniques/present market small/market uncertain Δ
Disadvantages: long company experience in Asia/potential for large volume of sales/difficulties of finding right agent/danger of losing expanding market/failure of agency policy in South America Δ
☐ The failure of the agency policy in South America. Even where mistakes were corrected, as in Brazil, the company had lost a lot of money. Δ

C Language Study

4 We refer to the number of the tool in our letter of the 21st September. The number is FC-3266. **b.** The machine-tool operators are working under highly undesirable conditions. This has been reported to the Union. **c.** The applicants were selected from a list. This list had been prepared by the Personnel Manager. **d.** The Safety Officer has a book. He enters a daily report in the book. **e.** Landseer will have to deal with the marketing problems. These problems are complex.

D Listening

1 Product Manager 2 7478 3 2.5 metric tonne of machine oil 4 PB/344/72/040 5 Noon on Friday 6 AO/TS-346-81 7 16.8.81 8 In about two hours

E Using Information in Different Ways

1. 10.30 **2.** 14.45; late departure Bristol **3.** 18.00; 18.30; rough weather **4.** 08.30; rough weather **5.** quick clearance at Customs **6.** early Le Havre departure **7.** 14.00; 13.30 **8.** 18.00; 21.45; mechanical problems **9.** 08.30; on schedule
10. 14.00; traffic hold-up at Cosne
11. 14.30; late arrival at Moulins
12. 17.00; light traffic conditions

F Writing

In April the Canpan factory produced 5,000 more units than the scheduled 40,000 because of overtime work for the purpose of building up stocks. In the following month, the production total of 40,000 units was 5,000 fewer than planned due to a reduction in demand. In June, a strike in the toolroom reduced the 40,000 target figure by 7,000 units. Another strike, this time by truck drivers, meant that the July production figure of 33,000 was 1,000 units below the schedule . . . Δ

Review Unit 2

2 **a.** (*l.*3) uncertainty (*l.*7) businessmen (*l.*10) improvement, deviation, potential, evaluation, design (*l.*18) the information (*l.*19) identifying and assessing a problem (*l.*28) identifying, assessing, objective setting, selecting policy, planning and control (*l.*29) as in f (*l.*31) end of the first problem solving sequence
b. (1), (2), (3) and (4) in paragraph one.
c. (1) An improvement problem is one that tries to improve the performance of a product, process, system or employee. (2) A deviation problem is one that sets new objectives owing to . . . Check with the table.
e. As a means of reducing uncertainty in business to reasonable limits. By means of problem-solving procedures.
f. Identify and assess the problem in order that the real problem is dealt with.
g. The quantity and quality of information and how well it is analysed.
h. Management's ability to forecast events and management's capacity for identifying the possibilities and potentialities of a situation.
i. Planned production, for example, is the expected or scheduled production, whereas actual production is the amount produced. The difference may be caused by machine breakdowns, strikes etc. Δ
j. When a problem remains unsolved after the process of problem-solving.

3 *verbs:* press, locate, consider, expand, deliver, deviate, instruct *nouns:* influence, offer, improvement, signification, identification, transfer, consumption, competition, installation, subtraction, justification, suggestion, implementation

4 **a.** conclusions **b.** effect **c.** total **d.** implement **e.** viable **f.** reason **g.** acquired **h.** justify

6 United Kingdom, United States of America, fahrenheit, company, centigrade, limited, Kelvin, arrival, departure, December, centimetre, specification, that is, Russia, European Economic Community, etcetera, established, programme evaluation and review technique, two and a half million pounds, March, organisation and methods,

carbon copy, for example, research and development, thousands.

7 **a.** (3) **b.** (2) **c.** (4) **d.** (1) **e.** (3) **f.** (1) **g.** (3) **h.** (4) **i.** (1) **j.** (2)

8 **a.** was pointed out **b.** looking around for **c.** put . . . through **d.** will . . . hand over **e.** go ahead with **f.** had broken down **g.** took over **h.** changed over **i.** to build up **j.** were held up

9 Check with paragraphs one and two in the Reading Passage in Unit 7.

10 **a.** (7) **b.** (1) **c.** (2) **d.** (1) **e.** (5) **f.** (3) **g.** (1) **h.** (4) **i.** (6)

11 **a.** owing to **b.** because **c.** although **d.** owing to **e.** unless **f.** if **g.** if **h.** because **i.** owing to **j.** although

12 **a.** A degree and job related experience. They are both senior appointments.
b. Purchases–Implement purchasing policy of utilizing local sources by managing existing and evaluating potential suppliers. Systems Designers–Implement computer-based management systems/Design, prepare and review written purchasing procedures/Train staff.
c. Excellent salaries/renewable contracts/low cost accommodation/free medical care/sports facilities/40 days holiday/return air fares to UK
d. They are job reference numbers to be quoted on correspondence.
e. Nigeria
f. Norman MacIntyre . . . The Netherlands
g. Company headquarters are in the Netherlands.

Unit 11

A Reading Comprehension

1 By ten per cent.
2 **a.** ex-factory sales figures **b.** Markham's **c.** the analysis of the market **d.** before Markham's entered the market **e.** launching a new sales campaign **f.** information on product range, packaging, users and market trends
g. Countryfresh
3 Because of an increase in the overall size of the market.
4 It increased the overall size of the market.
5 By March 1980 Markham's had achieved 3% of a total market of 5,050,000 tins. Between March and May sales rose from 3% to 9% which represented 477,000 tins. By July the figure had reached 633,600 tins or 11% of the total market . . . Δ
6 633,600. Countryfresh sold 3,168,000 and others 1,958,400.
7 They will increase with Markham's taking a larger share.
8 They should have launched a new sales campaign. They were looking at their ex-factory sales figures and not at their market share. Δ
9 Products must be packaged in such a way that customers can easily identify and associate themselves with the design. Δ
10 If user characteristics are known then advertising, for example, can be aimed at specific groups. Δ
11 (1) evaluation of a competitor's product compared with your own (2) the real situation (3) the consumers (4) a reason for worrying

B Listening

1 1. = Radley 2. = Pilger 3. = Sloane
2 Markham's entry into the soup market.
☐ **1** Under-estimates have 'a habit of coming true'. **2** His sales staff.

C Language Study

1 Future Time
b. If Radley's prediction comes true, sales will have reached over 2.5m by the end of 1981. If Pilger's prediction comes true, sales will have reached 2.25m. If Sloane's prediction comes true, sales will have been reduced to fewer than 1.5m.

2 Probability
a. Markham's must have known that the soup market was ready for expansion.
b. Countryfresh must have underestimated Markham's ability to penetrate the market.
c. Countryfresh's target sales for '79 and '80 must have been too optimistic.
d. Radley's marketing trip to Belgium must have been a busy one, since . . . . **e.** Dan Sloane must have had an excellent record in sales, if they . . . .

3 Referring to Mistakes or Failure
a. Markham's ability to penetrate the market should not have been underestimated in the report. **b.** Work should have been done on investigating the characteristics of Countryfresh's product. **c.** The operator should have worn safety glasses when working. **d.** A low estimate of our competitor's sales should not have been made. **e.** The stock list should have been checked at the end of the month.

D Listening

1 **a.** freezer compartment **b.** egg rack **c.** bottle rack **d.** vegetable container **e.** shelves
2 **a.** difficult to pull out and push back
b. covering starting to break and discolour
c. holes too small **d.** not high enough
3 **a.** Value for money **b.** Good performance

E Using Information in Different Ways

Types of Marketing Research
1. Product Research: 3, 6, 9, 11
2. User Market Research: 1, 12, 13, 18
3. Sales Operations Research: 2, 4, 5, 8, 16, 17
4. Economic and Business Research: 15, 19

G Writing

Manufacturing companies need to make . . . of their products. In a developing technical world . . . knowledge improves. As a result, some manufacturers . . . and equipment. Therefore, they will . . . in the market.

Unit 12

A Reading Comprehension

1 **a.** Too low **b.** Realistic **c.** Packaging, design and display **d.** Price cuts, trade discounts and consumer special offers
2 **a.** Alpine **b.** spending a high percentage of anticipated sales revenue on advertising **c.** high advertising expenditure to the extent of not meeting costs in the first year **d.** impact, frequency and coverage **e.** an advertising campaign **f.** a full campaign against half the market **g.** coupons **h.** Mr. Mayer **i.** promotional policy **j.** promotional policy
3 An advertising agency.
4 When marketing a high-turnover product.
5 Companies must decide how big advertisements should be; how long they should run on television; how often they should appear; and in what areas of the country they should be seen. Δ
6 That a full campaign should be run against half the market.
7 More details of what needs to be said and to whom. Mr. Stanton will provide the information by the end of the week following the meeting.
8 At the next meeting.
9 **a.** False. **b.** False. **c.** True. **d.** False. **e.** True.

B Listening

1 It has a new lightweight frame and Machet six-speed gearing.
2 Less than a hundred pounds.
3 She aims to sell to all sections of the market. She will promote the bike on its points of general interest and also market for the specialist buyer. Δ
☐ 1 He thinks that they won't have a defined market group to aim at. 2 He thinks that they will have an opportunity to extend the price range.

C Language Study

1 Habits
a. past practice **b.** present habit **c.** present habit **d.** present habit **e.** past practice

2 Reporting Statements
Check with parts three and four in the Reading Passage.

3 Suggesting
a. Why don't we evaluate the training programme? **b.** Shall we discuss it again tomorrow? **c.** What about launching a new sales campaign? **d.** Why don't we do some market research? **e.** What about having a drink? Δ

D Listening

1 **a.** Region One: Television advertising
b. Region Two: Press advertising
c. Region Three: Display material
2 To extend the product on a national basis.
☐ Because they need to know about what the competition is going to do, and what their media strategy will be.

E Using Information in Different Ways

2 **a.** 25% – newspaper advertising **b.** 15% – sales promotion **c.** 10% – magazine advertising
3 **a.** £935,000 **b.** £1,085,000 **c.** £1,100,000 **d.** £1,250,000 **e.** £1,382,500
4 TV: '76 = 500,000, '77 = 450,000, '78 = 550,000, '79 = 600,000, '80 = 650,000 '81 = 750,000
Press: '76 = 250,000, '77 = 275,000, '78 = 300,000, '79 = 225,000, '80 = 300,000 '81 = 325,000
Magazines: '76 = 100,000, '77 = 90,000, '78 = 100,000, '79 = 110,000, '80 = 120,000 '81 = 120,000
Promotion: '76 = 150,000, '77 = 120,000, '78 = 135,000, '79 = 165,000, '80 = 180,000 '81 = 187,500

G Writing

In the autumn of 1979, the company ran a limited sales training course, which lasted two weeks, in order to introduce part of the salesforce to the appropriate selling techniques for a new product called Ace. Then, restricted production of the new product was begun which was test marketed in two selected areas. Although completely satisfactory results were not achieved from the test areas, the decision was taken to go ahead with a national launch. Training programmes were introduced which all the salespeople had to complete. Next, existing production lines were altered so that they could be used for the new product, and full production began. Finally, a national advertising campaign was launched that was based on television and national newspapers and which aimed at maximum coverage of the market.

Unit 13

A Reading Comprehension

1 Because the results of the market analyses were late.
2 **a.** a reference; JR stands for Jean Renoir, and the other letters could refer to his secretary and the file reference. Δ
b. providing details of the campaign **c.** a wholesaler **d.** a UK television campaign for Rouen soaps **e.** week 24 **f.** the method of promotion **g.** a banded offer **h.** the campaign layout **i.** for the pre-launch meeting **j.** enclosures
3 In order that the product remains in stock.
4 2,000 a week.
5 **a.** bad for the up-market image **b.** a banded offer **c.** 2 The extra cost and banding not worthwhile
6 To introduce the product to important people in the market. Δ
7 So that fashion magazines will run articles on the product. Δ
8 Simpson Ltd. is the UK distribution company for Rouen. Δ
9 A pre-launch meeting.

B Listening

1 **a.** Supported small increase **b.** increase prices/marketing effort in cities/cut down salesforce **c.** reduce prices/provide retailer discounts/extra advertising/save on production costs
2 The picture territory by territory. In the large cities sales have been pretty stable. In the country districts and smaller towns there has been a sharp decline. Δ
☐ **a.** Maximum effort in marketing in cities because sales there have remained stable and consumers have been least affected by price considerations. **b.** Cut down the sales force by either limiting representation in less important regions or combining existing functions in fewer offices.

C Language Study

1 Reporting Questions

a. Mr. Bellamy asked if it would be possible to offer a banded pack. **b.** Mr. Renoir's assistant wanted to know if he might/could give out the details of the advertising theme. **c.** Renoir asked if they could be sure that Simpson Ltd would approve of their layout. **d.** M. Delmas asked his Sales Manager if his advertising support was going to continue after week 30. **e.** One of Renoir's salespeople asked if they had received anything from Bellamy on the pre-launch meeting they were planning. **f.** Renoir's secretary asked if Simpson wanted them to enclose the sales budget. **g.** He asked if the sales pack included an insert. **h.** He wanted to know if the truck had left Wilhelmshaven on schedule. **i.** He wanted to know why the truck had waited so long at Wilmhelmshaven. **j.** He wanted to know where the truck had stopped after Wilmhelmshaven.

2 Future Time

Tuesday: Discussions are to be held on the expansion plans.
Wednesday: The MD is to consider senior management appointments
Thursday: The MD is to hold an investigation of declining overseas sales.
Friday: The re-location plans will be evaluated. Δ

3 Comparing

a. 1978 **b.** yes **c.** early 1978 **d.** surplus of lamb caused a temporary fall in price Δ

D Listening

1 Name: Mr. Summers Quality of Work: 1
Accuracy: 4 Communicating: 1
Initiative: 1
2 Above average on all six assessment points.
☐ 1 He has joined an evening class to improve his maths. 2 He is very ambitious as he says he wants 'to go to the top'.

E Using Information in Different Ways

2 8, 1, 2, 9, 4, 3, 6, 5, 10, 7
3 (a) = 8 (b) = 4 (c) = 5 (d) = 3
(e) = 6 (f) = 9 (g) = 3 (h) = 9
(i) = 5 (j) = 2 (k) = 7 (l) = 1
(m) = 6 (n) = 2 (o) = 10 (p) = 2

G Writing

We need a new sales manager who must be able to build an effective salesforce in order to re-establish our position in the home market which we dominated until last year. The sales manager's first objective must be to produce a sales team wich utilizes the skills of all its members. All the individuals within the team must be encouraged not only to express their own opinions but also to contribute to the framing of proposals. This experience will enable everybody who shows interest and capacity to take a full part in discussions and decision-making. The effectiveness of the decisions and of the performance will depend both on the new sales manager's ability to establish and maintain close co-operation between all members of the team and on the quality of the individual skills and knowledge of the team members whose recruitment is the responsibility of the sales manager.

Unit 14

A Reading Comprehension

1 **a.** profits earned overseas **b.** Engineering Division **c.** MacGregors **d.** the Belgian subsidiary **e.** shareholder's **f.** 154p **g.** the expectations about the company's prospects in the current year **h.** that you be realistic in your expectations and remember the difficult trading conditions
2 The higher the inflation rate, the more difficult it will be to maintain their profit position.
3 They are the market value, earnings and dividend for ordinary shares.
4 £52 £1,540
5 9%. An increase in the proportion of profits earned overseas which attract a lower rate of tax than in the UK.
6 Either they performed as well or not as well as MacGregors.
7 Investment in new manufacturing facilities and a major overhaul of some existing equipment.
8 As a result of concentration on export markets.
9 They experienced a low volume of orders and made losses.
10 Check Word Study.
11 Liquidity is so strong that their borrowings are low, only 25% of share capital and reserves. This means that the company could borrow several million pounds if it wanted to.
12 The difficult economic conditions require the shareholders to be realistic in their expectations.
13 An improvement in trade.

B Listening

1 **a.** trading profit and loss **b.** overall profit and loss
2 An overseas tax charge of £5m and an unusual cost of £10m for closing down the Asian operation.
3 It is against the regulations.
4 That the company should be sold.
☐ The plan to sell Hamilton shares to their own employees at an attractive rate.

C Language Study

1 Comparing
c. The faster the speed of working, the higher the number of mistakes that are made.
d. The higher the production costs, the higher the price for which the goods are sold/the selling price. **e.** The greater the earnings, the greater is the amount of money spent.
f. The faster the rate of technological change, the faster the reduction in the number of people employed in manufacturing. Δ

2 Anticipated Response
a. Should the government decide to . . . at an attractive rate. **b.** Should the government take up . . . at an attractive rate. **c.** Should you ever need assistance, . . . on me.
d. Should a recession take place in . . . overseas sales. **e.** Should you require additional . . . sales office.

3 Degree
c. The number of imported cars sold is so large that domestic manufacturers are facing losses. **d.** There is so much pressure on plant facilities that it is necessary to acquire new land for extensions. **e.** The losses in the Asian market were so heavy that the company closed down the operation.
f. There is so much dependence on short-term loans that the future of the company is not secure. Δ

D Listening

1 **b.** Best on record **c.** More than doubled **c.** £20.2m
2 **a.** 4.86p **b.** 5.26p **c.** £5,324,000
☐ 1 UK: 55.2% Australasia: 14.6% Chemicals: 31.3% Paint: 20.3%

E Using Information in Different Ways

2 **a.** Is market value greater than the cost price? **b.** Is the selling price greater than the cost price? **c.** No tax either charged or allowed. **d.** Tax is allowed on the cost price less the selling price plus expenses. **e.** Tax is charged on the selling price less the market value less expenses. **f.** Tax is allowed on the market value less the selling price plus expenses.

G Writing

1 One of the functions of financial . . . its preference shares. This balance is known as capital gearing. If a company has . . . to be 'highly geared'. This may mean very high . . . in a bad one. In the case of . . . ordinary shareholders. They are often given . . . not been paid.
2 The general level of prices . . . make available. The fact that prices . . . value of output. The pressure on prices . . . the demand side. Supply conditions can change . . . wage costs increase. As a result . . . from consumers. On the other hand . . . to the market. This excess demand . . . general price level.

Unit 15

A Reading Comprehension

1 **a.** a common standard of comparability in company reporting **b.** accounting **c.** not using a common standard **d.** company reporting **e.** presenting themselves in the best way **f.** a company carrying assets at some anticipated value **g.** UK accounting **h.** a short qualification/all that is pointed out in the report
2 Because the account books of a company must balance.
3 By proper explanations in the notes to the accounts.
4 Lovett favours flexibility, Wright favours regulations and penalties.
5 Assets can be revalued at convenient times.
6 The avoidance of publishing inflation adjusted figures.
7 The way extraordinary costs are charged./ The valuation and depreciation of assets.
8 After they acquired it. To improve their asset position.
9 When a company revalues assets.
10 Current cost, historical cost, and the UK system.

B Listening

1 Because of their extensive financial experience of Morgans.
2 Because of pressure from the Board to find a solution to the recent poor performance.
3 A large number of investors.
☐ **a.** it is too simplistic. There are many reasons to explain the high turnover-rate. **b.** Barlow and Peters do not have the experience, and it would be a long and costly job.

C Language Study

1 Past Time

a. Having acquired a new tanker, Tyne Oil valued it at an optimum disposal price. **b.** Having compared the graph on the company's management turnover to the graph on its profit record, the investors concluded that personnel turnover was related to the company's overall performance. **c.** Having decided in favour of Barlow & Peter's proposal, the Board prepared a special statement for distribution to Morgan's investors. **d.** Having agreed on their approach to the Board, Royston and Klyne asked to meet with the MD to tell him what they intended to say. **e.** Having heard what Royston and Klyne intended to say to the Board, the MD tried to persuade them to change their minds.

2 Reporting Orders

a. Royston told Klyne not to forget about the meeting the following day. **b.** Mr. Tyler advised Mr. Brown to let the managers do the managing. **c.** He told them to report back to him as soon as they had reached a decision. **d.** He told her not to let anyone disturb them for the following few hours. **e.** He told the Representatives to tell them where the 150 million pounds was going to come from. **f.** Bob advised Harry to understand that the Board was serious about the proposal. **g.** He told Mr. Scott to be reasonable and to try to see the situation from the management's point of view.

3 Immediate Future and Past Time

a. The MD has just finished reading the report. **b.** The machine has just been repaired. **c.** The company is about to open their new factory extension. **d.** The management trainees have just completed their course. **e.** The train is about to leave.

D Listening

1 Because sales have been extremely good, the order book is filling up, and the staff are working well.
2 By keeping his liabilities to a minimum.
3 He needs detailed information on the costings of the new furnace compared to the current method, and he needs to look at the order book.
☐ **b.** £40,000 **c.** To purchase a gas furnace **d.** Hardening process done by outside firm. This is expensive, time-consuming, and not always of good quality.

E Using Information in Different Ways

a. Read down each of the six columns, beginning on the left:
Reserves (Capital); Loans; Taxation
2,850; 267,039 (total)
38,341; 9,615; 15,190; 117,990 (total)
Land and Buildings; Research; Stocks
102,018; 267,039 (total)
4,118; 2,460

b. Read down the 5 columns beginning on the left:
Plant; Cash; Share Capital; Proposed Dividend; Creditors
3,060; 2,658
59,068; 11,450; 7,291; 62,189; 30,202; 32,140; 39,000; 267,039 (total)
1,090; 1,760
26,115; 3,119; 117,990; 12,150; 117,990 (total)

G Writing

The aim of business managers is . . . of the company. There are basically three things . . . to do. First, they must obtain . . . on investment. Secondly, they must . . . unreasonable delay. Thirdly, they must pay . . . and customers. These objectives . . . management. In a large . . . company profits. For the management team . . . are achieved. To begin with . . . activity. It is also important . . . frequent intervals. Finally, corrective . . . the forecast. This process of . . . management accounting.

Review Unit 3

2 **a.** The range and weight of executive responsibility. **b.** Difficult decisions are hard to make, but critical decisions can mean the difference between success or failure of a project. Δ **c.** The manager is accountable for the results of work for which he is not directly involved. The weight of this responsibility can damage his health. Δ **e.** As a person acting in ways that are expected of him. **f.** By everyone playing the parts expected of them. When an executive moves too far or suddenly from his defined position. **g.** So that it does not interfere with his work. Δ **h.** Management specialists and writers. Their definitions share the elements of results, organisational objectives and managerial action. **i.** Environment, the organisation structure, the reward system and the manager's personal characteristics. **j.** Because of the factors listed in i above.

3 *verbs:* promote, restrict, penetrate, adjust, depreciate *nouns:* allocation, cover/coverage, constraint, lack, approval, excess, concentration, interpretation, penalty, response

4 **a.** a five-year bank loan **b.** after-tax Group profit **c.** Countryfresh soup marketing research report **d.** ten per cent market share **e.** UK television advertising campaign **f.** Rouen public relations pack **g.** Ford first-quarter sales figures **h.** sales personnel assessment form **i.** engineering division expansion plans **j.** UK metal prices

5 In 1971, production of Lalle red wine totalled 50m bottles, whereas sales totalled approximately 46m. In the following year, . . .

6 Graphs and Statistics: peak, level off, stable, trend, decline, fluctuations, trough Finance: dividend, audit, liquidity, liability, debtor, share, depreciation, reserves, interest Advertising and Promotion: launch, media, packaging, discounts, survey, sample, image, merchandise, coupons Production: furnace, plant, process, output, component, batch, lathe Personnel: incentive, grading, negotiations, award, recruit

7 **a.** are grouped/can be provided **b.** has been negotiated **c.** is being criticized **d.** were removed/could not be measured **e.** is expected **f.** will not be affected **g.** is expected **h.** will be asked **i.** have been reported/have been supplied **j.** had been taken over/were offered

8 **a.** a newspaper **b.** In response to a call to reduce the number of unemployed. – He informed the Inland Revenue – He received a number of forms. **c.** Because of the administrative work involved. – Administering her own social benefits. **d.** Reducing and simplifying paperwork. **e.** The unemployed will remain unemployed and small businesses remain small.

9 (1) the introduction to a campaign (2) more resources used on advertising (3) a low level at which income covers costs (4) the identification of a product with the mass market (5) a balance sheet which reflects good performance and a good overall position

10 **a.** of/in/of/of/to/in **b.** from/of/of/after/of/with **c.** of/to/of **d.** to/within **e.** of/of/to/in **f.** by/from/to/to/before **g.** in/of/on/for/of **h.** of/by/in

12 Harcourts: '76 = 20 '77 = 21 '78 = 40 '79 = 40 '80 = 50 Mathews: '76 = 50 '77 = 42 '78 = 10 '79 = 40 '80 = 20

Index

This is a list of the important items in the book which go beyond the lexical inventory of The Threshold Level. The number after each entry refers to the unit in which the word, expression or abbreviation first occurs. Two reference numbers after an entry indicate that this item has been used in different senses.